CONGRESSIONAL POLICIES, PRACTICES AND PROCEDURES

KEY CONGRESSIONAL REPORTS ON EDUCATION

CONGRESSIONAL POLICIES, PRACTICES AND PROCEDURES

Additional books and e-books in this series can be found
on Nova's website under the Series tab.

CONGRESSIONAL POLICIES, PRACTICES AND PROCEDURES

KEY CONGRESSIONAL REPORTS ON EDUCATION

GEORGIA TURNER
EDITOR

Copyright © 2019 by Nova Science Publishers, Inc.

All rights reserved. No part of this book may be reproduced, stored in a retrieval system or transmitted in any form or by any means: electronic, electrostatic, magnetic, tape, mechanical photocopying, recording or otherwise without the written permission of the Publisher.

We have partnered with Copyright Clearance Center to make it easy for you to obtain permissions to reuse content from this publication. Simply navigate to this publication's page on Nova's website and locate the "Get Permission" button below the title description. This button is linked directly to the title's permission page on copyright.com. Alternatively, you can visit copyright.com and search by title, ISBN, or ISSN.

For further questions about using the service on copyright.com, please contact:
Copyright Clearance Center
Phone: +1-(978) 750-8400   Fax: +1-(978) 750-4470   E-mail: info@copyright.com.

NOTICE TO THE READER

The Publisher has taken reasonable care in the preparation of this book, but makes no expressed or implied warranty of any kind and assumes no responsibility for any errors or omissions. No liability is assumed for incidental or consequential damages in connection with or arising out of information contained in this book. The Publisher shall not be liable for any special, consequential, or exemplary damages resulting, in whole or in part, from the readers' use of, or reliance upon, this material. Any parts of this book based on government reports are so indicated and copyright is claimed for those parts to the extent applicable to compilations of such works.

Independent verification should be sought for any data, advice or recommendations contained in this book. In addition, no responsibility is assumed by the Publisher for any injury and/or damage to persons or property arising from any methods, products, instructions, ideas or otherwise contained in this publication.

This publication is designed to provide accurate and authoritative information with regard to the subject matter covered herein. It is sold with the clear understanding that the Publisher is not engaged in rendering legal or any other professional services. If legal or any other expert assistance is required, the services of a competent person should be sought. FROM A DECLARATION OF PARTICIPANTS JOINTLY ADOPTED BY A COMMITTEE OF THE AMERICAN BAR ASSOCIATION AND A COMMITTEE OF PUBLISHERS.

Additional color graphics may be available in the e-book version of this book.

Library of Congress Cataloging-in-Publication Data

ISBN: 978-1-53615-731-4

Published by Nova Science Publishers, Inc. † *New York*

CONTENTS

Preface		**vii**
Chapter 1	"Affirmative Action" and Equal Protection in Higher Education *Christine J. Back and JD S. Hsin*	**1**
Chapter 2	Public Safety Officers' Benefits (PSOB) and Public Safety Officers' Educational Assistance (PSOEA) Programs *Scott D. Szymendera*	**71**
Chapter 3	The Closure of Institutions of Higher Education: Student Options, Borrower Relief, and Other Implications *Alexandra Hegji*	**87**
Chapter 4	School Meals Programs and Other USDA Child Nutrition Programs: A Primer (Updated) *Kara Clifford Billings and Randy Alison Aussenberg*	**129**
Chapter 5	Institutional Eligibility for Participation in Title IV Student Financial Aid Programs *Alexandra Hegji*	**179**

Chapter 6	Department of Education Funding: Key Concepts and FAQ	**217**
	Kyle D. Shohfi and Jessica Tollestrup	
Index		**253**
Related Nova Publications		**263**

PREFACE

This book is a comprehensive compilation of all reports, testimony, correspondence and other publications issued by the Congressional Research Service on education during the month of January and February.

Chapter 1 - When federal courts have analyzed and addressed "affirmative action" in higher education, they have done so in two distinct but related senses, both under the Fourteenth Amendment's guarantee of "equal protection." The first has its roots in the original sense of "affirmative action:" the *mandatory* use of race by public education systems to eliminate the remnants of state-imposed racial segregation. Because state-sanctioned race segregation in public education violates the Fourteenth Amendment's Equal Protection Clause, in certain cases involving a state's formerly *de jure* segregated public university system, a state's consideration of race in its higher education policies and practices may be an *affirmative obligation*. As the U.S. Supreme Court explained in its consequential 1992 decision *United States v. Fordice*, equal protection may *require* states that formerly maintained *de jure* segregated university systems to consider race for the purpose of eliminating all vestiges of their prior "dual" systems. Drawing upon its precedent addressing racially segregated public schools in the K-12 context, the Court established a three-part legal standard in *Fordice* for evaluating the sufficiency and effectiveness of a state's efforts in "dismantl[ing]" its formerly *de jure* segregated public university system. To that remedial end, mandatory race-conscious measures—in this *de jure* context—are not limited to admissions. Instead, remedies may also address policies and practices relating to academic programs, institutional missions, funding, and other aspects of public university operations. Outside this *de jure* context, "affirmative action" has come to refer to a different category of race-conscious policies. These involve what the Court at one time called the "benign" use of racial classifications—voluntary measures designed not to remedy past *de jure* discrimination, but to help racial minorities overcome the effects of their earlier exclusion. And for institutions of higher education, the Court has addressed one type of affirmative action policy in particular: the use of race as a factor in admissions decisions, a practice now widely observed by both public and private colleges and universities. The federal courts have come to subject these voluntary race-conscious policies—"affirmative action" in its perhaps more familiar sense—to a particularly searching form of review known as strict scrutiny. And even though this heightened judicial scrutiny has long been regarded as strict in theory but fatal in fact, the Court's review of race-conscious admissions policies in higher education has proved a notable exception, with the Court having twice upheld universities' use of race as one of many factors considered when assembling their incoming classes. The Court has long grappled with this seeming tension— between the strictness of its scrutiny and its approval of race-conscious admissions policies—beginning with its landmark 1978 decision in *Regents of the University of California v. Bakke* through its 2016 decision in *Fisher v. University of Texas*. Though the Equal Protection Clause generally concerns public universities and their constitutional obligations under the Fourteenth Amendment, federal statutory law also plays a role in ensuring equal protection in higher education. To that end, Title VI of the Civil Rights Act of 1964 prohibits recipients of federal funding—including private colleges and universities— from, at a minimum, discriminating against students and applicants in a manner that would violate the Equal Protection Clause. Federal agencies, including the Departments of Justice and Education,

Preface

ix

investigate and administratively enforce institutions' compliance with Title VI.

Chapter 2 - The Public Safety Officers' Benefits (PSOB) program provides cash benefits to federal, state, and local law enforcement officers; firefighters; employees of emergency management agencies; and members of emergency medical services agencies who are killed or permanently and totally disabled as the result of personal injuries sustained in the line of duty. The Public Safety Officers' Educational Assistance (PSOEA) program, a component of the PSOB program, provides higher-education assistance to the children and spouses of public safety officers killed or permanently disabled in the line of duty. The PSOB and PSOEA programs are administered by the Department of Justice (DOJ), Bureau of Justice Assistance (BJA). However, claimants dissatisfied with denials of benefits may pursue administrative appeals within DOJ and may seek judicial review before the United States Court of Appeals for the Federal Circuit. Each year, Congress appropriates funding for PSOB death benefits, which is considered mandatory spending, and for PSOB disability benefits and PSOEA benefits, which is subject to annual appropriations. For FY2019, the one-time lump-sum PSOB death and disability benefit is $359,316 and the PSOEA monthly benefit for a student attending an educational institution full-time is $1,224. In FY2017, the DOJ approved 399 claims for PSOB death benefits, 82 claims for PSOB disability benefits, and 601 claims for PSOEA benefits.

Chapter 3 - When an institution of higher education (IHE) closes, a student's postsecondary education may be disrupted. Students enrolled at closing IHEs may face numerous issues and may be required to make difficult decisions in the wake of a closure. Two key issues students may face when their IHEs close relate to their academic plans and their personal finances. The academic issues faced by students when their schools close include whether they will continue to pursue their postsecondary education, and if so, where and how they might do so. Students deciding to continue their postsecondary education have several options. They may participate in a teach-out offered by the closing institution or by another institution. A teach-out is a plan that provides students with the opportunity to complete their program of study after a school's closure. Students may also be able to transfer the credits they previously earned at the closed IHE to another IHE. If a student is able to transfer some or all of the previously earned credits, he or she would not be required to repeat the classes those credits represent at the new institution; if a student is unable to transfer previously earned credits, the student may be required to repeat the classes those credits represent at the new IHE. Decisions regarding the acceptance of credit transfers are within the discretion of the accepting IHE. The financial issues faced by students when their schools close include whether they are responsible for repaying any loans borrowed to attend a closed school and how they might finance any additional postsecondary education they pursue. In general, a closed school loan discharge is available to a borrower of federal student loans made under Title IV of the Higher Education Act (P.L. 89-329, as amended), if the student was enrolled at the IHE when it closed or if the student withdrew from the IHE within 120 days prior to its closure. Additionally, the student must have been unable to complete his or her program of study at the closed school or a comparable program at another IHE, either through a teach-out agreement or by transferring any credits to another IHE. Borrowers ineligible for a closed school discharge may be able to have eligible Title IV federal student loans discharged by successfully asserting as a borrower defense to repayment (BDR) certain acts or omissions of an IHE, if the cause of action directly relates to the loan or educational services for which the loan was provided. Whether a borrower may have discharged all or part of any private education loans borrowed to attend the closed IHE may depend on the loan's terms and conditions. Some students may also face issues regarding how they might finance future postsecondary educational pursuits. If a borrower receives a closed school discharge or has a successful BDR claim, the discharged loan will not count against the borrower's Subsidized Loan usage period, which typically limits certain borrowers' receipt of Direct Subsidized Loans for a period equal to 150% of the published length of his or her academic program, and a borrower's statutory annual and aggregate borrowing limits on Direct Subsidized and Direct Unsubsidized Loans are unlikely to be affected. Students who receive a Pell Grant for enrollment at a school that closed may have an equivalent amount of Pell eligibility restored. Likewise, if the student used GI Bill educational benefits from the Department of Veterans Affairs for attendance at a closed school, those benefits can be restored. Students may be reimbursed for payments on charges levied by closed IHEs that are not covered by other sources from a State Tuition Recovery Fund (STRF). The availability of and student eligibility for such funds vary by state, and not all states operate STRFs. Finally, the receipt of any of the above-mentioned benefits may have federal and state income tax implications, including the potential creation of a federal income tax liability for borrowers who have certain loans discharged.

Chapter 4 - The "child nutrition programs" refer to the U.S. Department of Agriculture's Food and Nutrition Service (USDA-FNS) programs that provide food for children in school or institutional settings. The best known programs, which serve the largest number of children, are the school meals programs: the National School Lunch Program (NSLP) and the School Breakfast Program (SBP). The child nutrition programs also include the Child and Adult Care Food Program (CACFP), which provides meals and snacks in day care and after school settings; the Summer Food Service Program (SFSP), which provides food during the summer months; the Special Milk Program (SMP), which supports milk for schools that do not participate in NSLP or SBP; and the Fresh Fruit and Vegetable Program (FFVP), which funds fruit and vegetable snacks in select elementary schools. Funding: The vast majority of the child nutrition programs account is considered mandatory spending, with trace amounts of discretionary funding for certain related activities. Referred to as open-ended, "appropriated entitlements," funding is provided through the annual appropriations process; however, the level of *spending* is controlled by benefit and eligibility criteria in federal law and dependent on the resulting levels of participation. Federal cash funding (in the form of per-meal reimbursements) and USDA commodity food support is guaranteed to schools and other providers based on the number of meals or snacks served and participant category (e.g., free meals for poor children get higher subsidies). Participation: The child nutrition programs serve children of varying ages and in different institutional settings. The NSLP and SBP have the broadest reach, serving qualifying children of all ages in school settings. Other child nutrition programs serve more-narrow populations. CACFP, for example, provides meals and snacks to children in early childhood and after-school settings among other venues. Programs generally provide some subsidy for all food served but a larger federal reimbursement for food served to children from low-income households. Administration: Responsibility for child nutrition programs is divided between the federal government, states, and localities. The state agency and type of local provider differs by program. In the NSLP and SBP, schools and school districts ("school food authorities") administer the program. Meanwhile, SFSP (and sometimes CACFP) uses a model in which sponsor organizations handle administrative responsibilities for a number of sites that serve meals. Reauthorization: The underlying laws covering the child nutrition programs were last reauthorized in the Healthy, Hunger-Free Kids Act of 2010 (HHFKA, P.L. 111-296, enacted December 13, 2010). This law made significant changes to child nutrition programs, including increasing federal financing for school lunches, expanding access to community eligibility and direct certification options for schools, and expanding eligibility options for home child care providers. The law also required an update to school meal nutrition guidelines as well as new guidelines for food served outside the meal programs (e.g., snacks sold in vending machines and cafeteria a la carte lines). Current Issues: The 114th Congress began but did not complete a 2016 child nutrition reauthorization, and there was no significant legislative activity with regard to reauthorization in the 115th Congress. However, the vast majority of operations and activities continue with funding provided by appropriations laws.

Chapter 5 - Title IV of the Higher Education Act (HEA) authorizes programs that provide financial assistance to students to assist them in obtaining a postsecondary education at certain institutions of higher education (IHEs). These IHEs include public, private nonprofit, and proprietary institutions. For students attending such institutions to be able to receive Title IV assistance, an institution must meet basic criteria, including offering at least one eligible program of education (e.g., programs leading to a degree or preparing a student for gainful employment in a recognized occupation). In addition, an IHE must satisfy the program integrity triad, under which it must be

- licensed or otherwise legally authorized to operate in the state in which it is physically located,
- accredited or preaccredited by an agency recognized for that purpose by the Department of Education (ED), and
- certified by ED as eligible to participate in Title IV programs.

These requirements are intended to provide a balance between consumer protection, quality assurance, and oversight and compliance in postsecondary education providers participating in Title IV student aid programs. An IHE must also fulfill a variety of other related requirements, including those that relate to institutional recruiting practices, student policies and procedures, and the administration of the Title IV student aid programs. Finally, additional criteria may apply to an institution depending on its control or the type of educational programs it offers. For example, proprietary institutions must meet HEA requirements that are otherwise inapplicable to public and private nonprofit institutions, including deriving at least 10% of their revenues from non-Title IV funds (also known as the 90/10 rule). While an institution is ineligible to participate in Title IV programs if more than 50% of its courses are offered by correspondence or if 50% or more of its students are enrolled in correspondence courses. This chapter first describes the types of institutions eligible to participate in Title IV programs and discusses the program integrity triad. It then discusses additional issues related to institutional eligibility, including program participations agreements, required campus safety policies and crime reporting, and distance and correspondence education.

Chapter 6 - Like most federal agencies, the Department of Education (ED) receives funds in support of its mission through various federal budget and appropriations processes. While not unique, the mechanisms by which ED receives, obligates, and expends funds can be complex. For example, ED receives both mandatory and discretionary appropriations; ED is annually provided forward funds and advance appropriations for some—but not all—discretionary programs; ED awards both formula and competitive grants; and a portion of ED's budget subsidizes student loan costs (direct loans and loan guarantees). As such, analyzing ED's budget requires an understanding of a broad range of federal budget and appropriations concepts. This chapter provides an introduction to these concepts as they are used specifically in the context of the congressional appropriations process for ED. The first section of this chapter provides an introduction to key terms and concepts in the federal budget and appropriations process for ED. In addition to those mentioned above, the report includes explanations of terms and concepts such as authorizations versus appropriations; budgetary allocations, discretionary spending caps, and sequestration; transfers and reprogramming; and matching requirements. The second section answers frequently asked questions about federal funding for ED or education in general. These are as follows:

- How much funding does ED receive annually?
- How much does the federal government spend on education?
- Where can information be found about the President's budget request and congressional appropriations for ED?
- How much ED funding is in the congressional budget resolution?
- What is the difference between the amounts in appropriations bills and report language?
- What happens to education funding if annual appropriations are not enacted before the start of the federal fiscal year?
- What happens if an ED program authorization "expires"?

The third section includes a brief description of, and links to, reports and documents that provide more information about budget and appropriations concepts.

In: Key Congressional Reports on Education   ISBN: 978-1-53615-731-4
Editor: Georgia Turner   © 2019 Nova Science Publishers, Inc.

Chapter 1

"AFFIRMATIVE ACTION" AND EQUAL PROTECTION IN HIGHER EDUCATION[*]

Christine J. Back and JD S. Hsin

SUMMARY

When federal courts have analyzed and addressed "affirmative action" in higher education, they have done so in two distinct but related senses, both under the Fourteenth Amendment's guarantee of "equal protection."

The first has its roots in the original sense of "affirmative action:" the *mandatory* use of race by public education systems to eliminate the remnants of state-imposed racial segregation. Because state-sanctioned race segregation in public education violates the Fourteenth Amendment's Equal Protection Clause, in certain cases involving a state's formerly *de jure* segregated public university system, a state's consideration of race in its higher education policies and practices may be an *affirmative obligation*. As the U.S. Supreme Court explained in its consequential 1992 decision *United States v. Fordice*, equal protection may *require* states that formerly maintained *de jure* segregated university

---

[*] This is an edited, reformatted and augmented version of Congressional Research Service, Publication No. R45481, dated January 31, 2019.

systems to consider race for the purpose of eliminating all vestiges of their prior "dual" systems. Drawing upon its precedent addressing racially segregated public schools in the K-12 context, the Court established a three-part legal standard in *Fordice* for evaluating the sufficiency and effectiveness of a state's efforts in "dismantl[ing]" its formerly *de jure* segregated public university system. To that remedial end, mandatory race-conscious measures—in this *de jure* context—are not limited to admissions. Instead, remedies may also address policies and practices relating to academic programs, institutional missions, funding, and other aspects of public university operations.

Outside this *de jure* context, "affirmative action" has come to refer to a different category of race-conscious policies. These involve what the Court at one time called the "benign" use of racial classifications— voluntary measures designed not to remedy past *de jure* discrimination, but to help racial minorities overcome the effects of their earlier exclusion. And for institutions of higher education, the Court has addressed one type of affirmative action policy in particular: the use of race as a factor in admissions decisions, a practice now widely observed by both public and private colleges and universities.

The federal courts have come to subject these voluntary race-conscious policies—"affirmative action" in its perhaps more familiar sense—to a particularly searching form of review known as strict scrutiny. And even though this heightened judicial scrutiny has long been regarded as strict in theory but fatal in fact, the Court's review of race-conscious admissions policies in higher education has proved a notable exception, with the Court having twice upheld universities' use of race as one of many factors considered when assembling their incoming classes. The Court has long grappled with this seeming tension— between the strictness of its scrutiny and its approval of race-conscious admissions policies—beginning with its landmark 1978 decision in *Regents of the University of California v. Bakke* through its 2016 decision in *Fisher v. University of Texas*.

Though the Equal Protection Clause generally concerns public universities and their constitutional obligations under the Fourteenth Amendment, federal statutory law also plays a role in ensuring equal protection in higher education. To that end, Title VI of the Civil Rights Act of 1964 prohibits recipients of federal funding—including private colleges and universities— from, at a minimum, discriminating against students and applicants in a manner that would violate the Equal Protection Clause. Federal agencies, including the Departments of Justice and Education, investigate and administratively enforce institutions' compliance with Title VI.

INTRODUCTION

The last several years have seen renewed debate over the role that race plays in higher education—a debate over "affirmative action." A high-profile lawsuit challenging Harvard University's consideration of race in admitting its incoming classes,[1] and the recent withdrawal of Obama Administration-era guidance addressing similar race-conscious policies,[2] have focused the debate on "affirmative action" in perhaps its more familiar sense: the *voluntary*[3] consideration of student applicants' race as a way of increasing the participation of racial minorities in higher education.[4] Meanwhile, a recent lawsuit involving Maryland's university system has brought renewed attention to "affirmative action" in its other, original sense: the *mandatory* use of race by public higher education systems to eliminate the remnants of state-imposed racial segregation.[5] This chapter addresses "affirmative action" in each of these two senses and discusses how the federal courts have analyzed them under the Fourteenth Amendment's guarantee of "equal protection."[6]

---

[1] *See, e.g.*, Nick Anderson, "Justice Department Criticizes Harvard Admissions in Case Alleging Bias against Asian Americans," WASH. POST (Aug. 30, 2018), https://www.washington post.com/education/2018/08/30/justice-deptcriticizes-harvard-affirmative-action-case.

[2] *See* Press Release, U.S. Dep't of Justice, Office of Public Affairs, "Attorney General Jeff Sessions Rescinds 24 Guidance Documents" (July 3, 2018), https://www.justice.gov/opa/pr/attorney-general-jeff-sessions-rescinds-24-guidance-documents.

[3] As used in this report, a "voluntary" race-conscious measure is one adopted by an institution apart from any legal obligation to do so.

[4] 28 C.F.R. § 42.104(b)(6)(ii) (Department of Justice regulation outlining a voluntary form of "affirmative action" permissible under Title VI of the Civil Rights Act of 1964).

[5] *See, e.g.*, Swann v. Charlotte-Mecklenburg Bd. of Educ., 402 U.S. 1, 22, 28 (1971) (stating that the remedy for state-enforced separation of the races is "to dismantle dual school systems" and approvingly discussing "affirmative action[s]" proper for achieving that end); *cf.* 28 C.F.R. § 42.104(b)(6)(i) (Department of Justice regulation providing, under Title VI of the Civil Rights Act of 1964, that "[i]n administering a program regarding which the recipient has previously discriminated against persons on the ground of race, color, or national origin, the recipient must take affirmative action to overcome the effects of prior discrimination").

[6] U.S. Const. amend. XIV, § 1 (providing that no state shall "deny to any person within its jurisdiction the equal protection of the laws"). This obligation applies with equal force, moreover, to the federal government. *See* Adarand Constructors, Inc. v. Peña, 515 U.S. 200, 217 (1995) (noting that under Supreme Court case law "the equal protection obligations imposed by the Fifth and the Fourteenth Amendments [are] indistinguishable," so that "the standards for federal and state racial classifications [are] the same").

The report first considers "affirmative action" in its original sense: the *mandatory* race-conscious measures that the federal courts have imposed on *de jure* segregated public university systems. The Supreme Court has made clear that a state that had a segregated system of education must eliminate all "vestiges" of that system, including through expressly race-conscious remedies.[7] In its consequential 1992 decision *United States v. Fordice*,[8] the Court charted a three-step inquiry for assessing whether a state has fulfilled that constitutional obligation, examining whether a current policy is traceable to the *de jure* segregated system, has continued discriminatory effect, and can be modified or practicably eliminated consistent with sound educational policy.[9]

Outside this *de jure* context, "affirmative action" has come to refer to a different category of race-conscious policies. These involve what the Court once called the "benign" use of racial classifications[10]—voluntary measures designed not directly to remedy past governmental discrimination, but to increase the representation of racial minorities previously excluded from various societal institutions.[11] And in the context of higher education the Court has addressed one type of policy in particular: the use of race as a factor in admissions decisions, a practice now observed by many public and private colleges and universities.

As this chapter explains, the federal courts have come to subject these voluntary "affirmative action" policies to a particularly searching form of review, known today as strict scrutiny. And they have so far upheld those policies under a single theory: that the educational benefits that flow from a diverse student body uniquely justify some consideration of race when deciding how to assemble an incoming class. To rely on that diversity rationale, however, the Court now requires universities to articulate in

---

[7] United States v. Fordice, 505 U.S. 717, 727-28 (1992).

[8] 505 U.S. 717 (1992).

[9] *Id.* at 731.

[10] Metro Broad., Inc. v. FCC, 497 U.S. 547, 564-65 (1990) (distinguishing "benign race-conscious measures," such as voluntary affirmative action programs, from those that are "'remedial' in the sense of being designed to compensate victims of past governmental or societal discrimination").

[11] *See* 28 C.F.R. § 42.104(b)(6)(ii) (Department of Justice regulation characterizing affirmative action policies as measures designed "to overcome the effects of conditions which resulted in limiting participation by persons of a particular race").

concrete and precise terms what their diversity-related goals are, and why they have chosen those goals in particular.[12] And even once those goals are established, a university must still show that its admissions policy achieves its diversity-related goals as precisely as possible, while ultimately "treat[ing] each applicant as an individual."[13]

Because both lines of cases discussed here have their roots in the Equal Protection Clause, this chapter focuses primarily on public universities, all of which are directly subject to constitutional requirements.[14] But those same requirements apply equally to private colleges and universities that receive federal funds pursuant to Title VI of the Civil Rights Act of 1964 (Title VI or the Act), which similarly prohibits recipients of federal dollars from discriminating on the basis of race.[15] This chapter concludes by discussing the role that Title VI plays in ensuring equal protection in higher education, both public and private, including several avenues for congressional action under the Act.

"AFFIRMATIVE ACTION" AS AFFIRMATIVE OBLIGATION: DISMANTLING *DE JURE* SEGREGATION

De Jure Segregation in Higher Ed and the Equal Protection Clause

Though government-sanctioned racial segregation in public education is commonly associated with primary and secondary schools, numerous

---

[12] Fisher v. Univ. of Texas (*Fisher II*), 136 S. Ct. 2198, 2211 (2016).

[13] Regents of Univ. of Cal. v. Bakke, 438 U.S. 265, 318 (1978).

[14] These obligations apply with equal force, moreover, to the federal government. *See* Adarand Constructors, Inc. v. Peña, 515 U.S. 200, 217 (1995) (noting that under Supreme Court case law "the equal protection obligations imposed by the Fifth and the Fourteenth Amendments [are] indistinguishable," so that "the standards for federal and state racial classifications [are] the same").

[15] 42 U.S.C. § 2000d (barring racial discrimination "under any program or activity receiving Federal financial assistance"); *see also* Alexander v. Sandoval, 532 U.S. 275, 281 (2001) ("tak[ing] as given" that Title VI "proscribes only those racial classifications that would violate the Equal Protection Clause or the Fifth Amendment") (quoting Regents of Univ. of Cal. v. Bakke, 438 U.S. 265, 287 (1978) (Powell, J., announcing judgment of the Court)).

6   *Christine J. Back and JD S. Hsin*

states had also mandated or permitted racial segregation in institutions of higher education, including through the latter part of the 20th century,[16] categorically excluding black students solely because of their race.[17] Though the Supreme Court held decades ago that state-sanctioned racial segregation in higher education violates the Equal Protection Clause,[18] such intentional segregation, or practices arising from formerly *de jure* segregated university systems and their discriminatory effects, may still persist.[19]

Addressing such circumstances, the Supreme Court has held the Equal Protection Clause to require states to eliminate all *vestiges* of their formerly *de jure* segregated public university systems that continue to have discriminatory effect.[20] As the Court concluded in *United States v. Fordice*, state actors "shall be adjudged in violation of the Constitution and Title VI [of the Civil Rights Act]" to the extent they have failed to satisfy this affirmative duty to dismantle a *de jure* segregated public university system.[21] A state actor therefore remains in violation of the Equal Protection Clause *today* if it maintains a policy or practice "traceable" to a formerly *de jure* segregated public university system that continues to

---

[16] *See, e.g., Fordice*, 505 U.S. at 722 (observing that Mississippi's segregated public university system "remained largely intact" through at least 1974).

[17] *See, e.g.*, Pearson v. Murray, 169 Md. 478, 590-91, 594 (1936) (addressing claim in which a black applicant to the state's law school met all standards for admission, but was denied admission "on the sole ground of his color" pursuant to the state's policy of segregating "the races for education"). *See also* Brown v. Board of Educ. of Topeka, Kan., 347 U.S. 483, 491-92 (1954) (explaining that in its cases preceding *Brown* concerning graduate school-level education, "inequality was found in that specific benefits enjoyed by white students were denied to Negro students of the same educational qualifications") (citing State of Missouri ex rel. Gaines v. Canada, 305 U.S. 337 (1938); Sipuel v. Bd. of Regents of Univ. of Okla., 332 U.S. 631 (1948); Sweatt v. Painter, 339 U.S. 629 (1950); and McLaurin v. Okla. State Regents for Higher Educ., 339 U.S. 637 (1950)).

[18] *Brown*, 347 U.S. at 495 (holding that racial segregation in "the field of public education" violates the Equal Protection Clause). *See also, e.g., Fordice*, 505 U.S. at 727-28 (stating that if a state has not discharged its duty to dismantle a segregated public university system, "it remains in violation of the Fourteenth Amendment. *Brown v. Board of Education* and its progeny clearly mandate this observation.").

[19] For example, as of the date of this report, a case pending before the Fourth Circuit alleges that the State of Maryland continues to maintain a variety of policies and practices traceable to its formerly *de jure* segregated higher education system. *See* Coal. for Equity and Excellence in Md. Higher Educ., Inc., et al. v. Md. Higher Educ. Comm'n, No. 17- 2451 (4th Cir.).

[20] United States v. Fordice, 505 U.S. 717, 727-28, 731 (1992).

[21] *Fordice*, 505 U.S. at 743.

"Affirmative Action" and Equal Protection in Higher Education   7

foster racial segregation.[22] Where such a violation is shown, race-conscious measures are not only constitutionally permissible, but may be constitutionally required to remedy and eliminate such unconstitutional remnants.[23]

Segregated Colleges and Universities Before 1954

As in the K-12 context,[24] a number of states maintained racially segregated public university systems and denied black students admission to post-secondary schools—including colleges, law schools, and doctoral programs[25]—on the basis that these institutions educated white students only. Prior to 1954—the year of the Supreme Court's landmark *Brown v. Board of Education* decision (*Brown I*)[26]—the Court had interpreted the Equal Protection Clause to permit state-sanctioned racially segregated public educational systems, provided that the separate schools for black students were substantially equal to those reserved for white students.[27]

---

[22] *See id.* at 731 (holding that a state has not satisfied its burden of proving that it has dismantled its prior system, if such policies are without sound educational justification and can be practicably eliminated).

[23] *See supra* section "The Affirmative Duty to Eliminate *De Jure* Segregation in Higher Education," pp. 6-11.

[24] *Compare* United States v. Montgomery Cty. Bd. Of Educ., 395 U.S. 225, 228 (1969) (discussing the intentional continuation of a racially segregated K-12 public school system in Alabama "in defiance of our repeated unanimous holdings that such a system violated the United States Constitution") *with* Knight v. Alabama, 14 F.3d 1534, 1538 (11th Cir. 1994) (discussing the state's denial of access to black persons to "college-level public higher education").

[25] *See, e.g.,* State of Missouri ex rel. Gaines v. Canada, 305 U.S. 337, 343, 349 (1938) (addressing a challenge to a state law school's refusal to admit a black student based on his race, though he was otherwise qualified for admission and there was no other law school in the state open to black students at the time; stating that "[b]y the operation of the laws of Missouri a privilege has been created for white law students which is denied to negroes by reason of their race.").
See also, e.g., McLaurin v. Okla. State Regents for Higher Educ., 339 U.S. 637, 638-40 (1950) (discussing the denial of plaintiff's admission to a doctoral program "solely because of his race," and his eventual admission to the white-only institution in the absence of a doctoral program at the black-only institutions in the state's segregated system).

[26] 347 U.S. 483, 495 (1954) (*Brown I*) (holding that racial segregation in "the field of public education" violates the Equal Protection Clause).

[27] *See, e.g., Missouri,* 305 U.S. at 344 (discussing the permissibility of a state's compliance with the Equal Protection Clause by providing equal facilities to black students and white

8   *Christine J. Back and JD S. Hsin*

For example, in its 1950 decision *Sweatt v. Painter*,[28] the Court addressed an equal protection claim raised by a black student challenging the University of Texas Law School's denial of his admission based on his race, pursuant to its white-only admissions policy.[29] At the time of the plaintiff's application in 1946, the state did not have a law school that admitted black students.[30] Denying the plaintiff's requested relief for admission, the state trial court instead granted additional time to Texas to create a law school for black students;[31] the state thereafter created a law school at the Texas State University for Negroes.[32] The Supreme Court, however, held that the law school—which, among other features, lacked accreditation[33]—did not offer an education "substantially equal" to that which the plaintiff would receive at the University of Texas Law School.[34] On that basis—the absence of a separate but equivalent legal education— the Court held that the Equal Protection Clause required the plaintiff's admission to the University of Texas Law School.[35]

A decisive turn in the Court's interpretation and application of the Equal Protection Clause, however, came by way of its 1954 decision in *Brown I*.[36] There, the Court held for the first time that race-based segregation "in the field of public education" violates the Equal Protection Clause.[37] The Court concluded that race-based segregation in public

---

students in separate schools) (citing Plessy v. Ferguson, 163 U.S. 537, 544 (1896) and other cases). *See, e.g., Plessy*, 163 U.S. at 548 (stating that "we think the enforced separation of the races, as applied to the internal commerce of the state, neither abridges the privileges or immunities of the colored man ... nor denies him the equal protection of the laws").

[28] 339 U.S. 629 (1950).

[29] *Id*. at 631 (stating that the petitioner's "application was rejected solely because he is a Negro").

[30] *Id*.

[31] *Id*. at 632.

[32] *Id*. at 633 (noting that the state reported the opening of a law school at the Texas State University for Negroes after the trial in that case).

[33] *Id*. (describing the law school as "apparently on the road to full accreditation").

[34] *Id*. at 633-34.

[35] *Id*. at 635-36.

[36] 347 U.S. 483 (1954). *See also* Brown v. Board of Educ. of Topeka, Kan., 349 U.S. 294 (1955) (*Brown II*).

[37] Brown v. Board of Educ. of Topeka, Kan., 347 U.S. 483, 494-95 (1954) ("We conclude that in the field of public education the doctrine of 'separate but equal' has no place. Separate educational facilities are inherently unequal. Therefore, we hold that the plaintiffs and others similarly situated for whom the actions have been brought are, by reason of the segregation complained of, deprived of the equal protection of the laws guaranteed by the

"Affirmative Action" and Equal Protection in Higher Education   9

schools deprives minority students of equal educational opportunities,[38] and observed that segregation commonly denotes inferiority of the minority group.[39] Segregated educational facilities, the Court concluded, are "inherently unequal."[40]

The Court's holding in *Brown I*[41] applies with equal force to public *higher* education—that is, to public colleges and universities[42]—as does the Court's subsequent 1955 decision in the same case ("*Brown II*"),[43] in which the Court addressed how school authorities and federal courts were to implement the mandate of *Brown I*.[44] Indeed, one of the Court's earliest applications of *Brown I* and *Brown II* was in the higher education context. In that case, *State of Fla. Ex. Rel. Hawkins v. Board of Control*,[45] the Supreme Court vacated[46] a Florida supreme court decision that declined to order the state's white-only law school to admit a black student.[47] Relying on language in *Brown II* that courts could consider practical obstacles to a school's transition to desegregation, the Florida court refused to order the

---

Fourteenth Amendment."). *See also id.* (rejecting "[a]ny language in *Plessy v. Ferguson* contrary to this finding").

[38] *Id.* at 493.

[39] *Id.* at 494 (discussing effect of segregation and approvingly quoting a lower court decision finding that the detrimental effect of segregation is "greater when it has the sanction of the law").

[40] *Id.* at 495.

[41] *Id.* (holding that "the plaintiffs and others similarly situated for whom the actions have been brought are, by reason of the segregation complained of, deprived of the equal protection of the laws guaranteed by the Fourteenth Amendment.").

[42] *See, e.g., Fordice*, 505 U.S. at 727-28 ("*Brown v. Board of Education* and its progeny clearly mandate" that a state has a constitutional duty to dismantle its formerly segregated system of higher education, and "remains in violation of the Fourteenth Amendment" if it has not discharged this duty).

[43] *Brown II*, 349 U.S. at 299-301 (addressing the same set of cases at issue in *Brown I*, but directing school districts and courts on the implementation of the Court's holding in *Brown I*; stating that courts should enter orders and decrees "as are necessary and proper" to admit students to public schools on a racially nondiscriminatory basis "with all deliberate speed").

[44] *Id.*

[45] 350 U.S. 413, 414 (1956).

[46] *Id.* at 413-14 (vacating the state court judgment and remanding pursuant to *Brown I* and *Brown II*).

[47] *See* State eN rel. Hawkins v. Bd. of Control, 83 So.2d 20, 21-22, 24-25 (Fla. 1955) (state court decision). *See id.* at 21 (describing its previous holding which had denied the black plaintiff's request to be admitted to the University of Florida's law school on the basis that he had "adequate opportunity for legal education at the Law School of the Florida A & M University, an institution supported by the State of Florida for the higher education of Negroes").

plaintiff's admission.[48] The Supreme Court vacated the state court's decision, concluding that in the case of admitting a black student "to a graduate professional school, there [wa]s no reason for delay" and that he was "entitled to prompt admission under the rules and regulations applicable to other qualified candidates."[49]

The Affirmative Duty to Eliminate *De Jure* Segregation in Higher Education

Following *Brown I* and *Brown II*, the Court's equal protection jurisprudence in the public education context expanded significantly to address questions regarding the *scope* and *sufficiency* of state actions to "dismantle" racially segregated systems in public school districts across the country,[50] and various challenges to district court-ordered remedies.[51] As the Court revisited these legal standards over time, it continued to describe the affirmative duty of formerly segregated public school entities

---

[48] *Hawkins*, 83 So.2d at 24-25 (concluding that *Brown II* did not require the university to admit the black plaintiff "immediately, or at any particular time in the future," but rather that "the state courts shall apply equitable principles in the determination of the precise time in any given jurisdiction"). *Cf. Brown II*, 349 U.S. at 299-301.

[49] *Hawkins*, 350 U.S. at 414.

[50] *See, e.g.*, Green v. Cty Sch. Bd. of New Kent Cty., Va., 391 U.S. 430, 433-34, 438-39 (1968) (holding that Virginia school district's "freedom of choice" plan allowing students to choose between attending a formerly white-only school or a formerly black-only school could "not be accepted as a sufficient step" to desegregate, in light of evidence including that in the three years under that plan, no white child had chosen to attend the formerly all-black school while some black children had chosen to attend the formerly all-white school; stating that the plan "has operated simply to burden children and their parents with the responsibility which *Brown II* placed squarely on the School Board."). *See generally*, Swann v. Charlotte-Mecklenburg Bd. of Educ., 402 U.S. 1, 18-21 (1971) (concluding that "the first remedial responsibility of school authorities is to eliminate invidious racial distinctions" with respect to matters such as faculty, the quality and maintenance of school buildings, equipment, transportation, support personnel, athletics, and extracurricular activities, and that local authorities and district courts must "see to it that future school construction and abandonment are not used and do not serve to perpetuate or re-establish the dual system.").

[51] *See, e.g.*, Missouri v. Jenkins, 515 U.S. 70, 86-94 (1995) (addressing a state's challenge to the scope of a district court's ordered desegregation remedy and discussing the Court's earlier precedent analyzing the permissible scope of a court's authority to fashion remedies for equal protection violations).

"Affirmative Action" and Equal Protection in Higher Education 11

as the duty to "take all steps necessary to eliminate the vestiges of the unconstitutional *de jure* system"[52] to the extent practicable.[53] Turning to the context of higher education, the Court addressed, in its 1992 decision *United States v. Fordice*,[54] how these equal protection principles and legal standards apply to a state's affirmative duty to dismantle a formerly *de jure* segregated public university system.

United States v. Fordice (1992)

Though it had "many occasions to evaluate whether a public school district has met its affirmative obligation to dismantle its prior *de jure* segregated system in elementary and secondary schools," the Court explained, *Fordice* presented the issue of "what standards to apply" in determining whether the state has met this obligation in the university context.[55]

At issue before the Court was Mississippi's prior *de jure* public university system. The Court observed that since establishing the University of Mississippi as an institution of "higher education exclusively of white persons" in 1848, Mississippi had created four more exclusively white institutions and three exclusively black institutions through 1950.[56] Thereafter, it continued to maintain its racially segregated public university system, and admitted its first black student to the University of Mississippi in 1962 "only by court order."[57] For the "next 12 years," the state's segregated university system "remained largely intact."[58] Around 1987,

---

[52] Freeman v. Pitts, 503 U.S. 467, 485 (1992); *Swann*, 402 U.S. at 15 ("The objective today remains to eliminate from the public schools all vestiges of state-imposed segregation.").

[53] *See* Bd. of Educ. of Okla. City Pub. Sch., Indep. Sch. Dist. No. 89, Okla. Cty., Okla, 498 U.S. 237, 249-50 (1991) (in order to determine whether the vestiges of *de jure* segregation have been eliminated "as far as practicable," instructing the district to examine student assignments, as well as "'every facet of school operations—faculty, staff, transportation, extra-curricular activities and facilities'") (quoting *Green*, 391 U.S. at 435).

[54] 505 U.S. 717 (1992).

[55] *Fordice*, 505 U.S. at 721.

[56] *Id.* (identifying the institutions exclusively for white persons as the University of Mississippi (1848), Mississippi State University (1880), Mississippi University for Women (1885), University of Southern Mississippi (1912), and Delta State University (1925); and identifying the institutions exclusively for black persons as Alcorn State University (1871), Jackson State University (1940), and Mississippi Valley State University (1950)).

[57] *Id.* at 722.

[58] *Id.*

when the case went to trial,[59] over 99 percent of the state's white students attended the five universities that had been formerly white-only, while the three formerly black-only institutions had student bodies between 92 percent to 99 percent black.[60]

Citing its precedent addressing *de jure* segregation in the K-12 context,[61] the Court stated that "[o]ur decisions establish that a [s]tate does *not* satisfy its constitutional obligations until it eradicates policies and practices traceable to its prior de jure dual system that continue to foster segregation."[62] Perhaps critically, in the context of remedying a formerly *de jure* segregated system, a state's "adoption and implementation of race-neutral policies *alone*" is not sufficient to demonstrate that it has "completely abandoned its prior dual system."[63] Aside from segregative admissions policies, the Court explained, a state's other policies may shape and determine student choice and attendance, and continue to foster segregation.[64]

Instead, to determine whether a state has satisfied its affirmative duty to dismantle its *de jure* public university system, the Court set out a three-step analysis. *First*, the analysis examines whether the challenged policy or practice maintained by the state is "traceable to its prior [*de jure*] system."[65] By way of example, the Court identified four policies[66] that, in its view, were "readily apparent" vestiges of *de jure* segregation:

---

[59] *Id.* at 723-25.

[60] *Id.* at 724-25.

[61] *Id.* at 728 (citing Freeman v. Pitts, 503 U.S. 467 (1992); Bazemore v. Friday, 478 U.S. 385, 407 (1986) (White, J., concurring); Pasadena City Bd. of Educ. v. Spangler, 427 U.S. 424, 434 (1976); Gilmore v. City of Montgomery, 417 U.S. 556, 566-67 (1974); Bd. of Educ. of Okla. City Pub. Sch. v. Dowell, 498 U.S. 237, 250 (1991); Swann v. Charlotte-Mecklenburg Bd. of Educ., 402 U.S. 1, 18 (1971); Green v. Cty. Sch. Bd. of New Kent Cty, 391 U.S. 430, 435-38 (1968)).

[62] *Fordice*, 505 U.S. at 728 (emphasis added).

[63] *Id.* at 729 (emphasis added). The Court agreed with the court of appeals below that there were relevant differences between the K-12 and higher education systems—namely, student choice as to which public university to attend, if one at all, in contrast to compulsory attendance for K-12, but expressly rejected the court of appeals' conclusion that because university attendance was largely a function of student choice, the state need only adopt race-neutral admissions policies to satisfy its affirmative duty. *See id.* at 727-29.

[64] *Id.*

[65] *See id.* at 731 ("If the State perpetuates policies and practices traceable to its prior system that continue to have segregative effects—whether by influencing student enrollment decisions or by fostering segregation in other facets of the university system—and such policies are

"Affirmative Action" and Equal Protection in Higher Education   13

- admissions standards based on a test-score range originally adopted for discriminatory reasons;[67]
- unnecessary program duplication throughout the university system (e.g., multiple institutions offering the same "nonbasic" courses);[68]
- the state's **academic mission** assignments to its higher education institutions (e.g., assigning the broadest academic missions to only formerly white-only institutions and the narrowest academic mission to a formerly black-only institution);[69] and
- the continued operation of all public universities established in the *de jure* segregated system.[70]

With respect to traceability, the Court's analysis reflects that where a current policy functions based on distinctions or a framework created in a formerly *de jure* system, traceability can be shown. For example, when concluding that the state's designation of academic missions to its universities was traceable to *de jure* segregation, the Court cited evidence that the state's current method of assigning its universities into three

---

without sound educational justification and can be practicably eliminated, the State has not satisfied its burden of proving that it has dismantled its prior system.").

[66] *Id.* at 733 (adding that it was "important to state at the outset that we make no effort to identify an exclusive list of unconstitutional remnants of Mississippi's prior *de jure* system," and that by highlighting four policies, "we by no means suggest that the Court of Appeals need not examine, in light of the proper standard, each of the other policies" that were challenged or are challenged on remand in light of the Court's articulation of the applicable standard).

[67] *See, e.g., Fordice,* 505 U.S. at 734-38 (analyzing the state's admissions policy based solely on minimum test scores and concluding the current policy was traceable to the *de jure* system and that the test score minimums had been discriminatorily set to exclude black students from admission to formerly white-only institutions; also concluding that the state had failed to show that its admissions standard was "not susceptible to elimination without eroding sound educational policy").

[68] *Id.* at 738 (explaining that unnecessary program duplication "was part and parcel of the prior dual system of higher education," as "the whole notion of 'separate but equal' required duplicative programs in two sets of schools").

[69] *Id.* at 740 (concluding that the state's "institutional mission designations adopted in 1981 have as their antecedents the policies enacted to perpetuate racial separation during the *de jure* segregated regime.").

[70] *Id.* at 741-42 (observing that the continued existence of all eight of the state's universities created in the *de jure* system, instead of a lesser number of universities, "was undoubtedly occasioned by state laws forbidding the mingling of the races" and thus traceable to *de jure* segregation; also noting the district court's finding that Delta State and Mississippi Valley State were 35 miles apart, while Mississippi State and Mississippi University for Women were "only 20 miles" apart).

academic missions levels[71] largely mirrored a three-tiered grouping of its universities in the *de jure* system.[72] In addition and more generally, an interim change or new, nondiscriminatory justification for a current policy does not necessarily sever its traceability to a *de jure* system.[73] Where the traceability of a policy or policies is shown, a party need not show discriminatory intent with respect to those challenged policies.[74]

Where traceability is *not* shown—that is, where the policies "do not have such historical antecedents" to *de jure* segregation—an equal protection challenge would then require "a showing of discriminatory purpose."[75] In those instances, the Court explained, "the question becomes whether the fact of racial separation establishes a new violation of the Fourteenth Amendment under traditional principles."[76]

Second, once traceability is shown, the analysis turns to whether those traceable policies have continued discriminatory or "segregative" effects in student choice, enrollment, or other facets of the university system.[77] At

---

[71] *Id.* at 740 (identifying the current academic mission designations as "comprehensive," "regional," and "urban").

[72] *Id.* at 739-41 (concluding that current academic mission assignments were traceable to *de jure* academic mission assignments, which had assigned three formerly white-only institutions the most expansive mission and programs, the formerly white-only liberal arts and women's colleges a more limited mission and programming, and the formerly black-only institutions the most limited mission and programming of all three).

[73] *Id.* at 734 (concluding that the state's "midpassage justification for perpetuating a policy enacted originally to discriminate against black students does not make the present admissions standards any less constitutionally suspect").

[74] *Id.* at 733 n.8 (explaining that the plaintiffs "need not show such discriminatory intent to establish a constitutional violation for the perpetuation of policies traceable to the prior *de jure* segregative regime which have continuing discriminatory effects"). *See also id.* at 746 (Thomas, J., concurring) (expressing the view that "we are justified in not requiring proof of a present specific intent to discriminate" when the three elements of the legal standard adopted in *Fordice* are met, as "[i]t is safe to assume that a policy adopted during the *de jure* era, if it produces segregative effects, reflects a discriminatory intent"). *See also, e.g.*, Knight v. Alabama, 14 F.3d 1534, 1540-41 (11th Cir. 1994) (explaining that "the burden of proof lies with the charging party to show that a challenged contemporary policy is traceable to past segregation").

[75] *Fordice*, 505 U.S. at 733 n.8 (explaining that in the absence of traceability, "a claim of violation of the Fourteenth Amendment cannot be made out without a showing of discriminatory purpose").

[76] *Id.* at 731 n.6 (citing Bd. of Educ. of Okla. City Pub. Sch. v. Dowell, 498 U.S. 237, 250-51 (1991); Arlington Heights v. Metro. Hous. Dev. Corp., 429 U.S. 252 (1977)). *See also supra* section "Racial Segregation and Discriminatory Intent," pp. 15-20.

[77] *Id. See also, e.g., id.* at 734 (after concluding that the admissions policy at issue was "traceable to the *de jure* system," finding that "they also have present discriminatory effects").

"Affirmative Action" and Equal Protection in Higher Education   15

this stage, the Court noted that a court should not consider "this issue in isolation," but rather examine the "combined effects" of all the challenged policies together "in evaluating whether the State ha[s] met its duty to dismantle its prior *de jure* segregated system."[78] In light of this instruction, it appears the focus of the second step of the test is not on establishing causation between specific racial disparities and specific policies—by this stage, a court has already found traceability—but rather to evaluate whether a state has sufficiently dismantled its formerly *de jure* system.[79] Consistent with the state's burden of proving it has dismantled its *de jure* segregated system, the state must show the absence of segregative effects;[80] plaintiffs are not required to establish this second element.[81]

Third, because traceable policies that have discriminatory effects "run afoul of the Equal Protection Clause,"[82] such policies must accordingly "be reformed to the extent practicable and consistent with sound educational practices."[83] Thus, at the third step, a court assesses whether traceable policies can be "practicably eliminated" "consistent with sound educational

---

[78] *Id.* at 738-39 (stating that the district court had "failed to consider the combined effects of unnecessary program duplication with other policies, such as differential admissions standards, in evaluating whether the State had met its duty to dismantle its prior *de jure* segregated system"; also noting that the district court's treatment of this issue was "problematic"). *See, e.g., Knight*, 14 F.3d at 1551 (instructing the lower court on remand to determine whether the traceable practice of discriminatory funding allocations, "in combination with other policies, has continuing segregative effects as required under the second part of the *Fordice* test.").

[79] *See Fordice*, 505 U.S. at 739 (describing the analysis of "combined effects" to "evaluat[e] whether the State ha[s] met its duty to dismantle its prior *de jure* segregated system.").

[80] *See id.* at 739 (stating that, as "*Brown* and its progeny" established that the burden of proof falls on the state "to establish that it has dismantled its prior *de jure* segregated system," it was erroneous for the district court to hold "that petitioners could not establish the constitutional defect of unnecessary duplication" which "improperly shifted the burden away from the State"). *See also, e.g., Knight*, 14 F.3d at 1541 (interpreting *Fordice* to require that the state prove that the challenged policy has no segregative effects to be "relieved of its duty to eliminate or modify" that policy).

[81] *Supra* note 80.

[82] *Fordice*, 505 U.S. at 731-32 ("Such policies run afoul of the Equal Protection Clause, even though the State has abolished the legal requirement that whites and blacks be educated separately and has established racially neutral policies not animated by a discriminatory purpose.").

[83] *Id.* at 729.

practices,"[84] with the burden on the state to show that the challenged policies are "not susceptible to elimination without eroding sound educational policy."[85] Because the Court remanded the case to the lower court to address practicable elimination, its analysis in *Fordice* on this point is limited.[86] The Court suggested, however, that if a current policy lacks sound educational justification, it reasonably follows that it can be practicably eliminated in part or in whole.[87] In addition, the Court observed that in some cases, a merger or closure of institutions could be constitutionally required to eliminate vestiges, should other methods fail to eliminate their discriminatory effects.[88] Finally, the Court repeatedly stated that so long as vestiges remain, which have discriminatory effects, the state remains in violation of the Equal Protection Clause unless it can show it cannot practicably eliminate those policies or practices.[89]

In addition, Justice O'Connor, in a separate concurring opinion in *Fordice*, emphasized the "narrow" circumstances under which a state could maintain a traceable policy or practice with segregative effects.[90] In her

---

[84] *Id.* at 731, 741 (stating that on remand, "the court should inquire whether it would be practicable and consistent with sound educational practices to eliminate" the discriminatory effects of the state's present policy).

[85] *See, e.g., id.* at 738 (concluding that the state had thus far failed to show that its admissions standard was "not susceptible to elimination without eroding sound educational policy."). *See also id.* at 744 (O'Connor, J., concurring) (expressing the view that even "if the State shows that maintenance of certain remnants of its prior system is essential to accomplish its legitimate goals, then it still must prove that it has counteracted and minimized the segregative impact of such policies to the extent possible").

[86] *See, e.g., id.* at 741 (stating that on remand, the court "should inquire whether it would be practicable and consistent with sound educational practices to eliminate any such discriminatory effects of the State's present policy").

[87] *Id.* at 739 (stating that "implicit" in the district court's finding that program duplication was "unnecessary" was the fact that the practice lacked "any educational justification" and "that some, if not all, duplication may be practicably eliminated.").

[88] *Id.* at 742 (noting that "certainly closure of one or more institutions would decrease the discriminatory effects of the present system" and observing that eliminating or revising other challenged policies "may make institutional closure unnecessary," but directing that on remand, "this issue should be carefully explored").

[89] *See, e.g., id.* at 743 ("To the extent that the State has not met its affirmative obligation to dismantle its prior dual system, it shall be adjudged in violation of the Constitution and Title VI and remedial proceedings shall be conducted."). *See also, e.g., id.* at 730 ("Thus, even after a State dismantles its segregative *admissions* policy, there may still be state action that is traceable to the State's prior *de jure* segregation and that continues to foster segregation. The Equal Protection Clause is offended by 'sophisticated as well as simple-minded modes of discrimination.'").

[90] *Id.* at 744 (O'Connor, J., concurring).

"Affirmative Action" and Equal Protection in Higher Education 17

view, courts may "infer lack of good faith" on the part of the state if it could accomplish educational objectives through less segregative means, and the state has a "'heavy burden'" to explain its preference for retaining the challenged practice.[91] Moreover, even if the state shows that retaining certain traceable policies or practices is "essential to accomplish its legitimate goals," Justice O'Connor asserted that the state must still prove it has "counteracted and minimized the segregative impact of such policies to the extent possible."[92]

Flagship Universities and Historically Black Colleges and Universities (HBCUs)

The Court in *Fordice* observed that the closure or merger of certain institutions may be constitutionally required,[93] consistent with its holding that any vestige of a *de jure* segregated system that continues to have discriminatory effect must be eliminated to the extent practicable and consistent with sound educational policy.[94] Yet that invited a new—and more difficult—set of questions: which institutions would be most subject to closure or merger, and under what circumstances would such action be required?

Significantly, the Court did not categorically identify which institutions would be most subject to such remedial action[95]—a state's flagship, formerly white-only institutions from which a *de jure* system originated, for example, or formerly black-only institutions created to preserve white-only admission at other institutions. Instead, the Court concluded that it was unable to determine—on the record presented in *Fordice*—whether closures or mergers were required in that case[96] and directed the lower court on remand to "carefully explore" several considerations.[97] This instruction to the lower court, while not part of the

---

[91] *Id.* (O'Connor, J., concurring).
[92] *Id.* (O'Connor, J., concurring).
[93] *Id.* at 742.
[94] *Id.* at 731, 741-42.
[95] *See id.* at 741-42.
[96] *Id.* at 742 (noting that the "[e]limination of program duplication and revision of admissions criteria may make institutional closure unnecessary").
[97] *Id.*

holding in *Fordice*, suggests that several factors are relevant for determining whether merger or closure is constitutionally required.[98] In addition, the Court observed that maintaining all eight higher education institutions in Mississippi was "wasteful and irrational," particularly in light of the close geographic proximity between some of the universities.[99] This observation suggests that close proximity between institutions offering similar programs could be a relevant factor in assessing remedial closure or merger as well.[100]

Regarding the fate of a state's historically black institutions, Justice Thomas, in a concurring opinion, did not read *Fordice* to "forbid[]" those institutions' continued operation or "foreclose the possibility that there exists 'sound educational justification' for maintaining historically black colleges *as such*."[101] Justice Thomas emphasized that "[d]espite the shameful history of state-enforced segregation," historically black colleges and universities were and remain institutions critical to the academic flourishing and leadership development[102] of many students, and observed that "[i]t would be ironic, to say the least, if the institutions that sustained blacks during segregation were themselves destroyed in an effort to combat its vestiges."[103] In his view, though a state is not constitutionally required

---

[98] *Id.* (instructing the lower court to consider (1) whether the retention of all institutions itself affects student choice and perpetuates segregation; (2) "whether maintenance of each of the universities is educationally justifiable"; and (3) whether one or more "can be practicably closed or merged with other existing institutions").

[99] *Id.* at 741-42 (noting district court findings that two institutions were "only 35 miles apart," while another two institutions were "only 20 miles" from each other).

[100] *Id. Cf.* Geier v. Univ. of Tenn., 597 F.2d 1056, 1064-71 (6th Cir. 1979). In *Geier*, a pre-*Fordice* decision, the Sixth Circuit affirmed a district court's order of a merger of two geographically proximate institutions as a remedy for the state's failure to satisfy its affirmative duty to dismantle its segregated higher education system. *Id.* at 1068-69. The approved merger was of the Nashville campus of the formerly white-only University of Tennessee (UT-N) and the formerly black-only Tennessee State University (TSU), also located in Nashville. *Id.* at 1068-70. The court of appeals noted that the "core of the problem" was that UT-N, as a four-year degree-granting institution in Nashville, created competition for white students in the Nashville area and "greatly inhibited the efforts to desegregate TSU." *Id.* at 1068. The two institutions merged in 1979 to become one institution under TSU. *See History of Avon Williams Campus*, Tenn. State Univ., http://www.tnstate.edu/library/avonwilliamslibrary/history.aspx (last visited Sept. 19, 2018).

[101] *Fordice*, 505 U.S. at 748-49 (Thomas, J., concurring) (emphasis in original).

[102] *Id.* at 748 (Thomas, J., concurring).

[103] *Id.* at 749 (Thomas, J., concurring).

"Affirmative Action" and Equal Protection in Higher Education   19

to maintain its historically black institutions as such, their continued operation is constitutionally permissible, so long as admission is open to all students "on a race-neutral basis, but with established traditions and programs that might disproportionately appeal to one race or another."[104]

Legal Challenges Following Fordice

Following *Fordice*, plaintiffs, including the United States in Title VI enforcement actions,[105] have brought suit challenging practices allegedly traceable to a state's *de jure* segregated university system. Challenged practices have included unnecessary program duplication,[106] which the Court identified in *Fordice* as one of the "readily apparent" remnants of *de jure* segregation, as well as others such as scholarship policies,[107] funding practices,[108] and the use of curricula at formerly white-only institutions with little representation of black history and culture.[109] More recently, in 2018, a legal challenge against the State of Maryland alleged that practices

---

[104] *Id.* (Thomas, J., concurring) (adding that a state's operation of "a diverse assortment of institutions," including historically black institutions, contributes to institutional diversity among a state's higher education institutions, and that such institutional diversity is not "even remotely akin to program *duplication*, which is designed to separate the races for the sake of separating the races").

[105] *See, e.g.*, Knight v. Alabama, 14 F.3d 1534, 1539 (11th Cir. 1994) (describing procedural history of case; explaining that the United States filed suit under Title VI, and was later joined by private plaintiffs). *See also* Ayers v. Fordice, 111 F.3d 1183, 1190-92 (5th Cir. 1997) (explaining history of challenge to Mississippi's public university system, including the Supreme Court's *Fordice* decision and later proceedings on remand; stating that private plaintiffs initiated the class action, and the United States intervened as plaintiff alleging violations of Title VI and the Equal Protection Clause).

[106] *See Ayers*, 111 F.3d at 1217-1221; *Knight*, 14 F.3d at 1539 (stating that plaintiffs had challenged policies such as program duplication; certain admissions standards; the underrepresentation of blacks in faculty, administration, and on governing boards; campus environments hostile to black students; the denial of adequate funding and facilities to formerly black-only institutions, and the denial of graduate and other desirable programs based on restrictive institutional missions, among others).

[107] *See, e.g., Ayers*, 111 F.3d at 1203-09 (analyzing challenge to scholarship policies).

[108] *See id.*, 111 F.3d at 1216-17 (analyzing challenge to state's allocation of land grant funding); *Knight*, 14 F.3d at 1546-52 (same).

[109] *See Knight*, 14 F.3d at 1552-53 (analyzing curriculum claim and rejecting argument that public universities' First Amendment right to academic freedom is as an absolute bar to a *Fordice* challenge to curriculm; on remand, noting it was possible that "First Amendment concerns should be considered when assessing whether relief should be granted," but declining to address "whether the curriculum claim indeed implicates First Amendment concerns and, if so, what form of legal analysis ought to be applied to take those concerns into account").

relating to capital and operational funding, unnecessary program duplication, and the limited institutional missions of the state's formerly black-only institutions[110] are traceable to the state's formerly *de jure* segregated higher education system.

To date, however, only a few federal appellate courts have had occasion to analyze *Fordice*-based claims,[111] and the Supreme Court has not, since its 1992 decision, addressed claims challenging higher education policies or practices as unconstitutional vestiges of *de jure* segregation. Though development of the *Fordice* standard in federal case law is limited, the few appellate decisions applying *Fordice* provide at least some analytical examples and reflect discernible differences in approach, particularly with respect to the evidence sufficient to satisfy the third element of the *Fordice* standard—that elimination of a practice is not possible, despite being traceable and having continued discriminatory effect.

---

[110] *See* Coal. for Equity and Excellence in Md. Higher Educ., Inc. et al. v. Md. Higher Educ. Comm'n, 977 F. Supp. 2d 507, 523-34 (D. Md. 2013) (analyzing traceability with respect to plaintiffs' claims). As of the publication date of this report, the case is pending before the U.S. Court of Appeals for the Fourth Circuit. *See* Coal. for Equity and Excellence in Md. Higher Educ., Inc., et al. v. Md. Higher Educ. Comm'n, No. 17-2451 (4th Cir.).

[111] *See, e.g.*, United States v. Louisiana, 9 F.3d 1159, 1165-68 (5th Cir. 1993) (applying *Fordice* to analyze claims challenging unnecessary program duplication throughout the university system, a four-board governing structure, and an "open admissions" policy); Knight v. Alabama, 14 F.3d 1534, 1542-53 (11th Cir. 1994) (applying *Fordice* to analyze claims challenging academic mission assignments, allocations of federal land grants and state funding, the underrepresentation of African American thought, culture, and history in the general curriculum of formerly white-only institutions, and a continued climate of racial hostility at those institutions); Ayers v. Fordice, 111 F.3d 1183, 1197- 1228 (5th Cir. 1997) (applying *Fordice* on remand to analyze remaining claims, including the admissions policy, scholarship policies, allocations of federal land grants and state funding, and the underemployment of black faculty beyond entry-level hires, among other challenged practices). *See also* Geier v. Univ. of Tenn., 597 F.2d 1056, 1064-71 (6th Cir. 1979) (pre-*Fordice* decision holding that the state has an affirmative duty to eliminate the vestiges of a dual system in the context of higher education and affirming the district court's order of a merger of two institutions as a remedy for the state's failure to satisfy its affirmative duty). The case ultimately resolved in a consent decree in 2001, with the stated objective of the agreement being to—pursuant to *Fordice*—eradicate policies traceable to the state's *de jure* segregated system that continue to foster segregation. Geier v. Sundquist, 128 F. Supp.2d 519, 521 (M.D. Tenn. 2001).

Unnecessary Program Duplication: Program Transfers to Mergers

As discussed above, the Supreme Court in *Fordice* identified "unnecessary program duplication" as a practice traceable to the prior *de jure* segregated system of higher education at issue in that case,[112] stating that "it can hardly be denied" that such duplication was a requisite feature of the prior dual system because "the whole notion of 'separate but equal' required duplicative programs in two sets of schools."[113] Drawing upon that rationale, courts that have addressed unnecessary program duplication have generally had little difficulty tracing duplicative courses and degree programs to prior *de jure* segregation.[114] On the matter of if and how program duplication might be eliminated, however, there is lesser consensus.[115] Generally, federal courts have considered several methods for eliminating program duplication, such as transferring existing programs from one institution to another, eliminating certain programs altogether, creating cooperative programs, and—perhaps most drastically—merging institutions.[116]

---

[112] *See Fordice*, 505 U.S. at 733 (emphasizing that its identification of certain remnants of Mississippi's *de jure* system was not an "exclusive list of unconstitutional remnants," and highlighting program duplication as one such remnant made "readily apparent" from the district and appellate courts' findings of fact in that case).

[113] *Id.* at 738.

[114] *See, e.g., Ayers*, 111 F.3d at 1220-21 (accepting finding that unnecessary program duplication between geographically proximate institutions was traceable to *de jure* segregation); United States v. Louisiana, 9 F.3d at 1165 66 (explaining that when racially segregated institutions were established under state law, "program duplication was intentional—to insure that the two sets of schools were 'separate but equal.'"). *See also Ayers*, 111 F.3d at 1218 (explaining that the district court, when analyzing program duplication in general, found that duplicative offerings between racially identifiable institutions supported a "'serious inference'" that the duplication continued to promote segregation) (quoting Ayers v. Fordice, 879 F. Supp. 1419, 1445 (N.D. Miss. 1995)).

[115] *Cf. Louisiana*, 9 F.3d at 1168-70 (holding that there were factual questions on the practicability of transferring programs to eliminate program duplication; citing evidence including that faculty would be reluctant to transfer to another university); with *Ayers*, 111 F.3d at 1220-21 (with respect to remedying unnecessary program duplication, concluding that the district court should order the Board of Trustees to study and report to a monitoring committee on program duplication between two universities, and noting that the district court had also ordered such a study of a third university in the system).

[116] *See, e.g., Ayers*, 111 F.3d at 1221; *Louisiana*, 9 F.3d at 1169 (stating that suggested remedies before the district court had included program transfers from one institution to another, merger, cooperative programs, and the elimination of certain programs to establish new programs). *See also Geier*, 597 F.2d at 1068-1071 (approving merger of two institutions and expressing no concern over possible disruption that could result from the proposed remedy). As the 1979 *Geier* decision predates *Fordice*, the Sixth Circuit did not expressly analyze

Challenges to Disproportionate Allocations of Federal and State Land Grants

Plaintiffs have also raised equal protection challenges to state funding practices that allocate all or most of their federal and state land grants to institutions that were formerly white-only in a *de jure* system while dedicating significantly less or no funds to formerly black-only institutions.[117] More specifically, these cases have concerned a state's allocation of federal land grants provided annually to support research on agricultural issues and the dissemination or "extension" of that research.[118]

At issue in *Knight v. Alabama*, for example, was the State of Alabama's allocation of federal funds between its two land grant universities, Auburn University, formerly white-only in the *de jure* system, and Alabama A&M University (A&M), formerly established as black-only.[119] The state allocated to Auburn the entirety of Alabama's approximately $4 million in federal aid for agricultural research, and allocated an additional $14 million to Auburn in state funds.[120] Meanwhile, the state had "for years" allocated no federal aid to A&M[121] and given state funds for agricultural research in amounts that "today still totals less than $200,000 each year."[122] The U.S. Court of Appeals for the Eleventh Circuit held that the state's current funding allocation was traceable to *de jure*

---

unnecessary program duplication or practicable elimination as later set forth in *Fordice*. Nonetheless, the court of appeals discussed district court findings that the continued operation of both schools impeded desegregation, *Geier*, 597 F.2d at 1059-63, 1068, and evidence supporting the workability and need for a merger. *Id.* at 1064, 1068-71.

[117] *Ayers*, 111 F.3d at 1215-17, 1221-25 (analyzing claim challenging the State of Mississippi's allocation of federal land grant aid and state funding through general legislative appropriations annually and line item appropriations); *Knight*, 14 F.3d at 1546-52 (analyzing claim challenging Alabama's allocation of federal land grant and state funding).

[118] *Ayers*, 111 F.3d at 1215-16 (discussing federal land grant aid for research pursuant to the Hatch Act, and federal land grant aid for "extension services" pursuant to the Smith-Lever Act); *Knight*, 14 F.3d at 1546-47 (same).

[119] *Knight*, 14 F.3d at 1546. *See also id.* at 1538-39, 1542 (describing the founding of the state's universities).

[120] *Id.* at 1547.

[121] *Id.* (explaining that federal aid to A&M changed in the late 1960s, "mostly pursuant" to a federal law that expressly designated A&M as a recipient and denied the State of Alabama discretion to reallocate the approximately $1.4 million in aid elsewhere).

[122] *Id.*

"Affirmative Action" and Equal Protection in Higher Education 23

segregation[123] and instructed the lower court on remand to make determinations with respect to the second and third parts of the *Fordice* test.[124] On the issue of practicable elimination, the Eleventh Circuit observed that reduced efficiency would not necessarily render a proposed modification impracticable or educationally unsound.[125]

By contrast, the Fifth Circuit affirmed a district court's ruling that permitted a state to retain its traceable funding practices.[126] There, despite finding traceability and discriminatory effects,[127] the district court had concluded, based on inefficiencies related to running more than one agricultural research program, that it was not practicable for the state to eliminate its exclusive funding allocation to its formerly white-only land grant institution.[128]

Open Questions after *Fordice*

The Supreme Court has not revisited its analysis in *Fordice*, leaving open questions about the permissible applications of its three-part legal standard to an array of fact patterns and legal theories. Similarly, as discussed above, few courts of appeals have addressed claims under *Fordice*, limiting the development and interpretation of *Fordice* in federal case law.

---

[123] *Knight,* 14 F.3d at 1551-52 (holding that, based on the district court's factual findings, traceability was established).

[124] *Id.* at 1551.

[125] *Id.* at 1551 ("In other words, even if it were true that partial reallocation of the land grant funds would result in a research and extension system somewhat less efficient than the one currently operating under Auburn's monopoly, it would not inescapably follow that such inefficiency would render the proposed modified system impracticable or educationally unsound."). *See also id.* at 1541 (concerning practicable elimination generally, discussing *Fordice* and concluding that a state can retain a traceable practice only "where, in effect, it simply is not possible" to eliminate or modify it).

[126] *Ayers,* 111 F.3d at 1217.

[127] *Id.* at 1216 (discussing district court findings).

[128] *See id.* (discussing district court findings that the creation of two separate agricultural research programs would be "inefficient," as "fewer and fewer" persons were entering the field of agriculture, and that two distinct programs would create "difficulties in communication among the participating scientists, and inefficient duplication.").

One such unresolved question is under what circumstances, if any, traceability can be established under *Fordice* when a state makes changes to an originally discriminatory policy such that the current policy functions differently, but there is still *some* evidence of traceability between the two, or perpetuation of similar segregative effects under the changed policy as under the original policy.[129] In addition, the Supreme Court and circuit courts have not yet expressly addressed how far a district court may go in remedying an unconstitutional vestige or remnant of a prior *de jure* public university system.[130] In the K-12 context, the Supreme Court has upheld district court orders that set certain faculty and student ratios at schools in noncompliant school districts, to desegregate them pursuant to *Brown* and its progeny.[131] It remains unclear, however, whether the district courts enjoy similar authority under *Fordice* to order similarly extensive remedies. Indeed, the few cases alleging *Fordice*-type claims that did reach

---

[129] Such circumstances appeared to be at issue in *Ayers*, where the Fifth Circuit analyzed a challenge to the state's general and line item legislative appropriations, and the "dearth" of black faculty and administrators at formerly white-only institutions. *See Ayers*, 111 F.3d at 1221-27. On the faculty issue, for example, the Fifth Circuit affirmed the district court's conclusion that there were no current employment or hiring practices traceable to *de jure* segregation, though the district court had also found that the racial predominance of faculty and administrators at formerly white-only institutions was "'to some extent attributable to *de jure* segregation.'" *Id.* at 1226-27.

[130] Settlements resolving these cases reflect agreement to take actions related to student enrollment and faculty representation. For example, the settlement resolving the *Ayers* case set a student enrollment goal at formerly black institutions of 10% other-race students (with other-race referring to persons who are not African American), though the agreement does not appear to have required a student enrollment goal for the formerly white-only institutions. *See* Ayers v. Musgrove, No. 75-9 (N.D. Miss. 2001) (Settlement Agreement, pp. 10-12). *See also, e.g.*, Geier v. Sundquist, 128 F. Supp.2d 519, 536-37 (M.D. Tenn. 2001) (directing that state funds be made available to recruit African American scholars as visiting professors).

[131] *See, e.g.*, United States v. Montgomery Cty. Bd. of Educ., 395 U.S. 225, 231-36 (1969) (reversing court of appeals' judgment striking aspects of district court remedial order requiring a ratio of black to white faculty in each school; the district court had ordered, for example, that with respect to full-time faculty, each school with fewer than 12 teachers was required to have at least one full-time teacher whose race was different from the race of the majority of the faculty). *See also Swann*, 402 U.S. at 18-19, 22 (discussing a school board's argument that it was unconstitutional for a district court to order assignment of teachers to achieve a certain degree of faculty desegregation and stating "[w]e reject that contention."; reviewing another district court order and concluding that the court "properly followed" the principles of the Supreme Court's *Montgomery* decision, as the district court's ratios were "no more than a starting point" in the remedial process "rather than an inflexible requirement," and "the very limited use made of mathematical ratios" was within the court's discretion).

the federal appellate courts ultimately resolved in settlements,[132] thus leaving little judicial guidance on the scope of a court's authority to mandate specific remedies if a state fails to dismantle its formerly *de jure* segregated public university system.[133] With respect to these unresolved questions, the Supreme Court's express reliance in *Fordice* on precedent addressing *de jure* segregation in the primary and secondary school context suggests that at least some of this same precedent should inform future analyses, with adaptation to the higher education context.[134]

RACIAL SEGREGATION AND DISCRIMINATORY INTENT

A finding of a state entity's intent to segregate students by race in the higher education context is critical to showing a violation of the Equal Protection Clause,[135] and has significant legal consequences. In such cases of *de jure*—that is, intentional, state-imposed[136]—segregation, the state has

---

[132] For example, after the Court remanded *Fordice*, that case went through further proceedings from 1992 through 2004, at which point the Fifth Circuit upheld the settlement agreement reached by the parties and challenged on appeal. *See* Ayers v. Thompson, 358 F.3d 356, 360-64, 375 (5th Cir. 2004). *See also id.* at 359 (also noting that "nearly thirty years of litigation" had transpired until a settlement agreement was reached between the plaintiffs, the federal government as intervenor in support of the private plaintiffs, and the State of Mississippi).

[133] *But see* Geier v. Univ. of Tenn., 597 F.2d 1056, 1068-69 (6th Cir. 1979) (rejecting the state's argument that the district court's order of a merger of two racially segregated universities was beyond its equitable power). *See also* United States v. Louisiana, 692 F. Supp. 642, 658 (E.D. La. 1988) (acknowledging that "drastic" changes might be required, including creating a system of junior colleges with open admission to all high school graduates and vesting state supervision to a single board.).

[134] *See, e.g.*, U.S. v. *Fordice*, 505 U.S. 717, 728 (1992) (citing, among other cases, Freeman v. Pitts, 503 U.S. 467 (1992); Gilmore v. City of Montgomery, 417 U.S. 556, 566-567 (1974); Bd. of Educ. of Okla. City Pub. Sch. v. Dowell, 498 U.S. 237, 250 (1991); Swann v. Charlotte-Mecklenburg Bd. of Educ., 402 U.S. 1, 18 (1971); and Green v. Cty Sch. Bd. of New Kent County, Va., 391 U.S. 430, 435-38 (1968). *See also id.* at 730, 739.

[135] *See, e.g.*, *Swann*, 402 U.S. at 22 ("The constant theme and thrust of every holding from *Brown I* to date is that state-enforced separation of races in public schools is discrimination that violates the Equal Protection Clause. The remedy commanded was to dismantle dual school systems.").

[136] *See, e.g.*, Keyes v. Sch. Dist. No. 1, Denver, Colo., 413 U.S. 189, 205, 208 (1973) (describing *de jure* segregation as "'stated simply, a current condition of segregation resulting from intentional state action,'" and emphasizing that the "differentiating factor" between *de jure* segregation and "so-called de facto segregation" is the purpose or intent to segregate).

an affirmative duty under the Equal Protection Clause to eliminate all vestiges of its *de jure* system by dismantling the infrastructure and other mechanisms that produced the discriminatory segregation.[137] According to the Supreme Court's 1992 *Fordice* decision, this duty commands more than just the repeal of state laws sanctioning racial segregation in higher education.[138] The state must also uproot or reform any policy or practice "traceable" to its formerly *de jure* system that continues to have discriminatory effect.[139]

In *Fordice*, the state's intent to racially segregate its higher education system was plain: with the founding of the University of Mississippi in 1848, Mississippi explicitly set out to create a public university "dedicated to the higher education exclusively of white persons," and racially segregated its public university system over the next 100 years through the creation of other "exclusively white institutions" and "solely black institutions."[140] Nor was Mississippi's system unique in this regard. "[D]ual system[s]"[141] of public higher education—one for black students, another for white—were codified in other state and local laws throughout

---

[137] *See id.*; *Fordice*, 505 U.S. at 728 ("Our decisions establish that a State does not discharge its constitutional obligations until it eradicates policies and practices traceable to its prior *de jure* dual system that continue to foster segregation."). *See generally* Green v. County School Bd. of New Kent County, Va., 391 U.S. 430, 437-38 (1968) (stating that school boards that operated "state-compelled dual systems" have "the affirmative duty to take whatever steps might be necessary to convert to a unitary system in which racial discrimination would be eliminated root and branch."). Though outside the scope of this report, the Supreme Court has addressed how to evaluate a state's compliance with this duty and determine whether a formerly segregated system may be found "unitary." *See, e.g.,* Freeman v. Pitts, 503 U.S. 467, 491-92 (1992) (identifying factors by which a court can evaluate whether to withdraw its supervision over the desegregation of a school system; also identifying its *Green* decision as setting forth "the elements of a unitary system" in the K-12 context).

[138] *See Fordice*, 505 U.S. at 731-32 ("Such policies run afoul of the Equal Protection Clause, even though the State has abolished the legal requirement that whites and blacks be educated separately and has established racially neutral policies not animated by a discriminatory purpose.").

[139] *Id.* at 731.

[140] *Id.* at 721-22. In addition, the Court observed that the state's racially segregated system of higher education "remained largely intact" at least two decades after the Court's 1954 *Brown v. Board of Education* decision. *Id.* at 722.

[141] *Id.* at 727 (reflecting that Mississippi's laws had once mandated a "dual school system"). *See* Bd. of Educ. of Okla. City Public Sch. v. Dowell, 498 U.S. 237, 246 (1991) (explaining that "[c]ourts have used the terms 'dual' to denote a school system which has engaged in intentional segregation of students by race").

"Affirmative Action" and Equal Protection in Higher Education 27

the country.[142] Thus far, federal courts that have addressed *de jure* segregation in higher education have done so in the context of such codified segregation,[143] as in *Fordice*.[144]

The absence of a codified dual system of higher education, however, may not mean that a university system was not or is not intentionally segregated. As reflected in the Supreme Court decision *Keyes v. School District No. 1, Denver, Colorado*,[145] even when state authorities have not segregated their public schools by statute, they may still have engaged in unconstitutional racial segregation.[146] Thus, in the K-12 context, federal courts have found *de jure* segregation based on evidence reflecting a state

---

[142] *See, e.g.*, Knight v. Alabama, 14 F.3d 1534, 1538-39 (11th Cir. 1994) (discussing *de jure* segregation of Alabama's public higher education system through state law from 1819 onward, which *inter alia* criminalized education of enslaved black persons and later excluded blacks from universities attended by white students following the abolition of slavery); Geier v. Univ. of Tenn., 597 F.2d 1056, 1058 (6th Cir. 1979) (explaining that public higher education in Tennessee had been segregated by law); United States v. Louisiana, 9 F.3d 1159, 1162 (5th Cir. 1993) (indicating that racial segregation had been codified in school segregation laws, and which plaintiffs argued continued in the state's system of higher education after those laws were officially repealed). More recently, as of the publication date of this report, a case pending before the Fourth Circuit raises a *Fordice* challenge to practices that the plaintiffs contend are traceable to the State of Maryland's formerly *de jure* segregated public university system. *See* Coal. for Equity and Excellence in Md. Higher Educ., Inc., et al. v. Md. Higher Educ. Comm'n, No. 17-2451 (4th Cir.); Coal. for Equity and Excellence in Md. Higher Educ., Inc. et al. v. Md. Higher Educ. Comm'n, 977 F. Supp. 2d 507, 512-13 (D. Md. 2013) (describing Maryland's dual system of public education as having operated under statute, with no public higher education offerings available to black students before 1920).

[143] *See supra* note 142.

[144] *Fordice*, 505 U.S. at 727 (noting that the State of Mississippi's laws had mandated a "dual school system").

[145] 413 U.S. 189 (1973).

[146] *See Keyes*, 413 U.S. at 198-201 (explaining that though a statutory dual system never existed in Denver, Colorado, a finding of *de jure* segregation may be established by evidence that school authorities carried out a "program of segregation affecting a substantial portion of the students, schools, teachers, and facilities within the school system"; stating that petitioners had proved that "for almost a decade after 1960 respondent School Board had engaged in an unconstitutional policy of deliberate racial segregation in the Park Hill schools."). Evidence of segregative intent can be used to show contemporaneous or new acts of state-imposed segregation, as opposed to historical *de jure* segregation only. *See, e.g.*, Diaz v. San Jose Unified Sch. Dist., 733 F.2d 660, 661-64, 675 (9th Cir. 1984) (en banc) (in a case where plaintiffs, the parents of Spanish-surnamed children, alleged that the school district intentionally segregated schools by race, holding that evidence was sufficient to show the school board's segregative intent).

actor's impermissible segregative intent.[147] This line of cases would appear to apply in the context of higher education as well. As the Court noted in *Fordice*, where a plaintiff is unable to show that a policy or practice is a vestige of prior *de jure* segregation, she may nonetheless prove a "new" constitutional violation with evidence of a present-day intent to racially segregate students "under traditional principles" governing discriminatory intent.[148] This would be consistent with the Court's application of *Brown* and its progeny broadly across "the field of public education,"[149] including higher education, as reflected in *Fordice*.[150]

Because the Supreme Court has yet to address segregative intent in higher education, it is unclear what intent evidence would be sufficient to establish a *de jure* segregated public university or institution, apart from a

---

[147] *See, e.g.*, *Keyes*, 413 U.S. at 199-209 (discussing evidence and allegations of segregative intent and establishing a burden-shifting test by which a state entity is presumed to have acted with segregative intent system-wide, once a finding has been made that a state entity acted with segregative intent as to a meaningful portion of a given school system). *See also infra* note 158. *See generally*, Spurlock v. Fox, 716 F.3d 383, 396 (6th Cir. 2013) (stating that to prove *de jure* segregation, a plaintiff must show "'1) action or inaction by public officials 2) with a segregative purpose 3) which actually results in increased or continued segregation in the public schools'") (quoting NAACP v. Lansing Bd. of Educ., 559 F.2d 1042, 1046 (6th Cir. 1977)).

[148] *Fordice*, 505 U.S. at 732 n.6 (citing Bd. of Educ. v. Dowell, 498 U.S. 237, 250-251 (1991) and Arlington Heights v. Metro. Housing Development Corp., 429 U.S. 252 (1977)). Applying such "traditional principles," it appears that a party could also offer nonstatutory evidence to prove a state actor's past segregative intent, in order to show the existence of a prior *de jure* segregated system and the state's present-day failure to eliminate vestiges of that prior system. *See, e.g.*, Dayton Bd. of Educ. v. Brinkman, 443 U.S. 526, 534-37 (1979) (discussing and upholding court of appeals' finding of *de jure* segregation based on evidence of segregative intent, where plaintiffs alleged the existence of a prior *de jure* segregated system before and in 1954—the year of the Supreme Court's *Brown I* decision— and the continued maintenance of that segregated system through the 1970s).

[149] *See, e.g.*, *Fordice*, 505 U.S. at 721 (describing *Brown I* and *Brown II* as holding that "the concept of 'separate but equal' has no place in the field of public education" and ordering "an end to segregated public education 'with all deliberate speed'") (quoting *Brown I*, 347 U.S. at 495 and *Brown II*, 349 U.S. 294, 301 (1955); Swann, 402 U.S. at 22 ("The constant theme and thrust of every holding from *Brown I* to date is that state-enforced separation of races in public schools is discrimination that violates the Equal Protection Clause."); *Brown I*, 347 U.S. at 491-92 (discussing its precedent involving segregation "in the field of public education," and including in that discussion four cases at the public graduate school level).

[150] *See Fordice*, 505 U.S. at 728-29 (citing and discussing its Equal Protection Clause jurisprudence addressing racial segregation in the K-12 context; acknowledging that though there are operational differences between a state university system and primary and secondary schools, rejecting the view that the adoption of a race-neutral admissions policy alone is sufficient to satisfy a state's affirmative obligation to dismantle a prior *de jure* segregated university system).

law codifying such segregation.[151] As a general matter, though, a court's determination of discriminatory intent is a fact-intensive, "sensitive inquiry."[152] And the Supreme Court has observed that this is even more so in cases alleging *de jure* segregation in public education.[153] Where the evidence indicates, for example, that a state actor undertook a policy or practice knowing that doing so would have the "foreseeable" effect of segregating students by race, that evidence may support an inference of *de jure* segregation.[154] In addition, at least in the K-12 context, a finding of a state entity's segregative intent in one part of a school system creates a rebuttable presumption that segregation found in other parts of the same system was also intentional.[155] *De jure* segregation proved by such nonstatutory evidence generally triggers the same affirmative obligation on

---

[151] The question of whether racial segregation was *de jure* was not at issue in *Fordice*. *See Fordice*, 505 U.S. at 721-22. In addition, there do not appear to be any cases in the federal appellate courts involving *de jure* segregation in a public university or public university system based on evidence other than its codification in state law. *See supra* note 142.

[152] *See generally Arlington Heights*, 429 U.S. at 266 (stating that the determination as to whether discrimination was a motivating factor in state action "demands a sensitive inquiry into such circumstantial and direct evidence of intent as may be available").

[153] *See* Dayton Bd. of Educ. v. Brinkman, 433 U.S. 406, 414 (1977) (observing, in a case alleging *de jure* segregation in a K-12 system, "that the task of factfinding in a case such as this is a good deal more difficult than is typically the case," while also noting that the question of whether "racial concentration occur[s] from purely neutral public actions or were instead the intended result of actions which appeared neutral on their face but were in fact invidiously discriminatory is not an easy one to resolve.").

[154] Columbus Bd. of Educ. v. Penick, 443 U.S. 449, 464-65 (1979) (explaining that evidence of a state entity's adherence to a policy or practice, with knowledge that adherence to that policy would have the foreseeable effect of racially segregating schools, is one type of evidence from which an inference of segregative intent may be drawn; describing the district court's analysis of such foreseeability evidence as "well within the requirements of *Washington v. Davis* and *Arlington Heights*"); Dayton Bd. of Educ. v. Brinkman, 443 U.S. 526, 536, n. 9 (1979) (stating that the Court has never held that the foreseeability of segregative consequences establishes a prima facie case of segregative intent, but acknowledging that "as we hold in Columbus today, 443 U.S., at 464–465, proof of foreseeable consequences is one type of quite relevant evidence of racially discriminatory purpose").

[155] *See Keyes*, 413 U.S. at 208 (holding that a finding of intentionally segregative state action "in a meaningful portion of a school system" establishes a prima facie case of "unlawful segregative design" with respect to segregation existing in other parts of the system as well; discussing the "high probability" that where school authorities intended to racially segregate a meaningful part of the school system, "similarly impermissible considerations" also motivated their actions in other parts of the same system). *See also Columbus*, 443 U.S. at 467 (describing *Keyes* as holding that "purposeful discrimination in a substantial part of a school system furnishes a sufficient basis for an inferential finding of a systemwide discriminatory intent unless otherwise rebutted").

the state to eliminate the vestiges of its state-imposed segregation, as when *de jure* segregation is shown through state or local laws.[156]

Though segregative intent analyses at the K-12 level may be instructive, the guidance these decisions provide may be limited by the nature of the evidence at issue in those particular cases:[157] the method of student assignment to elementary or secondary schools, for example, or the drawing of attendance zones to create racially segregated schools.[158] It appears unlikely that such evidence would be at issue or directly applicable in cases alleging segregative intent at the collegiate or graduate level. Nonetheless, these decisions generally suggest that categorical distinctions—between evidence indicative of *de jure* segregation and evidence of existing segregation insufficiently linked to state intent—are difficult to draw.[159] Indeed, given the difficulties that can arise in a court's

---

[156] *See, e.g., Keyes*, 413 U.S. at 203 (explaining that in cases where a finding of state-imposed segregation has been made based on nonstatutory evidence, such a finding, "as in cases involving statutory dual systems," triggers an affirmative duty on the part of the state to desegregate).

[157] *See, e.g., Keyes*, 413 U.S. at 198-202 (in a district where racial segregation in public schools was never codified in law, discussing other evidence that may be indicative of "segregative intent" on the part of the school board, such as the assignment of faculty and staff on racially identifiable bases, gerrymandering attendance zones and designating feeder schools on the basis of race, and the specific site selection for new school construction).

[158] *See, e.g.,* United States v. Yonkers, 197 F.3d 41, 47 (2d Cir. 1999) (summarizing district court findings of segregative intent, including evidence that the city had pursued a discriminatory housing policy in part motivated by an intent to maintain racially identifiable schools); United States v. Sch. Dist. of City of Ferndale, Mich., 616 F.2d 895, 897-99, 902-04 (6th Cir. 1980) (rejecting contention that attendance boundaries for an elementary school were race-neutral applications of the district's neighborhood school policies; holding that creation of school "was intentionally segregative in purpose and effect" based on evidence including that the school's attendance zone was precisely mapped to the only residential area that had not excluded black occupancy through restrictive housing covenants). *Cf., e.g., Spurlock*, 716 F.3d at 396-402 (analyzing evidence of segregative intent and affirming district court finding that the evidence was insufficient to establish that a school rezoning plan was undertaken with segregative purpose).

[159] Federal court decisions analyzing allegations of *de jure* segregation in the K-12 context have involved highly fact-intensive determinations regarding the interrelationship between schools' racial compositions and evidence regarding student assignment policies, the drawing of school attendance zones, site selection for school construction and closures, and racially segregated residential patterns (which, in some cases, had resulted from subdivision covenants that restricted occupancy in certain neighborhoods to white-only residents or from allegedly discriminatory state action with respect to housing). *See generally Swann*, 402 U.S. at 21-22 (discussing influence and impact of school location on patterns of residential development and neighborhood composition, and observing that a state authority's decisions relating to student assignment, school construction, and school

"Affirmative Action" and Equal Protection in Higher Education   31

analysis of "segregative intent," over the years a number of Justices have called into question the rationale and basis for the distinction between *de jure* and so-called *de facto* segregation,[160] though the majority of the Court has recognized and continues to recognize this distinction.[161]

Whatever the open questions may be regarding the evidence sufficient to show segregative intent, particularly in the higher education context, *Fordice* instructs that a plaintiff need not provide evidence of *new* discriminatory intent when alleging that a state has failed to eliminate vestiges of a prior *de jure* segregated system.[162] And with respect to remedying intentional racial segregation, the Court has repeatedly held that a state not only *may* use a broad array of explicit race-conscious policies

---

closures "have been used as a potent weapon for creating or maintaining a state-segregated school system). *See also supra* note 158.

[160] *See, e.g.*, Parents Involved in Community Sch. v. Seattle Sch. Dist. No.1, 551 U.S. 701, 820-22 (2007) (Breyer, J., dissenting) (questioning the basis for the legal distinction between *de jure* and *de facto* school segregation; also contending that the crucial difference between the two cannot be the fact of a court's *de jure* finding, given that numerous school districts had been segregated by law but desegregated without court order); *Keyes*, 413 U.S. at 215 (Douglas, J., concurring) (expressing that there should be "no constitutional difference between de jure and de facto segregation"; asserting that though certain state actions are "quite distinct from the classical de jure type of school segregation," it "is a misnomer" to categorize such actions—like a school board decision to close schools in certain areas and build new schools in "black areas and in distant white areas"—as *de facto*, "as they are only more subtle types of state action that create or maintain a wholly or partially segregated school system."). *See also id.* at 224 (Powell, J., concurring in part and dissenting in part) (stating that the *de jure/de facto* distinction cannot be "justified on a principled basis," and characterizing as "tortuous" the burden of identifying and proving segregative intent). In *Keyes*, Justice Powell would instead have held that where racial segregation exists to a substantial degree in a school system, there is a prima facie case that the school board or other public authorities "are sufficiently responsible to warrant imposing upon them a nationally applicable burden to demonstrate they nevertheless are operating a genuinely integrated school system." *Id.*

[161] *See, e.g.*, *Parents Involved*, 551 U.S. at 736 (stating that the distinction between *de jure* and *de facto* discrimination "has been central to our jurisprudence in this area for generations") (citing Milliken v. Bradley, 433 U.S. 267, 280, n. 14 (1977); Freeman v. Pitts, 503 U.S. 467, 495-96 (1992)).

[162] *See* United States v. Fordice, 505 U.S. 717, 733 n.8 (1992) (explaining that plaintiffs "need not show such discriminatory intent to establish a constitutional violation for the perpetuation of policies traceable to the prior *de jure* segregative regime which have continuing discriminatory effects"). *See also id.* at 746 (Thomas, J., concurring) (expressing the view that "we are justified in not requiring proof of a present specific intent to discriminate" when the three elements of the legal standard adopted in *Fordice* are met, as "[i]t is safe to assume that a policy adopted during the *de jure* era, if it produces segregative effects, reflects a discriminatory intent"). *See also Knight*, 14 F.3d at 1540-41 (explaining that "the burden of proof lies with the charging party to show that a challenged contemporary policy is traceable to past segregation").

32 *Christine J. Back and JD S. Hsin*

and practices to remedy its constitutional violation, but often *must* do so.[163] By themselves, race-neutral measures simply may not be enough, the Court has explained, to provide equitable, make-whole relief for intentionally segregative acts.[164]

This affirmative obligation to consider race arises, however, only in the context of *de jure* segregation. Outside that *de jure* context, institutions of higher education subject to the Equal Protection Clause[165] have no such duty to remedy racial segregation.[166] Nor may they—or the federal courts, for that matter—use the same broad array of race-conscious measures available for remedying *de jure* segregation.[167]

---

[163] *See, e.g., Fordice*, 505 U.S. at 729 (explaining that the adoption and implementation of race-neutral policies alone does not suffice to demonstrate that a state has eliminated its prior dual system; concluding that a race-neutral admissions policy does not cure the constitutional violation of a segregated university system given other policies that may continue to foster segregation); *Swann*, 402 U.S. at 27-28 (affirming the district court's remedial order assigning students to schools on a racial basis as an interim corrective measure so as to desegregate all-white and all-black schools in a formerly *de jure* segregated system; stating that race-neutral plans "may fail to counteract the continuing effects" of a state's intentional separation of students by race). *See also, e.g., Parents Involved*, 551 U.S. at 737 (stating that "no one questions that the obligation to disestablish a school system segregated by law can include race-conscious remedies—whether or not a court had issued an order to that effect").

[164] *See supra* note 163. In addition, the Court in *Fordice* observed that a state's current policies that are *traceable* to *de jure* segregation "may be race neutral on their face" but nevertheless foster racial segregation by "contribut[ing] to the racial identifiability" of a state's public universities. *See Fordice*, 505 U.S. at 733 (instructing that in such instances, the state "must justify these policies or eliminate them").

[165] Though the Equal Protection Clause applies only to state actors, Title VI of the Civil Rights Act similarly prohibits private recipients of federal funding from discriminating based on race. *See* 42 U.S.C. § 2000d. Moreover, the Supreme Court has read Title VI to proscribe the same conduct prohibited by the Equal Protection Clause. *See* Alexander v. Sandoval, 532 U.S. 275, 281 (2001) ("tak[ing] as given" that Title VI "proscribes only those racial classifications that would violate the Equal Protection Clause or the Fifth Amendment") (quoting Regents of Univ. of Cal. v. Bakke, 438 U.S. 265, 287 (1978) (Powell, J., announcing judgment of the Court)).

[166] *See, e.g., Fordice*, 505 U.S. at 727-28 (describing a state's affirmative obligation as arising from a showing that racial segregation is attributable to the state); *Keyes*, 413 U.S. at 200 (stating that in cases involving *de jure* segregation, the state "automatically assumes an affirmative duty" to eliminate from public schools within its system "'all vestiges of state-imposed segregation.'") (quoting Swann, 402 U.S. at 15).

[167] *See, e.g., Parents Involved*, 551 U.S. at 709-10, 736-37, 745-46 (holding unconstitutional voluntary race-conscious programs of student assignments in two public school systems, because one school district had never been segregated by law and the other district had been found to have eliminated the vestiges of its prior dual system). *See also Dayton*, 433 U.S. at 419-20 (stating that "[t]he power of the federal courts to restructure the operation of local and state governmental entities" may be exercised only on the basis of a constitutional

De jure segregation, however, is not the only context in which race-conscious measures in higher education may be used. For over forty years colleges and universities have considered race as a way of increasing the racial diversity of their student bodies, independent from a legal basis relating to *de jure* segregation. Thus far, however, the Supreme Court has addressed only one type of discretionary race-conscious measure in the higher education context: admissions policies. And when evaluating these discretionary policies, the Court reviews them under a notably different analytical lens, looking to their precision in achieving certain concretely defined and "compelling" educational interests, as explained more fully below.[168]

BEYOND *DE JURE*: JUDICIAL SCRUTINY OF RACIAL CLASSIFICATIONS

"Affirmative action" in its original sense grew out of the states' affirmative obligation under the Equal Protection Clause to rid their public institutions of the lingering vestiges of *de jure* segregation. But "affirmative action" has also come to refer to race-conscious policies developed outside this *de jure* context. These are policies *voluntarily* adopted by institutions to help racial minorities overcome the effects of their earlier exclusion.[169] And unlike the measures ordered by the courts to

---

violation); *Swann*, 402 U.S. at 15 ("If school authorities fail in their affirmative obligations under these holdings, judicial authority may be invoked. Once a right and a violation have been shown, the scope of a district court's equitable powers to remedy past wrongs is broad, for breadth and flexibility are inherent in equitable remedies.").

[168] *Compare Fordice*, 505 U.S. at 728, 733-43 (stating that a court must examine "[t]he full range of policies and practices" when evaluating the sufficiency of a state's efforts to dismantle its formerly *de jure* segregated public university system) *with* Fisher v. Univ. of Tex., 136 S.Ct. 2198, 2207-08 (2016) (setting forth "three controlling principles relevant to assessing the constitutionality of a public university's affirmative-action program" under strict scrutiny).

[169] *See* 28 C.F.R. § 42.104 (Department of Justice regulation characterizing affirmative action policies as measures designed "to overcome the effects of conditions which resulted in limiting participation by persons of a particular race"); *see also Metro Broadcasting*, 497 U.S. at 564-65 (distinguishing "benign race-conscious measures" from those meant "to compensate victims of past governmental ... discrimination").

right the wrongs of *de jure* segregation, these policies are strictly voluntary,[170] with their legality consequently turning on constitutional considerations unlike those involved in the *de jure* context.

"Affirmative action" in this more familiar, voluntary sense has also been among the most contentious subjects in constitutional law.[171] In the forty years since *Regents of the University of California v. Bakke*,[172] when the Court first addressed those programs' constitutionality, the Justices have divided sharply over when or whether such programs can survive constitutional scrutiny. And a major point of disagreement among the Justices—lingering to this day[173]—is how strictly to review those policies and what the government or other state entity must do to justify its use of "benign" racial classifications. In recent decisions, the Court has reviewed such classifications under a seemingly "elastic" regime of strict scrutiny,[174] accepting those classifications only where they have been narrowly tailored to serve compelling government interests.

---

[170] Not only are these voluntary race-conscious measures discretionary, but the Court has also held that states may forbid their use. *See* Schuette v. Coal. to Def. Affirmative Action, 134 S. Ct. 1623, 1638 (2014) (concluding that Michigan had the right to outlaw the use of "racial preferences" in the state).

[171] Erwin Chemerinsky, Constitutional Law: Principles Aad Policies 764 (5th ed. 2015) ("No topic in constitutional law is more controversial than affirmative action.").

[172] 438 U.S. 265 (1978).

[173] *See, e.g.*, Gratz v. Bollinger, 539 U.S. 244, 298 (2003) (Ginsburg, J., dissenting) (criticizing the Court for "once again maintain[ing] that the same standard of review controls judicial inspection of all official race classifications"); Grutter v. Bollinger, 539 U.S. 306, 346 (2003) (suggesting that in a different case the Court might revisit "whether all governmental classifications by race, whether designed to benefit or to burden a historically disadvantaged group, should be subject to the same standard of judicial review"); Fisher v. Univ. of Tex. (*Fisher I*), 570 U.S. 297, 337 (2013) (Ginsburg, J., dissenting) (suggesting the same); *see also* Parents Involved in Cmty. Sch. v. Seattle Sch. Dist. No. 1, 551 U.S. 701, 800-01 (2007) (Stevens, J., dissenting) (arguing that "a rigid adherence to tiers of scrutiny obscures *Brown* [*v. Board of Education*]'s clear message").

[174] Adarand Constructors, Inc. v. Peña, 515 U.S. 200, 268 (1995) (Stevens, J., dissenting) (observing that "the Court's very recognition [in that case] that strict scrutiny can be compatible with the survival of a classification so reviewed demonstrates that our concepts of equal protection enjoy a greater elasticity than the standard categories might suggest").

Equal Protection and Racial Classifications

The constitutional guarantee of equal protection broadly prohibits the government from employing "arbitrary classification[s]."[175] And the use of racial classifications in particular has long been of special concern for the courts. Indeed, this "heightened judicial solicitude"[176] for racial categorizing has roots nearly as old as the Fourteenth Amendment itself. As the Supreme Court explained in an early decision under the Amendment, the "spirit and meaning" of the Equal Protection Clause was "that the law in the States shall be the same for the black as for the white; that all persons, whether colored or white, shall stand equal before the laws of the States, and, in regard to the colored race, ... that no discrimination shall be made against them by law because of their color."[177] In the decades since, the Court has only made clearer that it regards the government's use of racial classifications as "inherently suspect" and therefore subject to more demanding scrutiny than other classifications,[178] which are typically reviewed only for basic rationality.[179]

---

[175] *See* Engquist v. Ore. Dep't of Agric., 553 U.S. 591, 597 (2008) (noting the Court's "traditional view of the core concern of the Equal Protection Clause as a shield against arbitrary classifications"). *See also* Willowbrook v. Olech, 528 U.S. 562, 564 (2000) ("Our cases have recognized successful equal protection claims brought by a 'class of one,' where the plaintiff alleges that she has been intentionally treated differently from others similarly situated and that there is no rational basis for the difference in treatment.").

[176] Graham v. Richardson, 403 U.S. 365, 372 (1971) (observing that "heightened judicial solicitude is appropriate" for classifications affecting "a 'discrete and insular minority'") (citing United States v. Carolene Products, 304 U.S. 144, 152-53 n.4 (1938)).

[177] Strauder v. West Virginia, 100 U.S. 303, 307 (1879).

[178] Graham v. Richardson, 403 U.S. 365, 371-72 (1971) (noting that "the Court's decisions have established that classifications based on ... race are inherently suspect and subject to close judicial scrutiny"); *Adarand*, 515 U.S. at 216 (internal quotation marks and citations omitted).

[179] Typically, but not always, some classifications not subject to strict scrutiny instead receive a milder but still heightened form of scrutiny, sometimes referred to as "intermediate." *Compare* Hodel v. Indiana, 452 U.S. 314, 331-32 (1981) ("Social and economic legislation ... that does not employ suspect classifications or impinge on fundamental rights must be upheld against equal protection attack.") *with* Clark v. Jeter, 486 U.S. 456 (1988) ("Between th[e] extremes of rational basis review and strict scrutiny lies a level of intermediate scrutiny, which generally has been applied to discriminatory classifications based on sex or illegitimacy.")

There has been significant disagreement, however, over just how rigidly the courts should scrutinize a racial classification, especially when the point of the classification is to benefit racial minorities, as in the case of affirmative action.[180] That issue came before the Court for the first time in *Bakke*,[181] involving a challenge to an affirmative action admissions program begun at the then newly created medical school at the University of California at Davis (the Medical School).

And the Court's fractured decision there prefigured the central disagreements that the Justices still face in reviewing so-called "benign" racial classifications.[182]

Bakke's Splintered Levels of Scrutiny

In the early 1970s, not long after the Medical School opened, it adopted a race-conscious admissions policy to increase its enrollment of certain "disadvantaged" students.[183] Under that policy, the school each year would set aside 16 seats in its entering class of 100 specifically for members of this "disadvantaged" group, to be admitted by a "special admissions" committee.[184] Although many white students sought admission under this "special" policy, the committee considered only

---

[180] *See, e.g.*, Whole Woman's Health v. Hellerstedt, 136 S. Ct. 2292, 2327-28 (2016) (Thomas, J., dissenting) (criticizing the Court's "tiers of scrutiny," especially as applied to affirmative action, as so many "labels [that] now mean little"); Williams-Yulee v. Fla. Bar, 135 S. Ct. 1656, 1673 (2015) (Breyer, J., concurring) (observing that, in his view, the "Court's doctrine referring to tiers of scrutiny [are] guidelines informing [its] approach to the case at hand, not tests to be mechanically applied"); Gratz v. Bollinger, 539 U.S. 244, 298-99 (2003) (Ginsburg, J., dissenting) (criticizing the Court for "once again maintain[ing] that the same standard of review controls judicial inspection of all official race classifications").

[181] In an earlier case—DeFunis v. Odegaard, 416 U.S. 312 (1974)—the Court declined to reach the merits of a similar challenge to an affirmation action admissions policy at the University of Washington's law school. *Bakke* was therefore the first case involving an affirmative action policy that the Court reviewed on its merits. *See* CHEMERINKSY, *supra* note 171, at 765 (noting the same).

[182] Metro Broad., Inc. v. FCC, 497 U.S. 547, 564-65 (1990) (distinguishing "benign race-conscious measures," such as voluntary affirmative action programs, from those that are "'remedial,' or designed to compensate victims of past governmental or societal discrimination").

[183] The Medical School apparently did not define what that category encompassed besides certain racial minorities. *See* Regents of Univ. of Cal. v. Bakke, 438 U.S. 265, 274-75 (1978) (describing the operation of the "special admissions program"). Unless otherwise indicated, citations of *Bakke* are of Justice Powell's opinion announcing the Court's judgment.

[184] *Id.*

"Affirmative Action" and Equal Protection in Higher Education   37

students of specifically identified racial minorities.[185] After Allan Bakke, a white male, twice sought—and was denied—admission to the school, he brought suit challenging the set-aside under the Equal Protection Clause as well as Title VI,[186] which prohibits institutional recipients of federal funds—like the Medical School—from discriminating on the basis of race.[187]

Bakke's case eventually found its way to the Supreme Court and into the hands of a divided bench. The Justices found themselves particularly at odds over the case's threshold question— what level of scrutiny the Court should apply in reviewing Bakke's challenge. Justice Stevens, writing for a quartet of Justices, concluded that the program violated Title VI, sidestepping the constitutional question.[188] Another four Justices would have reached the equal protection challenge,[189] and in doing so would have required the Medical School to point to "important governmental objectives" that justified its admissions policy's use of "remedial" racial classifications, along with evidence that their use was "substantially related to" achieving those important objectives.[190] Under that standard—a form of *intermediate scrutiny*[191]—these Justices would have upheld the policy.[192]

Justice Powell, announcing the Court's judgment but writing for himself, insisted that all "racial and ethnic distinctions" drawn by the government must be regarded as "inherently suspect," calling for "the most exacting judicial examination."[193] What that meant in *Bakke*, according to Justice Powell, was that the Medical School would need to prove that its

---

[185] Those included students who identified themselves as Asian, Black, "Chicano," or "American Indian." *Id.*

[186] The Act provides that "[n]o person in the United States shall, on the ground of race, color, or national origin, be excluded from participation in, be denied the benefits of, or be subjected to discrimination under any program or activity receiving Federal financial assistance." 42 U.S.C § 2000d.

[187] *Bakke*, 438 U.S. at 276-79.

[188] This group included Chief Justice Burger along with Justices Rehnquist, Stevens, and Stewart. *See id.* at 418 (Stevens, J., concurring in the judgment in part and dissenting in part).

[189] That group included Justices Brennan, Blackmun, Marshall, and White. *See id.* at 324.

[190] *Id.* at 359 (Brennan, J., concurring in the judgment in part and dissenting in part).

[191] *See* CHEMERINSKY, *supra* note 171, at 765 (characterizing this level of review as intermediate).

[192] *Bakke*, 438 U.S. at 325-26 (Brennan, J., concurring in the judgment in part and dissenting in part).

[193] *Id.* at 291.

use of the "special admissions" carve-out was "precisely tailored to serve a compelling governmental interest"—the standard of review now known simply as *strict scrutiny*.[194] And because, in his view, the school could come forward with no such proof,[195] Justice Powell concluded that its affirmative-action policy could not survive the Court's scrutiny, whether under the Fourteenth Amendment or the overlapping standards of Title VI.[196]

Settling on Strict Scrutiny

Because *Bakke* yielded no majority opinion, it could only hint at how the Court might treat other "benign" race-conscious policies that did not involve the sort of apparent quota[197] invalidated in that case or cases outside the unique context of higher education. That uncertainty would last another decade, as the Court, in another series of splintered decisions, weighed constitutional challenges to differently structured affirmative action policies in other contexts, each time without resolving the appropriate standard of review.[198]

That uncertainty appeared to abate with the Court's 1989 decision in *Richmond v. J.A. Croson, Co.*[199] There, for the first time,[200] five Justices

---

[194] *Id.* at 299.

[195] For a fuller discussion of Justice Powell's analysis of the Medical School's plan, *see infra* notes 144-148 and accompanying text.

[196] *Bakke*, 438 U.S. at 299. Justice Powell agreed with the four dissenting Justices that "Title VI must be held to proscribe only those racial classifications that would violate the Equal Protection Clause or the Fifth Amendment." *Id.* at 287; *see also id.* at 352 (Brennan, J., concurring in part and dissenting in part) (explaining the dissenters' view that "Title VI's definition of racial discrimination is absolutely coextensive with the Constitution's").

[197] *See Bakke*, 438 U.S. at 288 n.26 (noting that the lower courts there "found—and [the] petitioner d[id] not deny— that white applicants could not compete for the 16 places reserved solely for the special admissions program," leading the courts to "characterize[] this as a 'quota' system").

[198] *See* Fullilove v. Klutznick, 448 U.S. 448 (1980) (upholding a federal law that mandated 10 percent of federal funds granted for public work projects to be awarded to minority-owned and -controlled businesses, but expressly declining to adopt any of the analyses presented in *Bakke*); Wygant v. Jackson Bd. of Educ., 476 U.S. 267 (1986) (invalidating under the Fourteenth Amendment a collective bargaining agreement provision that protected minority public school teachers from layoff at the expense of more senior white faculty, again without reaching any consensus as to the standard of review); *see generally* CHEMERINSKY, *supra* note 171, at 766-68 (discussing the development of these cases in greater detail).

[199] 488 U.S. 469 (1989).

clearly signaled that they would apply strict scrutiny to affirmative action plans implemented at the state and local levels, including the program they invalidated in that case, involving the City of Richmond's set-aside of public work funds for minority-owned businesses.[201] But the next year, in *Metro Broadcasting, Inc. v. FCC*,[202] the Court, in another 5-4 ruling, suggested that it would review *federal* affirmative action plans differently. In the Court's view there, "benign race-conscious measures mandated by *Congress*" need only "serve important governmental objectives" and be "substantially related to the achievement of those objectives"—satisfying an intermediate level of scrutiny.[203]

Just a few years later, however, in *Adarand Constructors, Inc. v. Peña*,[204] the Supreme Court reversed course. There, in a federal contracting case, the Court drew a different lesson from its pre-*Metro* line of race-classification cases: in the view of the *Adarand* majority, "any person, of whatever race, has the right to demand that any governmental actor subject to the Constitution justify any racial classification subjecting that person to unequal treatment under the strictest judicial scrutiny."[205] That simple rule therefore precluded the divided regime upheld in *Metro Broadcasting*, subjecting the states' use of racial classifications to strict scrutiny, while relaxing the review of comparable classifications enacted by Congress. Instead, the *Adarand* Court held, "[f]ederal racial classifications, like those of a State, must serve a compelling governmental interest, and must be narrowly tailored to further that interest."[206] And to the extent that *Metro Broadcasting* was "inconsistent" with that uniform rule, it was accordingly overruled.[207]

---

[200] *Id.* at 551 (Marshall, J., dissenting) ("Today, for the first time, a majority of the Court has adopted strict scrutiny as its standard of Equal Protection Clause review of race-conscious remedial measures.").

[201] *See id.* at 499 (concluding that, "[w]hile there [was] no doubt that the sorry history of both private and public discrimination in this country ha[d] contributed to a lack of opportunities for black entrepreneurs, this observation, standing alone, cannot justify a rigid racial quota in the awarding of public contracts in Richmond, Virginia").

[202] 497 U.S. 547 (1990).

[203] *Id.* at 564-65 (emphasis added).

[204] 515 U.S. 200 (1995).

[205] *Id.* at 224.

[206] *Id.* at 227.

[207] *Id.*

After *Adarand* strict scrutiny therefore became the test of any classification that subjected individuals to unequal treatment based on their race, no matter which state actor was doing the classifying.[208] And the Court expressly extended that holding to the context of higher education.[209] As the Court reaffirmed in *Fisher v. University of Texas*, "because racial characteristics so seldom provide a relevant basis for disparate treatment," "[r]ace may not be considered [by a university] unless [its] admissions process can withstand strict scrutiny."[210]

It therefore appears that a classification that subjects individuals to unequal treatment because of their race, even if for a "benign" purpose, will have to satisfy strict scrutiny.[211] In its canonical formulation, that test calls for measuring such classifications along the two dimensions Justice Powell identified in *Bakke*: (1) the classification must serve a *compelling governmental interest* and (2) the use of that classification must also be *narrowly tailored* to achieving that interest.[212] The government has the burden of proving both,[213] and neither is easy to do.[214] Indeed, in the sixty

---

[208] *See, e.g.*, Johnson v. California, 543 U.S. 499, 505 (2005) ("We have held [in *Adarand*] that 'all racial classifications [imposed by government] ... must be analyzed by a reviewing court under strict scrutiny.'"). In several cases since *Adarand* the Court has suggested, as in *Johnson*, that the use of *any* racial classification by the government would be presumptively impermissible. A number of federal appeals courts, noticing some ambiguity in *Adarand*'s holding, have concluded that an express racial classifications need not, in every instance, draw strict scrutiny. *See* MD/DC/DE Broads. Ass'n v. FCC, 236 F.3d 13, 20 (D.C. Cir. 2001) ("assum[ing] ... that *Adarand* requires strict scrutiny only of governmental actions that lead to people being treated unequally on the basis of their race"); *see also* Safeco Ins. Co. of Am. v. City of White House, 191 F.3d 675, 692 (6th Cir. 1999) ("Outreach efforts may or may not require strict scrutiny.") Whether this distinction survives the Court's more recent rulings in Grutter v. Bollinger, 539 U.S. 306 (2003) and Fisher v. Univ. of Tex. (*Fisher I*), 570 U.S. 297, 309-10 (2013) remains to be seen.

[209] *See* Fisher v. Univ. of Tex. (*Fisher I*), 570 U.S. 297, 309-10 (2013) (citing Gratz v. Bollinger, 539 U.S. 244 (2003) and Grutter v. Bollinger, 539 U.S. 306 (2003) for the proposition that "[r]ace may not be considered [by a university] unless the admissions process can withstand strict scrutiny").

[210] Fisher v. Univ. of Tex. (*Fisher II*), 136 S. Ct. 2198, 2208 (2016).

[211] *See id.* ("Race may not be considered [by a university] unless [its] admissions process can withstand strict scrutiny."); *see also* Parents Involved in Cmty. Sch. v. Seattle Sch. Dist. No. 1, 551 U.S. 701, 720 (2007) ("It is well established that when the government distributes burdens or benefits on the basis of individual racial classifications, that action is reviewed under strict scrutiny.")

[212] Johnson v. California, 543 U.S. 499, 505 (2005) (citing Adarand Constructors, Inc. v. Peña, 515 U.S. 200, 227 (1995)).

[213] *Id.*

"Affirmative Action" and Equal Protection in Higher Education 41

years that separated the Court's now-repudiated decision in *Korematsu v. United States*[215] from *Grutter v. Bollinger*,[216] when the Court first upheld an affirmative action policy at a public university, the only other "racial classifications upheld under strict scrutiny [have been] race-based remedies for prior racial discrimination by the government."[217] To many commentators "strict scrutiny" has thus come to seem rather more "strict in theory, but fatal in fact"[218]—a point sometimes echoed by the Justices themselves.[219]

VOLUNTARY "AFFIRMATIVE ACTION" IN HIGHER EDUCATION: SCRUTINIZING ADMISSIONS

Strict scrutiny may typically be fatal in fact, but affirmative action policies in higher education have been a notable exception.[220] Partly this

---

[214] One study found, for example, that of all governmental actions reviewed by the federal courts under strict scrutiny to that point, only some 30% ended up surviving, including only 27% of challenged policies reviewed specifically for "suspect class discrimination." Adam Winkler, *Fatal in Theory and Strict in Fact: An Empirical Analysis of Strict Scrutiny in the Federal Courts*, 59 VAND. L. REV. 793, 815 (2006).

[215] 323 U.S. 214 (1944); *see* Trump v. Hawaii, 585 U. S. __, __ (2018) (slip op. at 38) (announcing that "*Korematsu* was gravely wrong the day it was decided, has been overruled in the court of history, and—to be clear—'has no place in law under the Constitution'").

[216] 539 U.S. 306 (2003).

[217] Suzanna Sherry, *Foundational Facts and Doctrinal Change*, 2011 U. ILL. L. REV. 145, 156, 156 n.27 (2011) (citing, as the only exceptions, United States v. Paradise, 480 U.S. 149 (1987) and Local 28 of the Sheet Metal Workers' Int'l Ass'n v. EEOC, 478 U.S. 421, 480 (1986)).

[218] Gerald Gunther, *In Search of Evolving Doctrine on a Changing Court: A Model for a Newer Equal Protection*, 86 HARV. L. REV. 1, 8 (1972).

[219] *See, e.g.*, Fullilove v. Klutznick, 448 U.S. 448, 507 (1980) (Powell, J., concurring) (acknowledging that "the failure of legislative action to survive strict scrutiny has led some to wonder whether our review of racial classifications has been strict in theory, but fatal in fact"); *Adarand*, 515 U.S. at 237 ("[W]e wish to dispel the notion that strict scrutiny is 'strict in theory, but fatal in fact.'"); Grutter v. Bollinger, 539 U.S. 306, 326 (2003) (explaining that "[s]trict scrutiny is not 'strict in theory, but fatal in fact.'"); Parents Involved in Cmty. Sch. v. Seattle Sch. Dist. No. 1, 551 U.S. 701, 832-33 (2007) (Breyer, J., dissenting) (explaining that strict scrutiny "is *not* in all circumstances 'strict in theory, but fatal in fact'").

[220] *See, e.g.*, Brett M. Kavanaugh, *Keynote Address: Two Challenges for the Judge as Umpire: Statutory Ambiguity and Constitutional Exceptions*, 92 NOTRE DAME L. REV. 1907, 1917 (2017) ("The Court has recognized a basic equal protection right not to be treated

has to do with the Equal Protection Clause itself, and the often crucial difference that a particular context makes in deciding cases under that "broad provision[]."[221] And for several Justices the context of affirmative action, involving the arguably "benign" use of race, has seemed particularly distinctive.[222] Yet, despite this contextual difference, the Court has made it clear that its scrutiny of race-conscious admission policies is still every bit as strict. Or, as Justice Kennedy put the point in the first *Fisher* case, even though "[s]trict scrutiny must not be 'strict in theory, but fatal in fact,'" it must also "not be strict in theory but feeble in fact."[223]

This seeming tension—between the strictness of the Court's scrutiny and its approval of race-conscious admissions policies—has led the Court to adjust its framework for scrutinizing similar policies over the years. And since *Bakke* that framework appears to have shifted in two significant respects, corresponding to each of the two prongs of strict scrutiny. First, the Court now requires public universities that adopt affirmative action admissions policies to explain in increasingly "concrete and precise" terms[224] what diversity-related educational goals those policies serve and why the university has chosen to pursue them.[225] Anything less, the Court has held, would fail to present an interest sufficiently compelling under strict scrutiny.[226] Second, the Court also now expects universities to prove that their policies achieve those "concrete and precise goals" in an appropriately "flexible" way, as most clearly exemplified by the Harvard

---

differently by the government on account of your race. But there is a longstanding exception for affirmative action, at least in the realm of higher education.").

[221] *Grutter*, 539 U.S. at 327 ("Context matters when reviewing race-based governmental action under the Equal Protection Clause.") (quoting Gomillion v. Lightfoot, 364 U.S. 339, 343-44 (1960)).

[222] *See, e.g.*, Richmond v. J. A. Croson Co., 488 U.S. 469, 551-52 (1989) (Marshall, J., dissenting) ("A profound difference separates governmental actions that themselves are racist, and governmental actions that seek to remedy the effects of prior racism or to prevent neutral governmental activity from perpetuating the effects of such racism.").

[223] Fisher v. Univ. of Tex. (*Fisher I*), 570 U.S. 297, 314 (2013).

[224] Fisher v. Univ. of Tex. (*Fisher II*), 136 S.Ct. 2198, 2211 (2016) (requiring the university to articulate "concrete and precise goals" to state a constitutionally compelling interest).

[225] *Fisher I*, 570 U.S. at 310 (requiring the university to provide "a reasoned, principled explanation for the academic decision" "to pursue 'the educational benefits that flow from student body diversity'").

[226] *Fisher II*, 136 S.Ct. at 2211 (requiring a university to state "goals" that are "sufficiently measurable to permit judicial scrutiny of the policies adopted to reach them").

plan that Justice Powell singled out in *Bakke*.[227] That model has yielded "five hallmarks" of an appropriately tailored affirmative action policy, criteria that have since guided lower courts in assessing other affirmative action plans.[228]

From "Student Body Diversity" to Concrete and Particular Diversity-Related Goals

For a university's affirmative action policy to survive strict scrutiny, a university must first "demonstrate with clarity that its 'purpose or interest is both constitutionally permissible and substantial.'"[229] The Court has recognized only a single interest that meets that standard: "the attainment of a diverse student body."[230] What exactly that interest amounts to—and how, consequently, a university should ensure it has appropriately tailored its policy to achieve that interest—has been a point of uncertainty since *Bakke*.[231] With its two decisions in *Fisher v. University of Texas*, however, the Court appears now to require a more "concrete and precise" articulation of the diversity-related educational goals a university hopes to achieve through its affirmative action admissions policy. In addition, the Court also now appears to expect a university to provide a reasoned and principled explanation of why the school believes it important to achieve those goals.

---

[227] *Grutter*, 539 U.S. at 334 (noting that "Justice Powell made clear in *Bakke* [that] truly individualized consideration demands that race be used in a flexible, nonmechanical way").

[228] *See, e.g.*, Smith v. Univ. of Wash., 392 F.3d 367, 373 (9th Cir. 2004) (applying *Grutter*'s "five hallmarks" to uphold the University of Washington Law School's affirmative action policy).

[229] *Fisher II*, 136 S.Ct. at 2208 (quoting *Fisher I*, 570 U.S. at 298).

[230] *Bakke*, 438 U.S. at 311-12.

[231] This appears to reflect more general uncertainty about the Court's use of strict scrutiny, a result of its having "largely ignored parallel questions involving the generality with which governmental interests should be specified." Richard H. Fallon, Jr., *Strict Judicial Scrutiny*, 54 UCLA L. REV. 1267, 1271 (2007).

44 Christine J. Back and JD S. Hsin

Bakke and the Diversity Interest

The diversity rationale emerged with the Court's first encounter with a voluntary affirmative-action policy, in *Bakke*.[232] There—in an opinion for the Court joined by no other Justice—Justice Powell explained what interests clearly would *not* count as compelling enough to satisfy strict scrutiny. Those included the Medical School's alleged interest in having "some specified percentage" of certain racial or ethnic groups in a student body and its interest in "remedying ... the effects of societal discrimination," as well as the school's particular interest in "the delivery of health-care services to communities currently underserved." None of these interests, Justice Powell concluded, provided a reason substantial enough to justify turning to race-conscious measures.[233] Nor has the Court said otherwise since.

But Justice Powell was also clear about what interest he believed *would* satisfy strict scrutiny: "student body diversity."[234] And just as importantly, he also explained why: colleges and universities, he suggested, had a uniquely academic interest in promoting an "atmosphere of speculation, experiment, and creation"—an interest, more simply, in "academic freedom."[235] That interest, Justice Powell observed, was not only "essential to the quality of higher education," but had also long "been viewed as a special concern of the First Amendment."[236] Thus the "right to select those students who will contribute the most to the robust exchange of ideas" not only allowed a university "to achieve a goal that is of paramount importance in the fulfillment of its mission,"[237] it also represented a "countervailing *constitutional* interest" that, in Justice Powell's view, called for the Court's respect.[238]

---

[232] *Bakke*, 438 U.S. at 306-12.

[233] *Id.*

[234] *See Gruffer*, 539 U.S. at 325 (endorsing "Justice Powell's view that student body diversity is a compelling state interest that can justify the use of race in university admissions"). No other Justice in *Bakke* joined Justice Powell's opinion or his explanation of the diversity rationale. Indeed, the term "diversity" does not even appear in any other Justice's opinion there.

[235] *Bakke*, 438 U.S. at 312-13 (internal quotation marks omitted).

[236] *Id.* (emphasis added).

[237] *Id.* (internal quotation marks omitted).

[238] *Id.* (emphasis added).

"Affirmative Action" and Equal Protection in Higher Education 45

In *Bakke*, Justice Powell set out the basic theory for why diversity could justify an affirmative action policy, at least "in the context of a university's admissions program.[239] But he gave few details about what that interest encompassed.[240] As he saw it, that interest must have its limits: pursuing diversity would not allow a university to resort to racial quotas,[241] for example, nor could the school disregard other "constitutional limitations protecting individual rights."[242] But Justice Powell declined to indicate where those other limitations fell or how they circumscribed the goals a university could permissibly seek in the name of a diverse student body. And because the *Bakke* Court fractured as it did, with no one opinion commanding a majority of the Justices' votes, the lessons of that case have been hard to discern, especially after the Court appeared to decline a similar diversity rationale in later cases outside higher education.[243] Perhaps unsurprisingly, the lower courts soon came to reflect this uncertain division of opinion in later cases involving affirmative action programs at other public universities.[244]

"Critical Mass" and Diversity

Some clarity over *Bakke*'s diversity theory came in 2003, with a pair of decisions reviewing affirmative action policies of the University of Michigan: *Grutter v. Bollinger*,[245] challenging the university's law school

---

[239] *Id.* at 314.

[240] In *Fisher II*, Justice Kennedy would make this concern explicit: "A university's goals cannot be elusory or amorphous—they must be sufficiently measurable to permit judicial scrutiny of the policies adopted to reach them." *Fisher II*, 136 S.Ct. 2198, 2211 (2016).

[241] *Bakke*, 438 U.S. at 307 ("If [the Medical School's] purpose is to assure within its student body some specified percentage of a particular group merely because of its race or ethnic origin, such a preferential purpose must be rejected not as insubstantial but as facially invalid.").

[242] *Id.* at 314.

[243] *See* Hopwood v. TeN., 78 F.3d 932, 944-45 (5th Cir. 1996), *cert. denied* 518 U.S. 1033 (1996) (striking down the University of Texas law school's affirmative action policy partly because "recent Supreme Court precedent"— including *Adarand*, *Metro Broadcasting*, and *Croson*—appeared to suggest that the "diversity interest will not satisfy strict scrutiny").

[244] *Compare Hopwood* 78 F.3d at 944 (concluding that the diversity interest was not compelling enough to survive strict scrutiny), *with* Smith v. Univ. of Wash. Law Sch., 233 F.3d 1188, 1200-01 (9th Cir. 2000) (concluding, based on Justice Powell's opinion in *Bakke*, that "educational diversity is a compelling governmental interest that meets the demands of strict scrutiny of race-conscious measures").

[245] 539 U.S. 306 (2003).

admission program, and *Gratz v. Bollinger*,[246] challenging the policy used by the university's undergraduate program. *Grutter*, especially, helped clarify what an interest in diversity involved, and how a university could rely on that interest to defend a race-conscious admissions policy.

Under the admissions policy of the University of Michigan Law School (the Law School) challenged in *Grutter*, applicants to incoming classes were admitted under a policy that weighed a composite of the applicant's LSAT score and undergraduate GPA along with several more individualized factors, including the applicant's race.[247] The Law School set out to create classes with what it called a "critical mass of underrepresented minority students,"[248] to ensure that those students felt "encourage[d] ... to participate in the classroom and not feel isolated."[249] The school, however, never explicitly assigned a numerical target for any particular racial group, though it did track, on an ongoing basis, "the racial composition of the developing class."[250] A rejected white applicant claimed the Law School's admission policy discriminated against her based on her race, in violation of the Equal Protection Clause and Title VI.[251] And her challenge eventually reached the Supreme Court, alongside its companion case, *Gratz*,[252] challenging the university's admissions policy for its undergraduate program.

Given the uncertainties surrounding *Bakke*'s bottom line,[253] the first major question in *Grutter* centered on the basic goal of the Law School's policy: Is achieving student diversity an interest compelling enough to justify a school's use of race at all in its admissions decisions? And for the first time the Supreme Court held that it was. Writing for a clear majority, Justice O'Connor adopted the view Justice Powell set out in *Bakke*:

---

[246] 539 U.S. 244 (2003).

[247] *Grutter*, 539 U.S. at 315.

[248] *Id.* at 319.

[249] *Id.* at 318.

[250] *Id.*

[251] *Id.* at 316-17.

[252] 539 U.S. 244 (2003).

[253] *Grutter*, 539 U.S. at 325 (noting that "[i]n the wake of [the Court's] fractured decision in *Bakke*, [lower] courts have struggled to discern whether Justice Powell's diversity rationale, set forth in part of the opinion joined by no other Justice, [was] nonetheless binding precedent").

"student body diversity is a compelling state interest that can justify the use of race in university admissions."[254]

More than that, the Court made clear that it was willing to defer to the Law School's understanding of that interest,[255] and its goal of "enroll[ing] a 'critical mass' of minority students.'"[256] As Justice O'Connor explained for the Court, by enrolling a "critical mass" of students, the Law School was trying to achieve the "substantial" "educational benefits that diversity is designed to produce"—benefits such as "promot[ing] cross-racial understanding," "break[ing] down racial stereotypes," "promot[ing] learning outcomes," and "better prepar[ing students] as professionals."[257] Achieving a "critical mass" of underrepresented students, the Court agreed, was simply one way that the Law School could try to vindicate those diversity-related educational benefits. And because this interest was deemed compelling enough to satisfy strict scrutiny, the Court was therefore willing to treat the school's use of the "critical mass" target as a permissible proxy for achieving those benefits.[258]

Not all the Justices agreed, however, that the university's invocation of "critical mass" made the diversity interest more concrete[259] or compelling.[260] In dissent, Justice Kennedy sided with Chief Justice Rehnquist's view that "the concept of critical mass [was] a delusion used by the Law School to mask its attempt to make race an automatic factor in most instances and to achieve numerical goals indistinguishable from

---

[254] *Id.* at 325.

[255] *Id.* at 328 ("The Law School's educational judgment that such diversity is essential to its educational mission is one to which we defer.").

[256] *Id.* at 329-30.

[257] *Id.*

[258] *Id.* at 333.

[259] *See id. at* 347 (Scalia, J., dissenting) (rejecting the "mystical 'critical mass' justification'" as "challeng[ing] even the most gullible mind").

[260] All four dissenting Justices—Chief Justice Rehnquist and Justices Kennedy, Scalia, and Thomas—wrote opinions, but only Justices Scalia and Thomas directly questioned whether the Law School had stated a sufficiently compelling interest. *See id.* at 357 (Thomas, J., dissenting) ("Justice Powell's opinion in *Bakke* and the Court's decision today rest on the fundamentally flawed proposition that racial discrimination can be contextualized so that a goal, such as classroom aesthetics, can be compelling in one context but not in another."); *id.* at 347 (Scalia, J., dissenting) (finding "particularly unanswerable" Justice Thomas's criticism of the "allegedly 'compelling interest'" advanced by the Law School).

quotas."[261] That "delusion," according to Justice Kennedy, did not just make the school's appeal to "critical mass" "inconsistent with [the] individual consideration" of applicants.[262] It also, in his view, turned the school's admissions policy into a veiled form of racial balancing.[263] And all four dissenting Justices found that result incompatible with the Equal Protection Clause.[264]

From "Critical Mass" to "Concrete and Precise Goals"

Grutter appeared to settle the major question left open by the fractured decision in *Bakke*: whether achieving student diversity was a compelling enough interest for a public university to justify its consideration of race in its admissions policies. *Grutter* confirmed not only that the Court still viewed student diversity as a compelling interest, but also that a school could vindicate that interest by seeking to enroll a "critical mass" of underrepresented minorities in its incoming classes.[265]

The ruling also effectively swept aside contrary lower court decisions that struck down other state universities' affirmative action policies, including in Texas.[266] In the wake of *Grutter*, the University of Texas (UT Austin) decided to revisit its applicant review process, eventually choosing to introduce race as one of the factors considered in its admissions policy. Under the revised policy, UT Austin would continue to admit all Texas high school students who graduated in the top ten percent of their class,[267] and fill in the rest of its incoming undergraduate classes[268] using an index score incorporating two assessments: (1) an "Academic Index" (AI) that weighed the applicant's SAT score and academic record; and (2) a "Personal Achievement Index" (PAI) that included a more holistic appraisal of the student's character and, following post-*Grutter* revisions,

---

[261] *Grutter*, 539 U.S. at 389 (Kennedy, J., dissenting).

[262] *Id.*

[263] *Id.*

[264] *See id.* at 387 (Rehnquist, C.J., dissenting).

[265] *Id.* at 335-36.

[266] *See Fisher II*, 136 S.Ct. 2198, 2205 (2016) ("In upholding this nuanced use of race, *Grutter* implicitly overruled *Hopwood*'s categorical prohibition.").

[267] *Id.*

[268] *Id.*

"Affirmative Action" and Equal Protection in Higher Education   49

also factored in the applicant's race.[269] Abigail Fisher, a white Texas student whose application to UT Austin was rejected under this process,[270] challenged the AI-PAI system.[271] That system, she argued, had discriminated against her as a white applicant by allegedly allowing race to figure in the decision to reject her application, in violation of the Equal Protection Clause.[272] Her challenge eventually made its way to the Supreme Court as *Fisher v. University of Texas*,[273] where the Supreme Court remanded the challenge to the lower court to review UT Austin's policy under strict scrutiny (*Fisher I*),[274] and then upon appeal upheld the school's admission policy (*Fisher II*).[275]

In her suit, Fisher did not challenge *Grutter*'s basic holding—that the university had a compelling interest in student diversity, or even that the school could pursue that interest in diversity by enrolling a "critical mass" of underrepresented minorities.[276] But when the Court finally took up her challenge on the merits in *Fisher II*, Justice Kennedy also took the occasion to revisit *Grutter*'s analysis, offering several "controlling principles"[277] on behalf of the four-Justice majority[278] that would guide its review of UT Austin's race-conscious admissions policy.

In *Fisher II*, as in *Fisher I*, Justice Kennedy confirmed that *Grutter*'s bottom line remained good law: "obtaining 'the educational benefits that flow from student body diversity,'" he confirmed, was still an interest

---

[269] This included essays submitted by the applicant, as well as other factors such as "leadership and work experience, extracurricular activities, community service, and other 'special characteristics.'" *Id.*

[270] Because Fisher did not graduate in the top ten percent of her high school class, her only chance for admission was through holistic review under the AI-PAI system. *Id.* at 2207.

[271] *Id.*

[272] *Id.*

[273] *Fisher I*, 570 U.S. 297 (2013).

[274] The Court held that the Fifth Circuit appellate panel in that case had misapplied the strict scrutiny standard by erroneously "deferring to the University's good faith in its use of racial classifications and affirming the grant of summary judgment on that basis." *Id.* at 314.

[275] *Fisher II*, 136 S.Ct. at 2215.

[276] *Fisher I*, 570 U.S. at 311 (noting that "the parties [did] not ask the Court to revisit that aspect of *Grutter*'s holding").

[277] *Fisher II*, 136 S.Ct. at 2207.

[278] Justice Kagan took no part in the case, and Justice Scalia had passed away before the case was decided, leaving only the seven Justices to consider Fisher's second appeal.

compelling enough to satisfy strict scrutiny.[279] But perhaps mindful of his dissent in *Grutter*, Justice Kennedy also clarified that "asserting an interest in the educational benefits of diversity writ large" would not suffice.[280] That, he explained, would make the "university's goals" too "elusory or amorphous" "to permit judicial scrutiny of the policies adopted to reach them."[281]

The Court thus cut two new benchmarks for reviewing a university's asserted interest in resorting to race as a factor in its admissions policy. First, the university had to articulate "precise and concrete goals" that its race-conscious policy served, goals "sufficiently measurable" under "judicial scrutiny."[282] And, second, the university had to provide a "'reasoned, principled explanation'" for its decision to pursue those goals"—a sound academic rationale, in other words, for wanting to achieve whatever diversity-related goals it set for itself.[283] In the majority's view, UT Austin's use of race in its admissions decisions measured up to both benchmarks.[284]

According to the Court, the first benchmark was straightforwardly met: the goals UT Austin articulated, Justice Kennedy pointed out, effectively "mirror[ed] the 'compelling interest' th[e] Court ha[d] approved in its prior cases."[285] And under *Grutter*, the majority concluded, those benefits passed constitutional muster.[286]

Notably, however, achieving critical mass was not among those Justice Kennedy listed. Nor did Justice Kennedy return to the question he raised in *Grutter*:[287] whether the "critical mass" concept even has a place among the

---

[279] *Id.* at 2210 (quoting *Fisher I*, 570 U.S. at 309).

[280] *Id.* at 2211.

[281] *Id.*

[282] *Id.*

[283] *Id.* at 2211 (quoting *Fisher I*, 570 U.S. at 310).

[284] *Id.*

[285] *Id.* at 2210 (reaffirming that "enrolling a diverse student body 'promotes cross-racial understanding, helps to break down racial stereotypes, and enables students to better understand persons of different races'").

[286] *Id.* at 2211 (rejecting the "contention that the University's goal was insufficiently concrete" based on its stated interest in obtaining the educational benefits approved in *Grutter*).

[287] *See Grutter*, 539 U.S. at 389 (Kennedy, J., dissenting) (describing the concept of "critical mass" as "a delusion used by the Law School to mask its attempt to make race an automatic factor in most instances and to achieve numerical goals indistinguishable from quotas").

"concrete and precise goals" that *could* survive strict scrutiny.[288] But that question was also arguably beside the point in *Fisher II*. As Justice Kennedy emphasized for the Court, the goals that UT Austin articulated were clearly constitutionally adequate, having come nearly verbatim from the Court's case law. And the university's officials had all offered "the same, consistent 'reasoned, principled explanation'" for pursuing them—meeting the Court's second benchmark.[289] That was apparently enough for the Court to conclude that a compelling interest justified the university's diluted use of race in its holistic review of applications.[290]

The Harvard Plan and the Five Hallmarks of Narrow Tailoring

With *Fisher I* and *II*, the Court reiterated that the educational benefits that come with a racially diverse student body count among the few interests compelling enough to survive strict scrutiny.[291] But *Fisher I* and *II* also narrowed that interest: seeking student body diversity had to involve objectives more specific than the simple desire for "diversity writ large."[292] Rather, under the *Fisher* formulation, the university must articulate the "concrete and precise goals" it expects its affirmative action policy to accomplish, along with a "reasoned, principled explanation" of why it has chosen to pursue them.[293] So long as a university does that, it will likely

---

[288] Justice Kennedy, writing for the majority, considered, but rejected, Fisher's argument that UT Austin allegedly "ha[d] no need to consider race because it had already 'achieved critical mass' by 2003 using the Top Ten Percent Plan and race-neutral holistic review." *Fisher II*, 126 S.Ct. at 2211. He did so, however, only because he concluded that UT Austin had carried its "heavy burden in showing that it had ... obtained the educational benefits of diversity before it turned to a race-conscious plan." *Id.* at 2211-12. He did not explain how—or whether—"achieving critical mass" mattered to that conclusion.

[289] *Id.*

[290] *Id.* at 2211. As Justice Kennedy emphasized in his opinion for the Court, "there [was] no dispute that race is but a 'factor of a factor of a factor' in the holistic-review calculus." *Id.* at 2207.

[291] *Id.* at 2210.

[292] *Id.* at 2211.

[293] *Id.*

have a strong case, under *Fisher I* and *II*,[294] that a compelling interest supports its use of a race-conscious admissions policy.

That, however, is only the first of two tests that a policy has to pass under strict scrutiny. The second—probing whether the university has narrowly tailored its policy to achieve those diversity-related benefits—has proved equally critical in the Court's review of affirmative action policies. And once again owing to Justice Powell's opinion in *Bakke*, the Court appears to have embraced a model of what a narrowly tailored policy looks like: Harvard College's admissions program endorsed in *Bakke*,[295] now more commonly known as the "Harvard plan."[296] The Harvard plan has also provided the Court with a basis for developing more specific criteria for evaluating other affirmative action policies—what one court has described as the "five hallmarks of a narrowly tailored affirmative action plan."[297]

A Narrowly Tailored Affirmative Action Policy: Bakke's Harvard Plan

The first affirmative action program to come before the Court—the policy challenged in *Bakke* at U.C. Davis's Medical School—was also the first to falter under the Court's scrutiny. But because the Justices were unable to cobble together a majority there, they also settled on no single rationale for why the Medical School's policy could not survive the Court's scrutiny. This uncertainty left the lower courts without clear

---

[294] The three dissenting Justices in *Fisher II*—Chief Justice Roberts along with Justices Alito and Thomas—voiced significant reservations about how compelling this interest was, or whether Justice Kennedy's new formulation of that interest, requiring "concrete and precise goals," really did anything to make it more concrete. As Justice Alito argued in the principal dissent, however "laudable" the university's goals may have been, they still were "not concrete or precise, and they offer[ed] no limiting principle for the use of racial preferences." *Fisher II*, 136 S.Ct. at 2233 (Alito, J., dissenting). That meant, in his view, that the Court could not "ensure than an admissions process is narrowly tailored," because it cannot "pin down the goals that the process is designed to achieve." *Id.* Justice Thomas, meanwhile, wrote to "reaffirm" his view "that 'a State's use of race in higher education admissions decisions is categorically prohibited by the Equal Protection Clause.'" *Id.* at 2215 (Thomas, J., dissenting) (quoting *Fisher I*, 570 U.S. at 315 (Thomas, J., concurring)).

[295] *See Bakke*, 438 U.S. at 316 (discussing the plan then in place at Harvard).

[296] Gratz v. Bollinger, 539 U.S. 244, 274 n.21 (2003) (analyzing "the individualized review ... discussed by Justice Powell and described by the Harvard plan in *Bakke*").

[297] Smith v. Univ. of Wash., 392 F.3d 367, 373 (9th Cir. 2004).

"Affirmative Action" and Equal Protection in Higher Education   53

guidance on the permissibility of race-conscious admissions policies structured differently than the one struck down in *Bakke*.[298]

In announcing the judgment in *Bakke*, however, Justice Powell offered a clear reason why, in his view, the Medical School's policy could not survive a challenge under the Equal Protection Clause. The school's 16-seat set-aside for minority students was not "the only effective means of serving [the school's] interest in diversity"[299]—in constitutional parlance, the set-aside was not narrowly tailored. And to explain why not, Justice Powell pointed to the Harvard plan as an example of an appropriately tailored affirmative action policy.[300]

That plan, according to Justice Powell, had several significant features that distinguished it— favorably—from the set-aside struck down in *Bakke*:

> In [Harvard's] admissions program, race or ethnic background [is] deemed a "plus" in a particular applicant's file, yet it does not insulate the individual from comparison with all other candidates for the available seats. The file of a particular black applicant may be examined for his potential contribution to diversity without the factor of race being decisive when compared, for example, with that of an applicant identified as an Italian-American if the latter is thought to exhibit qualities more likely to promote beneficial educational pluralism. Such qualities could include exceptional personal talents, unique work or service experience, leadership potential, maturity, demonstrated compassion, a history of overcoming disadvantage, ability to communicate with the poor, or other qualifications deemed important ... [And] the weight attributed to a particular quality may vary from year to year depending upon the 'mix' both of the student body and the applicants for the incoming class.[301]

Unlike this "flexible" system of review, the Medical School policy at issue in *Bakke* was rigid: reserving a predetermined number of seats for a

---

[298] Grutter v. Bollinger, 539 U.S. 306, 325 (2003) (noting the "courts ha[d] struggled to discern" what in Justice Powell's opinion was "binding precedent").

[299] Regents of Univ. of Cal. v. Bakke, 438 U.S. 265, 315 (1978).

[300] *See Bakke*, 438 U.S. at 316.

[301] *Id.* at 317-18.

"selected ethnic group." In Justice Powell's view, that technique effectively precluded a more holistic review, that "treats each applicant as an individual."[302] "[R]ace or ethnic origin," as he saw it, did not serve as "a single though important element" of an applicant's file in the Medical School's policy; it had instead become a factor that "foreclosed" other applicants "from all consideration for [certain] seat[s] simply because [they were] not the right color or had the wrong surname."[303] A program like that, Justice Powell concluded, could not be narrowly tailored—precisely because another more individualized and "holistic" model, like Harvard's, could serve instead.[304]

Ratifying the Harvard Model

Even if *Bakke* suggested that the Court's scrutiny of a race-conscious admissions policy would be every bit as strict as for other racial classifications, later cases have made clear that such scrutiny need not always be fatal. The companion cases of *Grutter v. Bollinger* and *Gratz v. Bollinger* offer clear examples: each involved affirmative action admissions policies at the University of Michigan, and each yielded a different bottom line, with the Court upholding the Law School's policy in *Grutter* while striking down the university's undergraduate admissions policy in *Gratz*.[305] But those diverging results appeared to proceed from a common starting point: how closely the challenged admissions policy resembled the Harvard plan.[306]

In the case of the Law School's admissions policy, the Court found the resemblance quite close. As Justice O'Connor explained for the Court in

---

[302] *Id.*

[303] *Id.*

[304] *See Grutter*, 539 U.S. at 337 (likening the University of Michigan Law School's "individualized, holistic review of each applicant's file" to "the Harvard plan Justice Powell referenced in *Bakke*").

[305] *Grutter*, 539 U.S. at 343-44; Gratz v. Bollinger, 539 U.S. 244, 275-76 (2003).

[306] *See Gratz*, 539 U.S. at 269, 271 (disagreeing with the university's contention that its "program 'hews closely' to both the admissions program described by Justice Powell and the Harvard College admissions program that he endorsed," while describing the Harvard plan as "instructive" in the Court's consideration of the undergraduate program); *Grutter*, 539 U.S. at 337 (concluding that the Law School's admissions policy conformed to "the Harvard Plan" that Justice Powell described in *Bakke*).

Grutter, "the Law School engages in a highly individualized, holistic review of each applicant's file, giving serious consideration to all the ways an applicant might contribute to a diverse educational environment."[307] It therefore did not award "mechanical, predetermined diversity 'bonuses' based on race or ethnicity."[308] And "[l]ike the Harvard Plan, the Law School's admissions policy" accorded each applicant the same sort of flexible consideration that Justice Powell had called for in *Bakke*.[309]

That "policy st[ood] in sharp contrast,"[310] however, with the way the Court viewed the university's undergraduate admissions policy in *Gratz*. Under the undergraduate policy, admissions officers automatically awarded "20 points, or one-fifth of the points needed to guarantee admission, to every single 'underrepresented minority' applicant solely because of race."[311] As Chief Justice Rehnquist explained for the Court, that policy therefore violated a basic feature of "[t]he admission program Justice Powell described" in *Bakke*—a program that "did not contemplate that any single characteristic automatically ensured a specific and identifiable contribution to a university's diversity."[312] The result was a policy that did not "offer applicants the individualized selection process described in Harvard's example," and that could consequently not pass strict scrutiny.[313]

On that point Justice O'Connor also agreed. As she explained in supplying her decisive fifth vote, the undergraduate policy simply did not "enable[] admissions officers to make nuanced judgments with respect to the contributions each applicant is likely to make to the diversity of the incoming class," unlike the Law School's more holistic policy.[314] This was true even though the undergraduate policy "assign[ed] 20 points to some 'soft' variables other than race," such as "leadership and service, personal

---

[307] *Grutter*, 539 U.S. at 337.
[308] *Id.*
[309] *Id.*
[310] *Gratz*, 539 U.S. at 279 (O'Connor, J., concurring).
[311] *Id.* at 270.
[312] *Id.* at 271.
[313] *Id.* at 273.
[314] *Id.* at 279.

achievement, and geographic diversity."[315] None of that, in Justice O'Connor's view, could counteract the more problematic effect of those factors' being "capped at much lower levels," so that "even the most outstanding national high school leader could never receive more than five points for his or her accomplishments—a mere quarter of the points automatically assigned to an underrepresented minority solely based on the fact of his or her race."[316] That weighting, though not problematic in all cases,[317] had all but ensured there "that the diversity contributions of applicants [could not] be individually assessed."[318] A thumb pressed that heavily on the racial scale, Justice O'Connor concluded, came too close to the "nonindividualized, mechanical" balancing condemned by *Bakke* to survive strict scrutiny.[319]

Five Hallmarks of a Narrowly Tailored Admissions Policy

Despite their contrasting results, *Gratz* and *Grutter* gestured at several basic criteria by which to assess a university's race-conscious admissions policy. Those criteria, as the U.S. Court of Appeals for the Ninth Circuit later described them, could be summed up in "five hallmarks of a narrowly tailored affirmative action plan."[320] And all five can be traced in one way or another to Justice Powell's analysis of the Harvard plan.

No Quotas

Perhaps the clearest violation of the requirement that a policy be narrowly tailored is the use of racial quotas. As Justice O'Connor explained in *Grutter*, a "'quota' is a program in which a certain fixed number or proportion of opportunities are reserved exclusively for certain minority groups," consequently "insulat[ing] the individual [applicant]

---

[315] *Id.*

[316] *Id.*

[317] *Id.* (contrasting the undergraduate policy's "automatic, predetermined point allocations" with the law school's admissions policy that "enable[d] admissions officers to make nuanced judgments").

[318] *Id.*

[319] *Id.* at 280.

[320] Smith v. Univ. of Wash., 392 F.3d 367, 373 (9th Cir. 2004).

"Affirmative Action" and Equal Protection in Higher Education 57

from comparison with all other candidates for the available seats."[321] And as Justice Powell emphasized in *Bakke*,[322] and as has been consistently reaffirmed by the Court since, "[t]o be narrowly tailored, a race-conscious admissions program cannot use a quota system."[323] This ban on quotas therefore precludes the use of a rigid set-aside like the one challenged in *Bakke*.[324] And it likewise rules out the sort of "mechanical," automatic points system that was once in place at the University of Michigan's undergraduate college and was later invalidated in *Gratz*.[325]

Individualized Consideration

The flip side of the Court's refusal to accept racial quotas has been its insistence on individualizing the consideration of applicants. As Justice Kennedy reaffirmed in *Fisher I*, echoing Justice Powell's description of the Harvard plan in *Bakke*,[326] an appropriately tailored program "must 'remain flexible enough to ensure that each applicant is evaluated as an individual and not in a way that makes an applicant's race or ethnicity the defining feature of his or her application.'"[327] And as the Court suggested in *Gratz* and *Grutter*, an acceptable plan will therefore engage in a "highly individualized, holistic review of each applicant's file, giving serious consideration to all the ways an applicant might contribute to a diverse educational environment."[328] Such review allows "the use of race as one of many 'plus factors' in an admissions program,"[329] like in the University of Michigan Law School's policy upheld in *Grutter*.[330] It also appears to bar a

---

[321] Grutter v. Bollinger, 539 U.S. 306, 335 (2003 (internal quotation marks and citations omitted).

[322] *See* Regents of Univ. of Cal. v. Bakke, 438 U.S. 265, 316 (1978) (quoting from a description of the Harvard College admissions plan that describes it as having "not set target-quotas for the number of blacks" or any other group).

[323] *Fisher I*, 570 U.S. at 309 (quoting *Grutter*, 539 U.S. at 334); *see also Smith*, 392 F.3d at 374 (discussing *Grutter*).

[324] *See Fisher II*, 136 S.Ct. at 2208 (quoting *Fisher I*, 570 U.S. at 311) ("A university cannot impose a fixed quota or otherwise 'define diversity as "some specified percentage of a particular group merely because of its race or ethnic origin."'").

[325] *See Gratz*, 539 U.S. at 280 (O'Connor, J., concurring).

[326] *See Bakke*, 438 U.S. at 316 (describing the Harvard plan as one that "treats each applicant as an individual").

[327] *Fisher I*, 570 U.S. at 309.

[328] *Grutter*, 539 U.S. at 337; *see also Smith*, 392 F.3d at 374 (quoting *Grutter* for the same).

[329] *Fisher I*, 570 U.S. at 305.

[330] *Id.* (citing *Grutter*).

58   *Christine J. Back and JD S. Hsin*

school from "automatically award[ing] points to applicants from certain racial minorities" as an effectively decisive factor, as it became under the university's undergraduate policy.[331]

Serious, Good-Faith Consideration of Race-Neutral or More Flexible Alternatives

Neither of these two criteria, however, implies that a university must exhaust "every conceivable race-neutral alternative" before turning to a race-conscious policy.[332] Instead, a university need only provide evidence that it undertook "serious, good faith consideration of workable race-neutral alternatives" before resorting to its choice of a race-conscious plan,[333] but that those alternatives either did not suffice to meet its approved educational goals[334] or would have required some sacrifice of its "reputation for academic excellence."[335] The same holds true, moreover, of more flexible race-conscious alternatives. Thus Justice Powell explained in *Bakke* that the Medical School's program was not narrowly tailored when the school could have adopted the more individualized, holistic program then in use at Harvard, an option the Medical School apparently did not consider.[336]

No Undue Harm

Even though the Court has allowed the use of race-conscious admissions policies under the exacting standard of strict scrutiny, it has also long "acknowledge[d] that 'there are serious problems of justice connected with the idea of preference itself.'"[337] In *Grutter*, Justice O'Connor drew another corollary from that apparent discomfort with racial preferences. "[A] race-conscious admissions program," she explained,

---

[331] *Id.* (citing *Gratz*).

[332] *Grutter*, 539 U.S. at 339.

[333] *Id.*

[334] *Fisher I*, 570 U.S. at 312.

[335] Fisher v. Univ. of Tex. (Fisher II), 136 S.Ct. 2198, 2213 (2016) (citing *Grutter*, 539 U.S. at 339).

[336] *See* Regents of Univ. of Cal. v. Bakke, 438 U.S. 265, 318-20 (1978) (concluding that the Medical School had not shown that "the challenged classification [was] necessary to promote a substantial state interest" given its departures from the Harvard plan).

[337] *Grutter*, 539 U.S. at 341 (quoting *Bakke*, 438 U.S. at 298).

"Affirmative Action" and Equal Protection in Higher Education 59

must "not unduly harm members of any racial group."[338] What this corollary means more specifically remains unclear; so far it has received only passing attention from the Court. At the least, Justice O'Connor suggested, a race-conscious admissions policy must not "unduly burden individuals who are not members of the favored racial and ethnic groups."[339] And in Grutter, Justice O'Connor put more flesh on that analysis: an affirmative action policy that closely resembled the Harvard plan, she suggested, would not "unduly harm" other applicants.[340] It remains to be seen, however, whether this principle might take on new life in the Court's review of other plans.[341]

Ongoing Review

In *Grutter*, Justice O'Connor also drew a fifth and final corollary from the basic premise that the Fourteenth Amendment was meant "to do away with all governmentally imposed discrimination based on race."[342] "[R]ace-conscious admissions policies," she concluded, "must be limited in time."[343] This requirement, Justice O'Connor explained for the Court,

---

[338] *Id.*

[339] *Id.* (internal quotation marks and citation omitted).

[340] *Id.* (concluding that "so long as a race-conscious admissions program uses race as a 'plus' factor in the context of individualized consideration, a rejected applicant" will have had her "qualifications ... weighed fairly and competitively," as required by the Equal Protection Clause); *see also Smith*, 392 F.3d at 374 (discussing this corollary).

[341] Justice Alito, dissenting in *Fisher II*, stressed just this concern about UT Austin's AI-PAI system, arguing that "the UT plan discriminates *against* Asian-American students," and contending that it "undeniably harms Asian-Americans" by effectively treating "the classroom contributions of Asian-American students as less valuable than those of Hispanic students" in deciding which group to give special consideration to during holistic review. *Fisher II*, 136 S.Ct. at 2227 (Alito, J., dissenting). Apparently as a result, the AI-PAI system was also "poorly tailored" under strict scrutiny. *Id.* This analysis may well have opened the door to the argument recently advanced by the U.S. Department of Justice (DOJ) in its intervention in the litigation involving Harvard's undergraduate admissions policy. Among the reasons that the policy should flunk strict scrutiny, DOJ has argued there, is that the policy has "work[ed] just such undue harm on Asian Americans," allegedly violating *Grutter*'s no-undue-harm principle. Statement of Interest in Opposition to Defendant's Motion for Summary Judgment at 12, Students for Fair Admissions, Inc. v. Harvard Corp., No. 1:14-cv14176-ADB (D. Mass. Aug. 30, 2018) (quoting *Grutter*).

[342] *Grutter*, 539 U.S. at 341-42.

[343] *Id.* (internal quotation marks and citation omitted). In *Fisher I*, the Court acknowledged the durational limit as a part of *Grutter*'s holding. *See* Fisher v. Univ. of Tex. (Fisher I), 570 U.S. 297, 313 (2013) ("In *Grutter*, the Court approved the plan at issue upon concluding that it was not a quota, was sufficiently flexible, *was limited in time*, and followed 'serious,

reflected a consideration apparently unique to racial classifications: "however compelling their goals, [they] are potentially so dangerous that they may be employed no more broadly than the interest demands."[344] Doctrinally, this meant there could be no "permanent justification" for race-conscious admissions policies in higher education; sooner or later they had to end, as the university conceded in its briefing.[345] Practically, this "logical end point" could come in one of several ways. It could take the form of an explicit "durational limit," such as a sunset provision.[346] Or it could arrive as a result of "periodic reviews to determine whether racial preferences are still necessary to achieve student body diversity."[347] But, however a university chooses to pursue that end, it has an "ongoing obligation to engage in constant deliberation and continued reflection regarding its admissions policies" and the role race plays in them, or whether it should continue to play one at all.[348]

For several Justices this ongoing obligation of review also pointed to something more definite— an expiration date, when "the use of racial preferences will no longer be necessary to further [the school's] interest" in student body diversity.[349] Looking back over the quarter-century since *Bakke*, Justice O'Connor "expect[ed]" that day to come twenty-five years after casting her deciding votes in *Gratz* and *Grutter*—ten years from this writing.[350] What exactly this meant, as either a practical or doctrinal matter, also remains unclear. Indeed, even then several of her fellow Justices seemed less sure, or simply unsure, what to make of that unusually specific

---

good faith consideration of workable race-neutral alternatives.'"). As the Court also expressly declined to "consider the correctness of that determination," with neither party having challenged it in *Fisher I* or *II*, a durational limit of some kind appears to remain good law. *Id.*

[344] *Id.* at 342.

[345] *Id.*

[346] *Id.*

[347] *Id.*; *see also Smith*, 392 F.3d at 375 (noting that, under *Grutter*, "race-conscious admissions programs must be limited in time, such as by sunset provisions or periodic reviews to determine whether the preferences remain necessary.").

[348] *Fisher II*, 136 S.Ct. at 2215.

[349] *Grutter*, 539 U.S. at 343.

[350] *Id.*

"Affirmative Action" and Equal Protection in Higher Education 61

constitutional deadline.[351] But with six Justices having since departed the Court,[352] Justices O'Connor and Kennedy included, it remains to be seen whether in the next ten years race-conscious admissions policies will reach this foreordained "logical end point."

What seems clear for now, however, is that the Harvard plan described in *Bakke* remains the Court's working model of a constitutionally satisfactory race-conscious admissions policy. And that, as the Court has consistently said since,[353] is a policy capable of achieving the diversity "essential" to the life of a modern university, while still "treat[ing] each applicant as an individual."[354]

TITLE VI AND HIGHER EDUCATION

Race has come to play two major doctrinal roles in higher education today, mirroring the two senses of "affirmative action" discussed in this chapter: the *mandatory* role, rooted in the affirmative obligation states have to eliminate the vestiges of *de jure* segregation, and the *voluntary* role, particularly in admissions decisions at selective colleges and universities. In the context of higher education, the Court has so far considered these two forms of "affirmative action" only in relation to public universities, and then primarily as a matter of constitutional law, under the Fourteenth Amendment's Equal Protection Clause. But many of those cases have also involved claims brought under Title VI of the Civil

---

[351] *See id.* at 346 (Ginsburg, J., concurring) ("From today's vantage point, one may hope, but not firmly forecast, that over the next generation's span, progress toward nondiscrimination and genuinely equal opportunity will make it safe to sunset affirmative action"); *id.* at 394 (Kennedy, J., dissenting) ("It is difficult to assess the Court's pronouncement that race-conscious admission programs will be unnecessary 25 years from now."); *but see id.* at 351 (Thomas, J., dissenting) (agreeing "with the Court's holding that racial discrimination in higher education admissions will be illegal in 25 years"); *id.* at 375-76 (Scalia, J., dissenting) (agreeing "that in 25 years the practices of the Law School will be illegal, [because] they are ... illegal now").

[352] This includes Chief Justice Rehnquist along with Justices O'Connor, Souter, Stevens, Scalia, and Kennedy. They have been replaced by, respectively, Chief Justice Roberts and Justices Alito, Sotomayor, Kagan, Gorsuch, and Kavanaugh.

[353] *See supra* section, "The Harvard Plan and the Five Hallmarks of Narrow Tailoring," pp.33-36.

[354] Regents of Univ. of Cal. v. Bakke, 438 U.S. 265, 312, 318 (1978).

Rights Act of 1964 (Title VI or the Act).[355] And while the Court has read Title VI's protections to overlap with the Equal Protection Clause,[356] Congress still has a significant say over the substantive scope of Title VI as well as its enforcement.

Agency Interpretation and Enforcement of Title VI

Title VI generally protects participants in federally funded "program[s] or activit[ies]" from discrimination based on their "race, color, or national origin."[357] To ensure that statutory right, the Act grants all federal funding agencies the authority to issue implementing regulations,[358] and the power to enforce the regulations they issue.[359] In practice, much of the interpretive authority falls to the U.S. Department of Justice (DOJ),[360] and for educational programs, the U.S. Department of Education (ED). Both DOJ and ED have also established their own processes for receiving and investigating complaints of suspected Title VI violations.[361] ED,

---

[355] 42 U.S.C. § 2000d.

[356] Alexander v. Sandoval, 532 U.S. 275, 281 (2001) ("tak[ing] as given" that Title VI "proscribes only those racial classifications that would violate the Equal Protection Clause or the Fifth Amendment") (quoting Regents of Univ. of Cal. v. Bakke, 438 U.S. 265, 287 (1978) (Powell, J., announcing judgment of the Court)).

[357] 42 U.S.C. § 2000d ("No person in the United States shall, on the ground of race, color, or national origin, be excluded from participation in, be denied the benefits of, or be subjected to discrimination under any program or activity receiving Federal financial assistance."). *See also id.* § 2000d-4a (defining program or activity).

[358] 42 U.S.C. § 2000d-1. Executive Order 12250 delegated functions that the statute had originally vested in the President to the Attorney General relating to the approval of rules, regulations, and orders of executive branch agencies that extend federal financial assistance. *See* Exec. Order No. 12250, 28 C.F.R. Part 41, Appendix A to Part 41 (Nov. 2, 1980).

[359] *See* 42 U.S.C. § 2000d-1.

[360] The Attorney General, pursuant to executive order, has been given broad authority to coordinate Title VI implementation and enforcement across executive branch agencies. *See* Exec. Order No. 12250 § 1-201(a), 28 C.F.R. Part 41, Appendix A to Part 41 (Nov. 2, 1980). DOJ has accordingly produced a comprehensive manual of Title VI guidance in addition to its own set of regulations under the Act. *See* U.S Dep't of Justice, Civ. Rights Div., *Title VI Legal Manual*, https://www.justice.gov/crt/case-document/file/934826/download; 28 CFR §§42.101-42.112 (DOJ regulations implementing Title VI).

[361] *See How to File a Complaint*, U.S. Dep't of Justice, https://www.justice.gov/crt/how-file-complaint#three (describing methods of reporting complaints to DOJ's Educational Opportunities Section); *Education and Title VI*, U.S. Dep't of Educ., Office for Civ. Rights, https://www2.ed.gov/about/offices/list/ocr/docs/hq43e4.html (explaining ED's enforcement

"Affirmative Action" and Equal Protection in Higher Education   63

meanwhile, has also issued its own set of rules to govern the federal education dollars it disburses each year, reaching some 4,700 colleges and universities.[362]

Every agency that awards federal funds—ED included—has the authority not just to issue implementing regulations but to enforce those rules against noncompliant recipients, including through an investigation that may, upon a finding of noncompliance, result in the termination, suspension, or refusal to grant federal funds.[363] Thus, for example, where ED finds a school in violation of Title VI or its implementing regulations the department may seek to cut off federal funding through an "administrative fund termination proceeding," as it has in at least some cases.[364] And since the passage of the Civil Rights Restoration Act of

---

of Title VI through its Office for Civil Rights, and describing the complaint procedure for reporting acts of discrimination based on "race, color or national origin, against any person or group, in a program or activity that receives ED financial assistance").

[362] *See Education and Title VI*, U.S. Dep't of Educ., Office for Civil Rights, https://www2.ed.gov/about/offices/list/ ocr/docs/hq43e4.html (identifying as DOE funding recipients: "50 state education agencies, their subrecipients, and vocational rehabilitation agencies; the education and vocational rehabilitation agencies of the District of Columbia and of the territories and possessions of the United States; 17,000 local education systems; 4,700 colleges and universities; 10,000 proprietary institutions; and other institutions, such as libraries and museums").

[363] 42 U.S.C. § 2000d-1 (stating that compliance "may be effected (1) by the termination of or refusal to grant or to continue assistance under such program or activity to any recipient as to whom there has been an express finding on the record, after opportunity for hearing, of a failure to comply with such requirement, but such termination or refusal shall be limited to the particular political entity, or part thereof, or other recipient as to whom such a finding has been made and, shall be limited in its effect to the particular program, or part thereof, in which such noncompliance has been so found, or (2) by any other means authorized by law").

[364] *See, e.g.*, Coal. for Equity & Excellence in Md. Higher Educ. v. Md. Higher Educ. Comm'n, 977 F. Supp. 2d 507, 516-17 (D. Md. 2013) (describing ED's earlier efforts to terminate funding for Maryland's higher education system); *see also Education and Title VI*, U.S. Dep't of Educ., Office for Civ. Rights, https://www2.ed.gov/about/offices/list/ ocr/docs/hq43e4.html ("If it cannot obtain voluntary compliance, OCR will initiate enforcement action, either by referring the case to the Department of Justice for court action, or by initiating proceedings, before an administrative law judge, to terminate Federal funding to the recipient's program or activity in which the prohibited discrimination occurred."). ED does not appear to have readily available data on how often it has initiated fund termination proceedings, or in how many cases such proceedings have resulted in the termination of funds.

1987,[365] the courts have read the scope of liability under Title VI broadly.[366] With respect to the termination of funds, a Title VI violation in one program at a college or university could therefore jeopardize funding for the institution as a whole.[367]

Withdrawing funds may be the ultimate means of enforcing Title VI, but it is far from exclusive.[368] DOJ, for its part, has also sought to achieve compliance through the federal courts, intervening in some private suits alleging Title VI violations[369] and otherwise representing executive branch agencies, such as ED, in lawsuits seeking enforcement of Title VI.[370] DOJ has participated in cases challenging practices of formerly *de jure* segregated public university systems as well as in settlements resolving such *Fordice*-related claims.[371] DOJ has also taken a position in cases challenging affirmative action admissions policies, most recently in the ongoing litigation surrounding Harvard College's admissions policies.[372] ED has ventured into this area as well, having recently opened

---

[365] Pub. L. No. 100-259 § 2 (finding that "legislative action [wa]s necessary to restore the prior consistent and longstanding executive branch interpretation and broad, institution-wide application of those laws as previously administered"). *See also* 42 U.S.C. § 2000d–4a.

[366] *See, e.g.*, Sharer v. Oregon, 581 F.3d 1176, 1178 (9th Cir. 2009) ("To honor Congress' intent, we 'interpret[] 'program or activity' broadly.'") (quoting Haybarger v. Lawrence County Adult Prob. & Parole, 551 F.3d 193, 200 (3d Cir. 2008)); *see also DOJ Title VI Legal Manual, supra* note 360, at 22-24, 27-28.

[367] *See* Ayers v. Allen, 893 F.2d 732, 754 (5th Cir. 1990) (noting that the Civil Rights Restoration Act of 1987 made it "possible to establish institution-wide discrimination under Title VI when there is federal financing that is program specific").

[368] *See* Nat'l Black Police Ass'n, Inc. v. Velde, 712 F.2d 569, 575 (D.C. Cir. 1983) (explaining that "fund termination was envisioned as the primary means of enforcement under Title VI," but that "Title VI clearly tolerates other enforcement schemes" including the "referral of cases to the Attorney General, who may bring an action against the recipient").

[369] *See generally* Alexander v. Sandoval, 532 U.S. 275, 279-80 (2001) (discussing the ability of private individuals to sue under Section 601 of Title VI).

[370] *See* U.S. Dep't of Justice, Educ. Opportunities Section, https://www.justice.gov/crt/educational-opportunitiessection (last visited Sept. 19, 2018).

[371] *See, e.g,* Geier v. Univ. of Tenn., 597 F.2d 1056, 1057-59 (6th Cir. 1979) (describing the procedural history of litigation and the intervention of the United States in the lawsuit alleging a violation of the Fourteenth Amendment). *See also* Geier v. Sundquist, 128 F.Supp.2d 519, 521 (M.D. Tenn. 2001) (settlement agreement).

[372] *See* Statement of Interest in Opposition to Defendant's Motion for Summary Judgment, Students for Fair Admissions, Inc. v. Harvard Corp., No. 1:14-cv-14176-ADB (D. Mass. Aug. 30, 2018).

investigations into the admissions decisions at several prominent private universities.[373]

Congress and Title VI

Congress continues to have considerable say over how Title VI works—at least within the parameters of the Supreme Court's equal protection jurisprudence. Perhaps the most direct way of doing so is by amendment. As a general matter, Congress could revise Title VI in one of two directions, to make the statute either (1) *more restrictive* than the Court's current Equal Protection jurisprudence or (2) *expressly permissive* of race-conscious measures that the Court has upheld or has thus far not addressed.

In the more restrictive direction, Congress could prohibit recipients of federal funds from using voluntary race-conscious measures at all—a result that four Justices in *Bakke* argued Title VI already requires, but which the Court has so far not embraced.[374] A statutory revision of that kind would also implicitly reject the Harvard Plan discussed in *Bakke*, by excluding race as a permissible factor in admissions decisions at the many universities subject to Title VI, including the many private universities that receive federal funds. And, consequently, an amendment along these lines would make unlawful the type of admissions policies that the Court has approved under the Equal Protection Clause, like those at issue in *Grutter* and *Fisher II*.

---

[373] *See, e.g.*, Benjamin Wermund, "Trump administration probes complaint that Yale discriminates against Asian-Americans," POLITICO (Sept. 26, 2018), https://www.politico.com/story/2018/09/26/trump-administration-probes-yalediscrimination-complaint-843581.

[374] *See* Regents of Univ. of Cal. v. Bakke, 438 U.S. 265, 414-15 (1978) (Stevens, J., concurring in the judgment in part and dissenting in part) (concluding from the legislative record that "under Title VI it is not 'permissible to say 'yes' to one person; but to say 'no' to another person, only because of the color of his skin").

On the other hand, Congress could expressly open other avenues for effectuating Title VI's antidiscrimination mandate. This could include incorporating a private right of action to bring suit under Title VI, which, at present, is an implied right with no statutorily defined remedies.[375] More consequentially, Congress could also amend Title VI to provide for disparate impact liability— that is, a Title VI violation based on a funding recipient's use of certain policies or practices that disproportionately and negatively impact members of a protected class, as already exists under Title VII of the same Act.[376] A provision addressing disparate impact liability—either its availability or foreclosure under Title VI—would resolve a significant and ongoing debate on the issue.[377] Such an addition would also be one way of clarifying whether Congress does in fact intend for Title VI to be read coextensively with the Equal Protection Clause.[378]

Beyond legislative amendments, Congress also exercises oversight over the agencies charged with carrying out Title VI's antidiscrimination mandate.[379] As discussed earlier, DOJ and ED are primarily responsible for enforcing Title VI in educational programs. For its part, ED investigates

---

[375] *See, e.g.*, Barnes v. Gorman, 536 U.S. 181, 185 (2002) ("Although Title VI does not mention a private right of action, our prior decisions have found an *implied* right of action."). *See also id.* at 187-90 (observing that "Title VI mentions no remedies—indeed, it fails to mention even a private right of action" and applying contract doctrine to conclude that remedies under Title VI include compensatory damages and injunctive relief, but not punitive damages).

[376] *See* 42 U.S.C. § 2000(k) (outlining the burden of proof in disparate impact cases under Title VII of the Civil Rights Act of 1964).

[377] During the Obama Administration, for example, the Office of Civil Rights issued a series of guidance premised on a disparate-impact theory under Title VI, to evaluate whether school districts were inappropriately disciplining minority students. The Trump Administration has proposed rescinding that guidance, however, arguing in a recent report that the guidance's disparate-impact theory rested on a "dubious" reading of Title VI, "at best." *See* Fed. Comm'n on School Safety, *Final Report* at 67-72 (Dec. 18, 2018) (discussing the earlier disparate-impact guidance and the Commission's reasons for urging their withdrawal).

[378] Because the Court has understood Equal Protection to forbid only acts of intentional discrimination, and not those solely with a "racially disproportionate impact," Washington v. Davis, 426 U.S. 229, 239 (1976), a statutory disparate-impact standard would necessarily broaden Title VI's protections beyond that constitutional minimum.

[379] For an overview of the oversight tools at Congress's disposal, see CRS Report R45442, *Congress's Authority to Influence and Control Executive Branch Agencies*, by Todd Garvey and Daniel J. Sheffner, at 30-36 (Dec. 19, 2018).

and seeks compliance through its Office for Civil Rights,[380] while the Educational Opportunities Section of the Department of Justice's (DOJ's) Civil Rights Division typically enforces Title VI in educational programs for the department.[381] Both offices maintain public archives documenting their past and current investigations,[382] as well as wider-ranging reports detailing thei r enforcement priorities and investigatory procedures.[383] And because Title V I applies to a wide variety of entities that receive federal financial assistance, not just colleges and universities, DOJ also publishes news and updates on Title V I enforcement activity in other programmatic areas, from agencies across the federal government.[384]

CONCLUSION

Race has come to play two major doctrinal roles in higher education today, reflecting the two senses of "affirmative action" discussed in this chapter. "Affirmative action" in its original sense grew out of the affirmative obligation imposed on the states by the Equal Protection Clause to eliminate the vestiges of *de jure* segregation from their public schools. And in that sense, "affirmative action" involves the *mandatory* use of race-conscious measures in higher education to right the enduring wrongs of

---

[380] The Office for Civil Rights has also published a detailed manual prescribing its procedures for handling complaints under Title VI, among other statutes with its purview. *See generally* U.S. Dep't of Educ., Office for Civ. Rights, *Case Processing Manual*, https://www2.ed.gov/about/offices/list/ocr/docs/ocrcpm.pdf.

[381] More recently, it has been reported that the Educational Opportunities Section is no longer exclusively handling certain enforcement matters in this area. *See* Charlie Savage, *Justice Dept. to Take On Affirmative Action in College Admissions*, N.Y. TIMES (Aug. 1, 2017), https://www.nytimes.com/2017/08/01/us/politics/trump-affirmative-actionuniversities.html.

[382] *See* U.S. Dep't of Justice, *Department of Justice Updates*, https://www.justice.gov/crt/fcs/DOJ-updates; U.S. Dep't of Educ., Office for Civ. Rights, *Pending Cases Currently Under Investigation at Elementary-Secondary and Post-Secondary Schools*, https://www2.ed.gov/about/offices/list/ocr/docs/investigations/open-investigations/index.html.

[383] *See* U.S. Dep't of Justice, *Title VI Legal Manual*, https://www.justice.gov/crt/fcs/T6manual; U.S. Dep't of Educ., Office for Civ. Rights, *Case Processing Manual* (Nov. 19, 2018), https://www2.ed.gov/about/offices/list/ocr/docs/ ocrcpm.pdf.

[384] *See, e.g.*, U.S. Dep't of Justice, *Title VI Enforcement and Updates by Agency*, https://www.justice.gov/crt/fcs/ Enforcement-updates-byagency.

state-sanctioned segregation. But "affirmative action" has also come to refer to race-conscious policies outside this *de jure* context—policies *voluntarily* adopted by institutions to help racial minorities overcome the effects of their earlier exclusion. In higher education, none has been more salient—or stirred more debate—than the race-conscious admissions policies that colleges and universities across the country have used to diversify their student bodies.

Thus far, remedial measures addressing *de jure* segregation, and voluntary measures designed to promote student-body diversity, have been the only race-conscious measures that the Court has approved under the Equal Protection Clause. And both remain areas of active litigation and administrative enforcement. Over the years, however, the Court has made it clear that it will subject *voluntary* "affirmative action" policies to especially close scrutiny, approving them only when they can be shown to be narrowly tailored to serve compelling educational goals. It has approved such polices twice already, most recently in 2016. Still, several Justices have suggested that the rationales supporting these voluntary race-conscious measures will one day run out. But for the time being, at least, these two lines of authority nevertheless provide a place for affirmative action in higher education today.

This authority, however, leaves questions as of yet unexplored. It appears to be an open question,[385] for example, whether a public institution[386] of higher education can cite its own history of intentional

---

[385] To date, there appears to be no federal court decision addressing an Equal Protection claim in which a litigant has challenged a public university's race-conscious admissions policy (or other race-conscious measure), and the institution has defended those race-conscious practices as necessary to correct or eliminate a vestige of prior *de jure* segregation, as *Fordice* mandates under the Equal Protection Clause. *Cf. Parents Involved*, 551 U.S. at 737 (stating that "no one questions that the obligation to disestablish a school system segregated by law can include race-conscious remedies— whether or not a court had issued an order to that effect").

[386] While intentional segregation is most commonly analyzed in terms of a public school *system* or district, it is less clear how a federal court might analyze segregation or segregative practices by a particular public *institution* as the basis for finding *de jure* segregation that triggers an affirmative duty. *Cf.* Keyes v. Sch. Dist. No. 1, Denver, Colo., 413 U.S. 189, 192-93, 198-205 (1973) (addressing claims alleging *de jure* segregation in one area ("Park Hill") within the Denver public school district, as well as *de jure* segregation with respect to the rest of the school district, "particularly heavily segregated schools in the core city area"); United States v. Sch. Dist. of City of Ferndale, Mich., 616 F.2d 895, 896 (6th Cir.

"Affirmative Action" and Equal Protection in Higher Education   69

exclusion,[387] or else its "past discrimination,"[388] as a basis for adopting a race-conscious admissions policy, among other measures. Whether—and how—the courts might assess such untested arguments would likely turn on a range of factors, including the further development of the two lines of authority addressed in this chapter. Regardless of those and other possible developments, however, Congress still has a significant say in in this area, through its authority not just to revise Title VI but to oversee the Act's enforcement.

1980) (holding that there was *de jure* segregation as to *one* public school in the district). *See also* Wessman v. Gittens, 160 F.3d 790, 795 (1st Cir. 1998) ("Of course, we know that [the government's use of a racial classification] is acceptable upon a showing, *inter alia*, that it is needed to undo the continuing legacy of an *institution*'s past discrimination.") (emphasis added).

[387] *See generally Fordice*, 505 U.S. at 728 ("Our decisions establish that a State does not discharge its constitutional obligations until it eradicates policies and practices traceable to its prior *de jure* dual system that continue to foster segregation.").

[388] *See, e.g., Wessman*, 160 F.3d at 800-807 (in a case challenging a race-conscious admissions policy at a selective K12 public "examination" school in Boston, applying an analysis "guided primarily by the [Supreme] Court's particularized analysis in [*City of Richmond v.*] *Croson*" that requires state actors to "muster a 'strong basis in evidence'" of "past discrimination" to justify race-conscious measures, where such measures must be narrowly tailored to remedy the specific harm at issue; noting there was no contention in the case that "any municipal actor ha[d] attempted intentionally to subvert the demographic composition" of the school); Podbersky v. Kirwan, 38 F.3d 147, 152-153 (4th Cir. 1994) (applying the "strong basis in evidence" test to a public university's scholarship program for African American students).

In: Key Congressional Reports on Education ISBN: 978-1-53615-731-4
Editor: Georgia Turner © 2019 Nova Science Publishers, Inc.

Chapter 2

PUBLIC SAFETY OFFICERS' BENEFITS (PSOB) AND PUBLIC SAFETY OFFICERS' EDUCATIONAL ASSISTANCE (PSOEA) PROGRAMS[*]

Scott D. Szymendera

SUMMARY

The Public Safety Officers' Benefits (PSOB) program provides cash benefits to federal, state, and local law enforcement officers; firefighters; employees of emergency management agencies; and members of emergency medical services agencies who are killed or permanently and totally disabled as the result of personal injuries sustained in the line of duty. The Public Safety Officers' Educational Assistance (PSOEA) program, a component of the PSOB program, provides higher-education assistance to the children and spouses of public safety officers killed or permanently disabled in the line of duty.

---

[*] This is an edited, reformatted and augmented version of Congressional Research Service, Publication No. R45327, dated February 1, 2019.

The PSOB and PSOEA programs are administered by the Department of Justice (DOJ), Bureau of Justice Assistance (BJA). However, claimants dissatisfied with denials of benefits may pursue administrative appeals within DOJ and may seek judicial review before the United States Court of Appeals for the Federal Circuit.

Each year, Congress appropriates funding for PSOB death benefits, which is considered mandatory spending, and for PSOB disability benefits and PSOEA benefits, which is subject to annual appropriations.

For FY2019, the one-time lump-sum PSOB death and disability benefit is $359,316 and the PSOEA monthly benefit for a student attending an educational institution full-time is $1,224.

In FY2017, the DOJ approved 399 claims for PSOB death benefits, 82 claims for PSOB disability benefits, and 601 claims for PSOEA benefits.

The Public Safety Officers' Benefits (PSOB) program provides cash benefits to federal, state, and local law enforcement officers; firefighters; employees of emergency management agencies; and members of emergency medical services agencies who are killed or permanently and totally disabled as the result of personal injuries sustained in the line of duty.[1] The Public Safety Officers' Educational Assistance (PSOEA) program, a component of the PSOB program, provides higher-education assistance to the children and spouses of public safety officers killed or permanently disabled in the line of duty.[2] Both programs are administered by the PSOB Office of the Department of Justice (DOJ), Bureau of Justice Assistance (BJA).[3]

Congress appropriates funds for these programs in the annual Departments of Commerce and Justice, Science, and Related Agencies Appropriations Act. For FY2019, the one-time lump-sum PSOB benefit is $359,316 and the monthly full-time attendance PSOEA assistance is $1,224. The PSOB and PSOEA benefit amounts are indexed to reflect changes in the cost of living.

---

[1] The Public Safety Officers' Benefits (PSOB) program is authorized in statute at Part L of Title I of the Omnibus Crime Control and Safe Streets Act of 1968 (34 U.S.C. §§10281-10288).

[2] The Public Safety Officers' Educational Assistance (PSOEA) program is authorized in statute at 34 U.S.C. §§10301 10308.

[3] The PSOB program website is at https://psob.bja.ojp.gov/.

Table 1. PSOB and PSOEA Claims and Approvals
(FY2015-FY2017)

	FY2015	FY2016	FY2017
PSOB Death Benefits			
Claims Filed	284	285	356
Claims Approved	266	330	399
PSOB Disability Benefits			
Claims Filed	64	61	77
Claims Approved	17	31	82
PSOEA Benefits			
Claims Filed	606	679	715
Claims Approved	453	549	601

Source: Department of Justice, Office of Justice Programs, *FY2019 Program Summaries*, February 2018, p. 108, https://www.justice.gov/jmd/page/file/1039211/download.

Note: Data is reported when a claim is filed and approved, thus claims filed in one year may be approved in another year.

Table 1 shows PSOB and PSOEA claims and approvals as reported by DOJ.

PUBLIC SAFETY OFFICERS' BENEFITS PROGRAM

Eligible Public Safety Officers

To be eligible for PSOB benefits for death or disability, a person must have served in one of the following categories of public safety officers:

- law enforcement officer, firefighter, or chaplain in a public agency;
- FEMA employee or a state, local, or tribal emergency management agency employee; or
- emergency medical services member.

There is no minimum amount of time a person must have served to be eligible for benefits.

74 Scott D. Szymendera

Law Enforcement Officer, Firefighter, or Chaplain

To be eligible for PSOB benefits as a law enforcement officer, firefighter, or chaplain, a person must have served in a "public agency" in an official capacity, with or without compensation.[4] For the purposes of PSOB eligibility, a public agency is defined as

- the federal government and any department, agency, or instrumentality of the federal government; and
- any state government, the District of Columbia government, and any U.S. territory or possession; and any local government, department, agency, or instrumentality of a state, the District of Columbia, or any U.S. territory or possession.[5]

Law Enforcement Officer

For the purposes of PSOB eligibility, a law enforcement officer is defined as "an individual involved in crime and juvenile delinquency control or reduction, or enforcement of the criminal laws (including juvenile delinquency), including, but not limited to, police, corrections, probation, parole, and judicial officers."[6]

Firefighter

For the purposes of PSOB eligibility, the definition of firefighter includes both professional firefighters and persons serving as an "officially recognized or designated member of a legally organized volunteer fire department."[7]

Chaplain

A chaplain is eligible for PSOB benefits (1) if he or she is either an "officially recognized or designated member of a legally organized volunteer fire department or legally organized police department" or public

---

[4] 34 U.S.C. §10284(9).
[5] 34 U.S.C. §10284(8).
[6] 34 U.S.C. §10284(6).
[7] 34 U.S.C. §10284(4).

employee of a police or fire department[8] and (2) only if he or she was performing the duties of a chaplain in an official capacity while responding to a police, fire, or rescue emergency.[9]

Emergency Management Agency Employee

Employees of the Federal Emergency Management Agency (FEMA) and state, local, or tribal emergency management agencies may be eligible for PSOB benefits under certain conditions provided in statute. A FEMA employee or an employee of a state, local, or tribal emergency management agency working with FEMA is eligible for PSOB benefits if he or she is performing official duties that are related to a major disaster or an emergency declared under the Robert T. Stafford Disaster Relief and Emergency Assistance Act (Stafford Act)[10] and that are considered hazardous by the FEMA Administrator or the head of the state, local, or tribal agency.[11]

Emergency Medical Services Member

A member, including a volunteer member, of a rescue squad or "ambulance crew" who is authorized or licensed by law and the applicable agency and is engaging in rescue services or providing emergency medical services may be eligible for PSOB benefits.[12] The rescue squad or ambulance service may provide ground or air ambulance services and may be either a public agency or a nonprofit entity authorized to provide rescue or emergency medical services.

---

[8] 34 U.S.C. §10284(2).

[9] 28 C.F.R. §32.3.

[10] The Stafford Act is in statute at 42 U.S.C. §§5121 et seq. For additional information on emergency and disaster declarations under the Stafford Act, see CRS Report R43784, *FEMA's Disaster Declaration Process: A Primer*. The definition of hazardous duty for the purposes of determining the eligibility of emergency management employees is not defined in statute or regulation. Rather, the determination of whether duty is hazardous is made by the FEMA Administrator or head of the relevant state, local, or tribal emergency management agency.

[11] 34 U.S.C. §§10284(9)(b) and (c).

[12] 34 U.S.C. §10284(9).

By PSOB regulation, eligible emergency medical services workers include rescue workers, ambulance drivers, paramedics, health care responders, emergency medical technicians, or others who are trained in rescue activity or emergency medical services and have the legal authority and responsibility to provide such services.[13]

Injury and Line of Duty Requirements

The PSOB program pays benefits if a public safety officer becomes permanently and totally disabled or dies "as the direct and proximate result of a personal injury sustained in the line of duty."[14]

Injury Requirement

To qualify for coverage under the PSOB program, a public safety officer's disability or death must have been the result of a personal injury. The PSOB regulation defines an injury for the purposes of benefit eligibility as

> a traumatic physical wound (or a traumatized physical condition of the body) directly and proximately caused by external force (such as bullets, explosives, sharp instruments, blunt objects, or physical blows), chemicals, electricity, climatic conditions, infectious disease, radiation, virii, or bacteria ...[15]

The regulation also provides that the definition of an injury does not include an occupational disease or a condition of the body caused by stress or strain, including psychological conditions such as post-traumatic stress disorder. However, the PSOB statute specifically provides for deaths caused by certain cardiovascular conditions.

---

[13] 28 C.F.R. §32.3.
[14] 34 U.S.C. §§10281(a) and (b).
[15] 28 C.F.R. §32.3.

Public Safety Officers' Benefits (PSOB) ...

Presumption of Injury Status for Heart Attack, Stroke, or Vascular Rupture

The death of a public safety officer due to a heart attack, stroke, or vascular rupture shall be presumed to be a death from a personal injury for the purposes of PSOB eligibility if the officer engaged in nonroutine stressful or strenuous physical activity as part of an emergency response or training exercise; and if the condition began during the physical activity, while the officer remained on duty after the physical activity, or within 24 hours of the physical activity.[16]

Line of Duty Requirement

The PSOB program covers a public safety officer's death or disability if it occurred as the result of an injury incurred in the line of duty. The PSOB regulations provide that an injury occurs in the line of duty if it (1) is the result of the public safety officer's authorized activities while on duty, (2) occurs while responding to an emergency or request for assistance, or (3) occurs while commuting to or from duty in an authorized department or personal vehicle.[17] In addition, if there is convincing evidence that the injury was the result of the individual's status as a public safety officer, that injury is covered by the PSOB program.

Benefit Amounts

The lump-sum PSOB death and disability benefit for FY2019 is $359,316. The benefit amount is adjusted annually to reflect changes in the cost of living using the annual percentage change in the Consumer Price Index for Urban Consumers (CPI-U) for the one-year period ending in the previous June.[18] If a public safety officer receives a disability benefit and later dies from the same injury, the officer's survivors may not receive a PSOB death benefit.

---

[16] 34 U.S.C. §10281(k).
[17] 28 C.F.R. §32.3.
[18] 34 U.S.C. §10281(h).

The payable benefit amount is based on the date of the public safety officer's death or the date of the injury that caused the disability, rather than on the date of application for benefits or disability determination. Thus, if a benefit increase occurs while an application is pending, the benefit is payable at the previous, lower, benefit level.

Death and disability benefits are not subject to the federal income tax.[19] In general, PSOB death and disability benefits are paid in addition to any other workers' compensation, life insurance, or other benefits paid for the death of a public safety officer. However, the PSOB death benefit is offset by the following benefits:[20]

- benefits under the Federal Employees' Compensation Act (FECA) payable to state and local law enforcement officers injured or killed while enforcing federal law;[21]
- benefits under the D.C. Retirement and Disability Act of 1916 for certain police officers and firefighters in the District of Columbia;[22] and
- payments from the September 11th Victim Compensation Fund (VCF).[23]

Payments to Survivors

PSOB death benefits are payable to the eligible spouse and children of a public safety officer. A spouse is the person to whom the officer is legally married, even if physically separated, under the marriage laws of the jurisdiction where the marriage took place. Pursuant to regulations issued after the Supreme Court struck down the federal Defense of

---

[19] Section 104(a)(6) of the Internal Revenue Code [26 U.S.C. §104(a)(6)].
[20] 34 U.S.C. §10281(f).
[21] 5 U.S.C. §8191. For additional information on FECA, see CRS Report R42107, *The Federal Employees' Compensation Act (FECA): Workers' Compensation for Federal Employees*. There is no offset for FECA benefits for federal employees.
[22] Section 12 of Act of Sept. 1, 1916, ch. 433, 39 Stat. 718.
[23] 49 U.S.C. §40101 note.

Marriage Act in *United States\ v. Windsor*,[24] the legally married spouse of a public safety office may be of the same sex as the officer.[25]

A child is defined as any "natural, illegitimate, adopted, or posthumous child or stepchild" of the public safety officer who, at the time of the public safety officer's fatal or catastrophic injury, is

- 18 years of age or under;
- between 18 and 23 years of age and a full-time student in high school or undergraduate higher education; or
- over 18 years of age and incapable of self-support because of physical or mental disability.[26]

PSOB death benefits are paid to eligible survivors in the following order:

1. if the officer is survived by only a spouse, 100% of the death benefits are payable to the spouse;
2. if the officer is survived by a spouse and children, 50% of the death benefits are payable to the spouse and the remaining 50% is distributed equally among the officer's children;
3. if the officer is survived by only children, the death benefits are equally distributed among the officer's children;
4. if the officer has no surviving spouse or children, the death benefits are paid to the individual or individuals designated by the officer in the most recently executed designation of beneficiary on file at the time of the officer's death; or if the officer does not have a designation of beneficiary on file, the benefits are paid to the individual or individuals designated by the officer in the most recently executed life insurance policy on file at the time of the officer's death;

---

[24] 570 U.S. 744 (2013).
[25] Department of Justice, "Public Safety Officers' Benefit Program," 79 *Federal Register* 35492, June 23, 2014.
[26] 34 U.S.C. §10284(3).

5. if the officer has no surviving spouse or eligible children, and the officer does not have a life insurance policy, the death benefits are equally distributed between the officer's surviving parents; or
6. if the officer has no surviving spouse, eligible children, or parents, and the officer did not have a designation of beneficiary or a life insurance policy on file at the time of his or her death, the death benefits are payable to surviving adult, nondependent, children of the officer.[27]

Definition of Disability

PSOB disability benefits are paid only in cases of permanent and total disability. There are no benefits payable for partial or short-term disabilities. A disability is considered permanent for the purposes of PSOB eligibility if, given the current state of medicine in the United States, there is a degree of medical certainty that the condition will remain constant or deteriorate over the person's lifetime or that the public safety officer has reached maximum medical improvement. A public safety officer is considered to be totally disabled for the purposes of PSOB eligibility if given the current state of medicine in the United States, there is a degree of medical certainty that the officer is unable to perform any gainful work. PSOB regulation defines gainful work as "full- or part-time activity that is compensated or commonly compensated."[28]

Application Process

Applications for PSOB death and disability benefits are filed with the PSOB office, which determines benefit eligibility and commences benefit payment. Unless extended for good cause, application deadlines must be met. Complete benefit applications must be filed no later than

---

[27] 34 U.S.C. §10281(a).
[28] 28 C.F.R. §32.23.

- for death benefits:
  - three years after the death;
  - one year after the determination of the officer's employing agency to award or deny death benefits payable by that agency; or
  - one year after certification by the officer's employing agency that the agency is not authorized to pay any death benefits;[29] and
- for disability benefits:
  - three years after the date of the injury;
  - one year after the determination of the officer's employing agency to award or deny workers' compensation or disability benefits payable by that agency; or
  - one year after certification by the officer's employing agency that the agency is not authorized to pay any workers' compensation or disability benefits.[30]

A lump-sum interim payment of up to $3,000 may be made if a PSOB death benefit will "probably be paid."[31] The interim payment amount reduces the final PSOB payment amount. If the ultimate decision is to deny death benefits, the interim payment must be returned to the federal government, unless this repayment is waived because it would create a hardship for the beneficiary.

Expedited Benefits in Terrorism Cases

Section 611 of the Uniting and Strengthening America by Providing Appropriate Tools Required to Intercept and Obstruct Terrorism Act of 2001 (USA PATRIOT Act; P.L. 107-56) provides for expedited payment of PSOB death and disability benefits if the officer's injury occurred "in connection with prevention, investigation, rescue, or recovery efforts

---

[29] 28 C.F.R. §32.12.

[30] 28 C.F.R. §32.22.

[31] 34 U.S.C. §10281(c). The amount of the interim payment is not subject to a cost-of-living adjustment.

82   *Scott D. Szymendera*

related to a terrorist attack."[32] In such cases, PSOB benefits must be paid within 30 days of certification from the officer's employing agency that the officer's death or disability was related to terrorism.

PUBLIC SAFETY OFFICERS' EDUCATIONAL ASSISTANCE PROGRAM

The Public Safety Officers' Education Assistance (PSOEA) program provides financial assistance with costs associated with higher education to the spouse or children of a public safety officer who is eligible for PSOB death or disability benefits.

Eligibility

The spouse or child of a public safety officer who is eligible for PSOB death or disability benefits may be eligible for PSOEA benefits. To be eligible for PSOEA benefits, a spouse must have been married to an eligible public safety officer at the time of the officer's death or injury. A child is eligible for PSOEA benefits until the age of 27. This age limit can be extended by the Attorney General in extraordinary circumstances, or, pursuant to Section 3 of the Public Safety Officers' Benefits Improvement Act of 2017 (P.L. 115-36), if there is a delay of more than one year in approving PSOB or PSOEA benefits.[33]

In addition, to be eligible for PSOEA benefits, the spouse or child must be enrolled at an eligible educational institution. For the purposes of PSOEA eligibility, an eligible education institution is one that meets the definition of an "institution of higher education" as provided by Section

---

[32] 34 U.S.C. §10486.
[33] 34 U.S.C. §10302(c).

Public Safety Officers' Benefits (PSOB) ... 83

102 of the Higher Education Act of 1965[34] and that is eligible for federal student aid.[35]

Amount of Benefits

PSOEA benefits are payable to the claimant and may be used only to defray costs associated with higher education attendance, including tuition, room, board, book and supplies, and education-related fees. The monthly PSOEA benefit amount is equal to the monthly benefit amount payable under the GI Bill Survivors' and Dependents' Educational Assistance (DEA) program, which is administered by the Department of Veterans Affairs (VA) for spouses and dependents of veterans with disabilities or who died as a result of service-connected conditions.[36] The PSOEA benefit amounts are adjusted annually to reflect changes in the cost of living in accordance with changes to the GI Bill DEA benefit amounts. For FY2019, the PSOEA monthly benefit for a student attending an educational institution full-time is $1,224.[37] The PSOEA benefit rates are prorated for less than full-time attendance.

Duration of Benefits

The maximum duration of PSOEA benefits for any person is 45 months of full-time education or a proportionate duration of part-time education. A person is ineligible for PSOEA if he or she is in default on a

---

[34] 20 U.S.C. §1002.

[35] 34 U.S.C. §10307(3). For additional information on institutional eligibility for federal student aid, see CRS Report R43159, *Institutional Eligibility for Participation in Title IV Student Financial Aid Programs*.

[36] For additional information on the GI Bill Survivors' and Dependents' Educational Assistance (DEA) program, see CRS Report R42785, *GI Bills Enacted Prior to 2008 and Related Veterans' Educational Assistance Programs: A Primer*.

[37] Current and historical GI Bill DEA benefit rates are available on the Department of Veterans Affairs (VA) website, at https://www.benefits.va.gov/GIBILL/resources/benefits_ resources/rate_tables.asp.

84 *Scott D. Szymendera*

federal student loan or is ineligible for federal benefits due to a drug trafficking or drug possession conviction. In addition, the Attorney General may discontinue PSOEA benefits for a student that fails to make satisfactory progress in his or her course of study as defined by Section 484(c) of the Higher Education Act of 1965.[38]

PSOB AND PSOEA APPEALS PROCESS

A claimant who is dissatisfied with a PSOB disability benefit denial may request a reconsideration.[39] There is no reconsideration offered for denials of PSOB death or PSOEA benefits. A claimant who is dissatisfied with a PSOB or PSOEA benefit denial may request a de novo hearing before a hearing officer assigned by the director of the DOJ PSOB Office.[40] The determination of a hearing officer may be appealed to the PSOB Office director.[41] The director's determination is considered the final agency determination and is not subject to any further agency administrative review or appeal. However, provided all administrative appeals remedies have been exhausted, the PSOB Office director's determination may be appealed to the United States Court of Appeals for the Federal Circuit.[42]

The PSOB statute authorizes the BJA to prescribe the maximum fee that an attorney or other representative may charge a claimant for services rendered in connection with a claim, with attorney fees generally limited to between 3% and 6% of the total benefit paid, depending on the level in the administrative appeals process the claim is approved.[43] Program regulation prohibits stipulated-fee and contingency-fee arrangements for PSOB representation.[44]

---

[38] 34 U.S.C. §10305. Section 484(c) of the Higher Education Act of 1965 is codified at 20 U.S.C. §1091(c).

[39] 28 C.F.R. §32.28.

[40] 28 C.F.R. §§32.41-32.45.

[41] 28 C.F.R. §§32.51-32.54.

[42] 34 U.S.C. §10287, and 28 C.F.R. §§32.8 and 32.55.

[43] 34 U.S.C. §10285(a) and 28 C.F.R. §32.7.

[44] 28 C.F.R. §32.7(d)(1).

Public Safety Officers' Benefits (PSOB) ... 85

BUDGET AND APPROPRIATIONS

Congress provides funding for PSOB and PSOE benefits and associated administrative expenses in the annual Departments of Commerce and Justice, Science, and Related Agencies Appropriations Act.[45] Funding for PSOB death benefits and associated administrative expenses is considered mandatory spending and Congress appropriates "such sums as may be necessary" for the payment of these benefits. Funding for PSOB disability and PSOEA benefits is considered discretionary and is subject to specific congressional appropriations. Annual appropriations language grants the Attorney General the authority to transfer from any available appropriations to the DOJ the funds necessary to respond to emergent circumstances that require additional funding for PSOB disability benefits and PSOEA benefits.[46]

---

[45] For additional information on this appropriations legislation, see CRS Report R44877, *Overview of FY2018 Appropriations for Commerce, Justice, Science, and Related Agencies (CJS)*.

[46] See, for example, Title II of Division B of the Consolidated Appropriations Act, 2018 (P.L. 115-141).

In: Key Congressional Reports on Education   ISBN: 978-1-53615-731-4
Editor: Georgia Turner   © 2019 Nova Science Publishers, Inc.

Chapter 3

THE CLOSURE OF INSTITUTIONS OF HIGHER EDUCATION: STUDENT OPTIONS, BORROWER RELIEF, AND OTHER IMPLICATIONS*

Alexandra Hegji

SUMMARY

When an institution of higher education (IHE) closes, a student's postsecondary education may be disrupted. Students enrolled at closing IHEs may face numerous issues and may be required to make difficult decisions in the wake of a closure. Two key issues students may face when their IHEs close relate to their academic plans and their personal finances.

The academic issues faced by students when their schools close include whether they will continue to pursue their postsecondary education, and if so, where and how they might do so. Students deciding to continue their postsecondary education have several options. They may

---

* This is an edited, reformatted and augmented version of Congressional Research Service Publication No. R44737, Updated February 5, 2019.

participate in a teach-out offered by the closing institution or by another institution. A teach-out is a plan that provides students with the opportunity to complete their program of study after a school's closure. Students may also be able to transfer the credits they previously earned at the closed IHE to another IHE. If a student is able to transfer some or all of the previously earned credits, he or she would not be required to repeat the classes those credits represent at the new institution; if a student is unable to transfer previously earned credits, the student may be required to repeat the classes those credits represent at the new IHE. Decisions regarding the acceptance of credit transfers are within the discretion of the accepting IHE.

The financial issues faced by students when their schools close include whether they are responsible for repaying any loans borrowed to attend a closed school and how they might finance any additional postsecondary education they pursue. In general, a closed school loan discharge is available to a borrower of federal student loans made under Title IV of the Higher Education Act (P.L. 89-329, as amended), if the student was enrolled at the IHE when it closed or if the student withdrew from the IHE within 120 days prior to its closure. Additionally, the student must have been unable to complete his or her program of study at the closed school or a comparable program at another IHE, either through a teach-out agreement or by transferring any credits to another IHE. Borrowers ineligible for a closed school discharge may be able to have eligible Title IV federal student loans discharged by successfully asserting as a borrower defense to repayment (BDR) certain acts or omissions of an IHE, if the cause of action directly relates to the loan or educational services for which the loan was provided. Whether a borrower may have discharged all or part of any private education loans borrowed to attend the closed IHE may depend on the loan's terms and conditions.

Some students may also face issues regarding how they might finance future postsecondary educational pursuits. If a borrower receives a closed school discharge or has a successful BDR claim, the discharged loan will not count against the borrower's Subsidized Loan usage period, which typically limits certain borrowers' receipt of Direct Subsidized Loans for a period equal to 150% of the published length of his or her academic program, and a borrower's statutory annual and aggregate borrowing limits on Direct Subsidized and Direct Unsubsidized Loans are unlikely to be affected. Students who receive a Pell Grant for enrollment at a school that closed may have an equivalent amount of Pell eligibility restored. Likewise, if the student used GI Bill educational benefits from the Department of Veterans Affairs for attendance at a closed school, those benefits can be restored.

Students may be reimbursed for payments on charges levied by closed IHEs that are not covered by other sources from a State Tuition

The Closure of Institutions of Higher Education 89

Recovery Fund (STRF). The availability of and student eligibility for such funds vary by state, and not all states operate STRFs. Finally, the receipt of any of the above-mentioned benefits may have federal and state income tax implications, including the potential creation of a federal income tax liability for borrowers who have certain loans discharged.

LIST OF ABBREVIATIONS

The following are abbreviations used throughout this chapter.

ACI	American Career Institutes
AOTC	American Opportunity Tax Credit
BDR	Borrower defense to repayment
CCI	Corinthian Colleges, Inc.
DL	Direct Loan
ED	U.S. Department of Education
FFEL	Federal Family Education Loan
HEA	Higher Education Act
IHE	Institution of higher education
IRC	Internal Revenue Code
IRS	Internal Revenue Service
LLC	Lifetime Learning Credit
SAP	Satisfactory Academic Progress
STRF	State Tuition Recovery Fund
TEACH Grant	Teacher Education Assistance for College and Higher Education Grant
VA	Department of Veterans Affairs

INTRODUCTION

In academic year (AY) 2017-2018, 6,700 institutions of higher education (IHEs), enrolling over 27 million postsecondary education

90 *Alexandra Hegji*

students in AY2016-2017,[1] participated in the federal student aid programs authorized under Title IV of the Higher Education Act of 1965 (HEA; P.L. 89-329, as amended).[2] These IHEs ranged in sector, size, and educational programs offered. They comprised all sectors (i.e., public, private nonprofit, and proprietary), with some IHEs enrolling as few as three students and others enrolling over 190,000 in a single year.[3] Offered educational programs varied from certificate programs in career and technical fields to doctoral and professional degree programs.

Most of these IHEs operate from year to year with few severe financial or operational concerns; however, each year, a few do face such concerns, which may cause them to cease or significantly curtail operations. The recent closure of multiple large, proprietary (or private, for-profit) IHEs has brought into focus the extent to which a postsecondary student's education may be disrupted by a school closure.[4] However, even in instances of a small IHE's closure, student concerns remain the same. Concerns include the following, among others: Can they continue their postsecondary education at another school? How will they finance future postsecondary educational pursuits? Are they liable for repaying loans they may have borrowed to pursue a postsecondary credential that they were unable to obtain because of an IHE's closure?

This chapter provides an explanation of the options a postsecondary student may pursue in the event the IHE he or she attends closes, any financial relief that may be available to such students, and other practical implications for students following a school's closure. First, this chapter describes the academic options available to such students, such as participating in a teach-out or transferring to a new IHE. Next, it discusses issues related to financing a postsecondary education, including the extent

---

[1] U.S. Department of Education, National Center for Education Statistics, Integrated Postsecondary Education Data System (IPEDS).

[2] 20 U.S.C. 1001, et seq.

[3] U.S. Department of Education, National Center for Education Statistics, Integrated Postsecondary Education Data System (IPEDS).

[4] For additional information on some of these closures, see CRS Report R44068, *Effect of Corinthian Colleges' Close on Student Financial Aid: Frequently Asked Questions*, archived, available to congressional clients upon request, and CRS Insight IN10577, *The Closure of ITT Technical Institute*, archived, available to congressional clients upon request.

The Closure of Institutions of Higher Education 91

to which borrowers may have any loans borrowed to finance educational expenses discharged due to a school closure and whether future financial assistance, including federal student loans, Pell Grants, and GI educational benefits, may be available to students should they decide to continue their postsecondary education at another IHE. This chapter then describes additional relief that may be available to students who attended IHEs that closed, such as the potential to have tuition paid reimbursed through a state tuition recovery fund. Finally, this chapter describes some potential income tax implications for students when their IHE has closed, including the extent to which they may incur a federal income tax liability for loans discharged and whether higher education tax credits remain available to them in future years. The Appendix provides a list of abbreviations used in this chapter.

ACADEMIC OPTIONS AND CONSEQUENCES

In the event of a school closure, currently enrolled students must consider their academic options, including whether they will continue pursuing their postsecondary education, and if so, where. Two options that may be available to students include teach-outs and credit transfer.

Teach-Out Plans and Agreements

To participate in the Title IV federal student aid programs, an IHE must, among other requirements, agree to submit a teach-out plan to its accrediting agency if it intends to close a location that provides 100% of at least one educational program offered by the IHE or if it intends to otherwise cease operations.[5]

---

[5] 34 C.F.R. §668.14(b)(31). In addition, IHEs are required to submit teach-out plans to their accreditors when ED initiates an emergency action against or limitation, suspension, or termination of an IHE's participation in an HEA Title IV program; when an IHE's

As part of a teach-out plan, an IHE may enter into a teach-out agreement with another IHE to provide the closing IHE's students with an educational program of similar content.

Teach-Out Plans

A teach-out plan is an institution's "written plan that provides for the equitable treatment of students if [the IHE] ceases to operate before all students have completed their program of study."[6] Accrediting agencies establish the criteria IHEs must meet when submitting a teach-out plan; thus, there are no standard components of a teach-out plan. Typically, however, in a teach-out plan, an IHE may be required to include provisions for students to complete their programs of study within a reasonable amount of time, a communication plan to affected parties (e.g., faculty and students) informing them of the impending closure, and information on how students may access their institutional records.[7]

Teach-Out Agreements

As part of a teach-out plan, an IHE may enter into a teach-out agreement with another IHE. A teach-out agreement is an agreement between the closing IHE and another IHE that provides the closing IHE's students with a reasonable opportunity to complete their programs of study at the new IHE. Teach-out agreements are used when an IHE ceases operations before all of its enrolled students are able to complete their programs of study.[8]

---

accrediting agency acts to withdraw, terminate, or suspend an IHE's accreditation or preaccreditation; or when the IHE's legal authorization to operate within a state is revoked.

[6] HEA §487(f)(2).

[7] See, for example, Higher Learning Commission, "Teach-Out Requirements: Provisional Plan and Teach-Out Agreements," https://downloadna11.springcm.com/content/Download Documents.ashx?Selection=Document%2C73d8aaaf-d1fb-df11-bf75-001cc448da6a% 3B&aid=5968, accessed October 29, 2018; and Southern Association of Colleges and Schools, Commission on Colleges, "Substantive Change For SACSCOC Accredited Institutions," pp. 22-23, http://www.sacscoc.org/pdf/081705/SubstantiveChange.pdf, accessed October 29, 2018.

[8] 34 C.F.R. §602.3.

The Closure of Institutions of Higher Education 93

Under a teach-out agreement, the new IHE must

- provide students with an educational program that is of an acceptable quality and reasonably similar in content, structure, and scheduling to that provided by the closing IHE;
- be accredited or preaccredited by a Department of Education (ED) recognized accrediting agency, remain stable, carry out its mission, and meet all obligations to its current students; and
- demonstrate that it can provide students with access to its services without requiring students to move or travel a substantial distance.[9]

In addition, teach-out agreements may establish the cost of attendance for students being taught out.[10]

When implemented, teach-out agreements may take a variety of forms. For instance, a teach-out agreement may provide that the teach-out institution will provide the faculty and student supports necessary to deliver the closing IHE's educational programs at the closing IHE's facilities for the remainder of the academic year in which the closing IHE ceases operations.[11] In other instances, a teach-out agreement may provide educational programs to the closing IHE's students at the teach-out IHE's facilities.

In the event an IHE closes without a teach-out plan or agreement in place, the IHE's accrediting agency must work with ED and appropriate state agencies to assist students in finding opportunities to complete their postsecondary education.[12]

---

[9] 34 C.F.R. §602.24(c).

[10] See, for example, Higher Learning Commission, "Teach-Out Requirements: Provisional Plan and Teach-Out Agreements", p. 3,https://downloadna11.springcm.com/content/Download Documents.ashx?Selection=Document%2C73d8aaaf-d1fb-df11-bf75-001cc448da6a% 3B&aid=5968, accessed October 29, 2018.

[11] See, for example, Southern New Hampshire University, "Southern New Hampshire University to Lead 'Teach-Out' of all Daniel Webster College Programs," press release, September 13, 2016.

[12] 34 C.F.R. §602.24(d).

Credit Transfer

In lieu of a teach-out, students of closed IHEs may be able to continue their postsecondary education by transferring some or all of the credits earned at the closed IHE to another IHE. In general, credit transfer is the process of one institution (the accepting institution) measuring a student's prior learning (typically via coursework) at another institution (the sending institution) and comparing that prior learning against educational offerings at the accepting institution. The accepting institution determines whether a student's prior learning meets its standards and whether the prior learning is applicable to its educational programs. If it determines the prior learning meets its standards, the accepting institutions gives credit toward its educational programs for the prior learning, such that a student transferring credits need not repeat all or part of a program's curriculum. Transfer-of-credit policies are determined by individual IHEs.

To smooth the credit transfer process, some IHEs have entered into articulation agreements. Articulation agreements are agreements between two or more IHEs demonstrating that a student's prior learning from a sending IHE meets the accepting IHE's standards. Typically, they guarantee acceptance of at least some credits earned at the sending institution by the accepting institution.

The HEA does not require Title IV participating IHEs to maintain transfer-of-credit policies nor does it specify requirements for transfer-of-credit policies for IHEs that do have them. The HEA does, however, require that Title IV participating IHEs make publicly available any transfer-ofcredit policies they may have in place.[13] In disclosing transfer-of-credit policies, accepting IHEs must include information on the criteria the institution uses in evaluating credit transfers, and all institutions that are parties to articulation agreements must disclose a list of IHEs with which it has articulation agreements.

Students who attended a closed IHE may decide to continue their postsecondary education at another IHE and may wish to transfer credits

---

[13] HEA §485(h).

earned at the closed IHE to the new IHE. Typically, students must initiate the credit-transfer process by expressing interest in transferring credit to another IHE.[14] The IHE would then inform the student of next steps the student must take to enroll. Because IHEs set their own credit transfer criteria, credit transfer may not be guaranteed.[15] Thus, some students may have all or a large proportion of their previously earned credits transferred to an accepting IHE and may experience little to no disruption or delay in their postsecondary educational pursuits, while others may have few or no credits transferred to an accepting IHE and may experience significant disruptions and delays in their postsecondary education. In addition, a student may incur greater financial obligations (e.g., student loans) if he or she must repeat coursework because credit from the closed school did not transfer.

Finally, students who successfully transfer some or all of their previously earned credits would be required to meet the accepting IHE's satisfactory academic progress (SAP) policies to maintain eligibility to receive Title IV funds at the accepting IHE.[16] IHEs may establish their own SAP policies, but these policies must meet minimum federal standards, which must establish a minimum grade point average (or equivalent) and a maximum time frame in which students must complete their education program (pace of completion).[17] Only transfer credits that count toward a student's educational program at the accepting IHE are included in the

---

[14] In some cases, a teach-out agreement may specify that the credits a student earned at the closed institution will transfer to the new IHE. See, for example, Higher Learning Commission, "Teach-Out Requirements: Provisional Plan and Teach-Out Agreements," March 2017, https://downloadna11.springcm.com/content/DownloadDocuments.ashx?Selection= Document%2C73d8aaaf-d1fb-df11-bf75-001cc448da6a%3B&aid=5968, accessed February 5, 2019.

[15] For information on how often credits transfer, see Sean Anthony Simone, *Transferability of Postsecondary Credit Following Student Transfer or Coenrollment: Statistical Analysis Report*, National Center for Education Statistics, NCES 2014-163, August 2014.

[16] HEA §484(c).

[17] 34 C.F.R. §668.34. A student's pace of completion is calculated by dividing the total number of credits a student has successfully completed by the number of credits the student has attempted. A student becomes ineligible for Title IV aid when it is mathematically impossible for him or her to complete their course of study within 150% of the length of the program (e.g., six years for a full-time, full-year four-year program) for undergraduate students and within the maximum time frame established by the IHE for graduate students.

accepting IHE's calculation of SAP.[18] Thus, if a student is unable to transfer any credits from a closed IHE to another IHE, the student's previously earned credits will not count toward the accepting IHE's SAP calculation and would not have the potential to affect the student's aid eligibility with respect to SAP at the new IHE. However, should some or all of a student's previously earned credits from a closed IHE transfer to another IHE, depending on the accepting IHE's specific SAP policy, a student's Title IV eligibility may be affected such that he or she may not be meeting the IHE's SAP policies and thus may be ineligible for Title IV aid at the accepting IHE.[19]

FINANCIAL OPTIONS AND CONSEQUENCES

Along with considering academic options in the event of a school closure, students may also need to consider the financial options available to them, as they may have received financial assistance to help finance their education at the closed school and may need to seek financial assistance should they decide to continue pursuing a postsecondary education. Considerations for students who borrowed funds (or parents who borrowed funds on behalf of a student) to finance their education at a closed school include whether they are responsible for repaying any loans borrowed to attend the school. Considerations for students who wish to continue their education at another IHE include the extent to which their eligibility for various forms of financial aid (e.g., Direct Loans, Pell

---

[18] U.S. Department of Education, *2018-2019 Federal Student Aid Handbook*, vol. 1, p. 16.

[19] In general, it appears that a student's pace of completion is unlikely to be affected by a credit transfer, as typically, only successfully completed courses at the original IHEs may be transferred to an accepting institution. However, successful course completion is defined by individual IHEs. Thus, should an accepting IHE define successful completion as any grade higher than an F (or its equivalent), then a student might be able to transfer credits from a class in which he or she earned, for instance, a D. This D would be included in the accepting IHE's calculation of the student's grade point average for purposes of determining SAP. Such grades may have the effect of bringing the student's GPA below the federally required C minimum, such that he or she may become ineligible for Title IV student aid at the accepting institution.

Loan Discharge

In some instances, individuals who borrowed funds to finance postsecondary education expenses may be provided some relief from being required to repay their loans, depending on the type of loan they seek to have discharged and specific borrower circumstances.

Federal Student Loans

Students who attended a school that closed (or the parents of students who attend a school that closed) may have borrowed federal student loans to help finance their postsecondary education at the closed school. For HEA Title IV federal student loans (i.e., loans made under the Direct Loan [DL], Federal Family Education Loan [FFEL], and Perkins Loan programs), borrowers may be provided some relief from being required to repay their federal student loans through a closed school loan discharge. In addition, borrowers who are ineligible for a closed school loan discharge may, in certain circumstances, seek debt relief on their Title IV student loans by asserting a borrower defense to repayment (BDR) for certain acts or omissions of an IHE, if the cause of action directly relates to the loan or educational services for which the loan was provided. The availability of a BDR claim may be closely related to a school's closure, as oftentimes, a BDR claim is predicated on misleading representations of an IHE relating to the educational services provided, and in recent years allegations of misrepresentation have played a part in the ultimate closure of some IHEs.[20]

---

[20] For instance, in 2014 ED placed restrictions to Title IV aid on IHEs owned by Corinthian Colleges, Inc. (CCI) to address concerns relating to a variety of practices, including inconsistencies in job placement rates that had been presented to students. In response to its limited access to federal student aid funds, CCI closed and sold many of its IHEs. CRS Report R44068, *Effect of Corinthian Colleges' Closure on Student Financial Aid: Frequently Asked Questions*, archived, available to congressional clients upon request.

Previously, regulatory provisions addressed closed school discharge standards and procedures. They also addressed BDR standards and procedures, but in a somewhat limited manner. On November 1, 2016, ED promulgated new regulations (hereinafter, "the 2016 regulations") intended to create a more robust set of standards and streamlined procedures for assessing BDR claims and to make some changes to the closed school discharge procedures.[21] These regulations were scheduled to take effect on July 1, 2017, but prior to the effective date, ED issued a Final Rule establishing July 1, 2019, as the new effective date for the regulations.[22] Following a series of lawsuits, however, a court vacated the delay of the 2016 regulations.[23] The 2016 regulations went into effect October 16, 2018, and ED is currently working to fully implement the 2016 regulations.[24] On July 31, 2018, ED issued a new Notice of Proposed Rulemaking to revise the BDR standards.[25] A Final Rule has not yet been issued, and it appears that the potential new BDR regulations would not go into effect until at least July 2020.[26]

The following section of the report describes the closed school discharge and BDR regulations, as in effect on October 16, 2018.[27]

---

[21] Department of Education, "Student Assistance General Provisions, Federal Perkins Loan Program, Federal Family Education Loan Program, William D. Ford Federal Direct Loan Program, and Teacher Education Assistance for College and Higher Education Grant Program," 81 *Federal Register* 75926, November 1, 2016.

[22] Department of Education, "Student Assistance General Provisions, Federal Perkins Loan Program, Federal Family Education Loan Program, William D. Ford Federal Direct Loan Program, and Teacher Education Assistance for College and Higher Education Grant Program," 83 *Federal Register* 6458, February 14, 2018.

[23] *Bauer v. DeVos*, 332 F. Supp. 3d 186 (D.C. Cir. 2018). See also, *Cal. Ass'n of Private Postsecondary Schs. v. DeVos*, 2018 U.S. Dist. LEXIS (D.C. Cir. 2018).

[24] CRS email communication with U.S. Department of Education personnel on October 31, 2018. See also U.S. Department of Education, Electronic Announcement, "Closed School Discharge Changes," December 13, 2018.

[25] Department of Education, "Student Assistance General Provisions, Federal Perkins Loan Program, Federal Family Education Loan Program, and William D. Ford Federal Direct Loan Program," 83 *Federal Register* 37242, July 31, 2018.

[26] Andrew Kreighbaum, "Missed Deadline Stalls DeVos Agenda," *Inside Higher Ed*, October 4, 2018.

[27] 81 *Federal Register* 75926, November 1, 2016.

Closed School Loan Discharge

Students who attended a school that closed (or their parents) may be eligible to have the full balance of the outstanding HEA Title IV loans they borrowed to attend the IHE discharged. In general, borrowers of Title IV loans may be eligible to have the full balance of their outstanding HEA Title IV loans discharged (including any accrued interest and collection costs) if they, or the student on whose behalf a parent borrowed in the case of Parent PLUS Loans, are unable to complete the program in which they enrolled due to the closure of the school.[28] Borrowers who have their loans discharged due to a school closure are also eligible to be reimbursed for any amounts previously paid or collected on those loans, and if any adverse credit history was associated with the loan (e.g., default), the loan discharge will be reported to credit bureaus so that they may delete the adverse credit history associated with the loan.[29]

Closed School Loan Discharge Eligibility

Typically, to be eligible for loan discharge due to school closure, a student must have been enrolled in an IHE when it closed or must have withdrawn from the IHE within 120 days prior to its closure.[30] In addition, the student must have been unable to complete his or her program of study at the closed school or in a comparable[31] program at another IHE, either

---

[28] HEA §437(c)(1); HEA §455(a)(1); HEA §464(g). In some instances, borrowers who are ineligible to have their federal student loans discharged due to school closure may be able to seek debt relief for their DL and FFEL program loans for a variety of other reasons. For additional information, see CRS Report R40122, *Federal Student Loans Made Under the Federal Family Education Loan Program and the William D. Ford Federal Direct Loan Program: Terms and Conditions for Borrowers*.

[29] 34 C.F.R. §§674.33(g)(2); 682.402(d)(2); 685.214(b).

[30] The Secretary may extend the 120-day period in exceptional circumstances.

[31] There is no formal definition of comparable program. However, information made available by ED to former Corinthian Colleges students provided an illustrative example of when a program might be considered comparable: "for instance, if you were taking a criminal justice program and you transferred to another criminal justice program, that would be a transfer to a similar program." Borrowers self-certify whether their new program of study is similar to their program of study at the closed school. See U.S. Department of Education, Office of Federal Student Aid, "Information About Debt Relief for Corinthian Colleges Students," https://studentaid.ed.gov/sa/about/announcements/corinthian, accessed October 25, 2018.

through a teach-out agreement or by transferring any credits to another IHE.[32]

If the closing school offers the option for students to complete their education through a teach-out agreement with another IHE, a student may refuse the option, and the borrower may still qualify for loan discharge. However, in general, a borrower may not qualify for a closed school discharge in the following scenario: a student refuses the teach-out, later enrolls at another IHE in a program comparable to the one in which he or she had been enrolled, receives transfer credit for work completed at the closed school, and completes the program at the new IHE.[33]

Alternatively, if a student transfers credits to a new school but completes an entirely different program of study at the new school, then the borrower is eligible for loan discharge, regardless of the fact that some credits from the closed IHE may have transferred to the new IHE. This is because the program at the new school is entirely different than the one for which the loans were intended at the previous school.[34]

Finally, to obtain discharge a borrower must cooperate with ED in any judicial or administrative proceeding brought by ED to recover amounts discharged from the school.[35] If a borrower fails to cooperate with ED, the loan discharge may be revoked.[36]

Closed School Loan Discharge Procedures

Borrowers may have their loans discharged in one of two ways: (1) by applying for a closed school loan discharge or (2) by having their loans automatically discharged by the Secretary of Education (the Secretary).

---

[32] 34 C.F.R. §§674.33(g)(4), 682.402(d)(3), 685.214(c)(1). See also, U.S. Department of Education, Federal Student Aid, "Frequently Asked Questions About Corinthian Colleges," Questions 9 and 10, https://studentaid.ed.gov/sa/about/announcements/corinthian/faq#loan-discharge, accessed October 29, 2018.

[33] Ibid.

[34] U.S. Department of Education, Federal Student Aid, "Q&A on Closed School Discharge," https://studentaid.ed.gov/ sa/repay-loans/forgiveness-cancellation/closed-school#q-and-a, accessed October 25, 2018.

[35] For instance, the borrower may be required to provide testimony supporting a request for discharge.

[36] 34 C.F.R. §§674.33(g), 682.402(d), 685.214(c) & (d).

The Closure of Institutions of Higher Education 101

Borrowers applying for a closed school discharge must fill out the closed school loan discharge application and return it to their loan servicer.[37] Generally, while a borrower's loan discharge application is being considered, the borrower's loan is placed in forbearance until a discharge decision is made.[38] Under forbearance, a borrower is able to temporarily stop making payments or reduce the monthly payments on his or her federal student loans. During this time, interest continues to accrue on both subsidized and unsubsidized loans. In addition, collections on an eligible defaulted loan cease, although a borrower may continue to make payments on the loan.

Borrowers may initiate the closed school loan discharge process on their own;[39] however, the Secretary[40] is required to identify all borrowers who may be eligible for a closed school discharge upon a school's closure and mail to each borrower a discharge application and an explanation of qualifications and procedures for obtaining a discharge, if the borrower's address is known.[41] After the Secretary sends notice to a borrower, the

---

[37] Ibid. See U.S. Department of Education, "Loan Discharge Application: School Closure," OMB No. 1845-0058.

[38] 34 C.F.R. §§674.33, 682.211, 685.205. Unlike the FFEL and DL programs, the Perkins Loan program regulations do not specify that an IHE must place a borrower's loan in forbearance while his or her closed school loan discharge application is being processed; however, the regulations do state than an IHE may place a borrower's loan in forbearance due to several specified reasons "or for other acceptable reasons." In addition, in certain stages of the closed school discharge application process, an IHE (or ED, in the case of Perkins Loans held by ED) may be required to suspend efforts to collect on a borrower's Perkins Loans.

[39] In certain circumstances, including when an IHE submits a teach-out plan to its accrediting agency because it intends to close a location at which 100% of at least one program is offered or otherwise cease operations, the IHE is required to provide to enrolled students a closed school discharge application and a written disclosure describing the benefits and consequences of a closed school discharge. 34 C.F.R. §668.14(b)(32).

[40] This paragraph generally describes the procedures associated with closed school loan discharges as specified in regulations. The descriptions herein are drawn from the regulations specific to the Direct Loan program (34 C.F.R. §685.214), but are generally applicable to the Perkins Loan and FFEL programs as well. However, because parties other than ED may be responsible for administrative functions associated with closed school discharges in the Perkins Loan and FFEL programs, the tasks described in this report may vary somewhat from what Perkins Loan and FFEL program loan holders other than ED may be required to undertake. Closed school discharge procedures specific to the Perkins Loan program and the FFEL program can be found at 34 C.F.R. §674.33 and 34 C.F.R. §682.402, respectively.

[41] If the borrower's address is unknown, ED attempts to locate the borrower by consulting with a variety of parties, including the closed school, the school's accrediting agency, and the school's licensing agency. 34 C.F.R. §685.214(f)(3).

102 *Alexandra Hegji*

Secretary suspends any effort to collect a borrower's defaulted loans. The borrower then has 60 days in which to submit a closed school discharge application. If the borrower fails to submit such an application within the 60-day time frame, the Secretary resumes collections[42] and again provides the borrower with another discharge application and an explanation of qualifications and procedures for obtaining a discharge. Should a borrower not submit a closed school discharge application within the 60-day time frame, he or she may still submit a closed school discharge application at any time for consideration.[43]

Alternatively, a borrower's loans will be automatically discharged by the Secretary, if with respect to schools that closed on or after November 1, 2013, the Secretary determines that the borrower did not subsequently reenroll in any Title IV eligible institution within three years after the school closed. A borrower's loans also may be automatically discharged if the Secretary determines the borrower qualifies for the discharge based on information within ED's possession.[44]

Relief Provided

If a borrower receives a closed school discharge, the full balance of the outstanding Title IV loan borrowed to attend the IHE is discharged and the borrower is qualified to be reimbursed for any amounts previously paid or collected on those loans. In addition, for loans that were considered in default, ED is to consider such loans not in default following discharge,

---

[42] Upon resuming collection on a borrower's loans, ED grants forbearance of principal and interest for the period during which the collection activity was suspended and may capitalize any interest accrued but not paid during that time. 34 C.F.R. §685.214(f)(4).

[43] 34 C.F.R. §685.214(f).

[44] In the instance of a FFEL program loan, ED may automatically discharge a borrower's FFEL program loan if he or she qualified for and received a closed school discharge of his or her Direct Loan program or Perkins Loan program loans. Similarly, ED may automatically discharge a borrower's Perkins Loan program loan if he or she qualified for and received a closed school loan discharge of his or her Direct Loan program or FFEL program loan and "was unable to receive a discharge on his or her ... Perkins Loan because the Secretary of Education lacked statutory authority to discharge the loan." See 34 C.F.R. §§682.402(d)(8), 674.33(g)(3). The Perkins Loan provisions appear to apply largely Perkins Loan program loans made prior to 1998, when ED did not have legal authority to discharge such loans due to a school's closure. The rationale behind the FFEL program loan provisions is not explicitly identified in materials located and reviewed for this report. See 64 *Federal Register* 41236, July 29, 1999.

The Closure of Institutions of Higher Education 103

and the borrower is to regain eligibility to receive additional Title IV assistance.[45] Finally, ED is to update reports to consumer reporting agencies so that they may delete any adverse credit history associated with the loan.[46]

Borrower Defense to Repayment

Even if borrowers who attended a closed school are ineligible for a closed school loan discharge, they may, in certain circumstances, seek debt relief on their Title IV student loans by asserting a borrower defense to repayment (BDR) certain acts or omissions of an IHE, if the cause of action directly relates to the loan or educational services for which the loan was provided. The availability of a BDR claim may be closely related to a school's closure, as oftentimes, a BDR claim is predicated on misleading representations of an IHE relating to the educational services provided, and in recent years, allegations of misrepresentation have played a part in the ultimate closure of some IHEs.[47] Whether a borrower may seek this type of relief depends on the type of Title IV loan borrowed. The standard under which a BDR may be reviewed also depends on the type of Title IV loan borrowed and when the loan was disbursed. Newly promulgated BDR procedures apply to many, but not all, BDR claims and vary depending on the type of Title IV loan.

If a borrower's BDR is successful, ED is to determine the amount of debt relief to which the borrower is entitled, which can include relief from repaying all or part of the outstanding loan balance and reimbursement for previous amounts paid toward or collected on the loan. Additionally, if an adverse credit history was associated with the loan (e.g., default), the loan

---

[45] Individuals become ineligible for additional Title IV student aid if they default on a Title IV loan. HEA §484(a)(3).

[46] 34 C.F.R. §§674.33(g)(2), 682.402(d)(2), 685.214(b).

[47] For instance, in 2014, ED placed restrictions to Title IV aid on IHEs owned by Corinthian Colleges, Inc. (CCI) to address concerns relating to a variety of practices, including inconsistencies in job placement rates that had been presented to students. In response to its limited access to federal student aid funds, CCI closed and sold many of its IHEs. CRS Report R44068, *Effect of Corinthian Colleges' Closure on Student Financial Aid: Frequently Asked Questions*, archived, available to congressional clients upon request.

104   *Alexandra Hegji*

discharge is to be reported to credit bureaus so that they may delete the adverse credit history associated with the loan.[48]

Applicable Borrower Defense to Repayment Standards

The HEA specifies that Direct Loan borrowers may assert as a defense to repayment certain "acts or omissions of an institution of higher education."[49] Although this statutory language is specific to Direct Loans, implementing regulations have expanded the instances in which a borrower of a non-Direct Loan may assert a BDR claim. Thus, loans that are potentially eligible for discharge under a BDR claim include Direct Loan program loans and Federal Family Education Loan program loans and Perkins Loans program loans, if they are first consolidated into a Direct Consolidation Loan.[50]

In addition, even if a FFEL program loan is not consolidated into a Direct Consolidation Loan, FFEL program regulations specify instances in which a FFEL program loan may not be legally enforceable, such that a borrower need not repay it. ED has stated that the claims a borrower could bring as a defense against repayment under the FFEL program are the same as the pre-July 1, 2017, standards (discussed later in this chapter) that could be brought under the DL program.[51] Perkins Loan program loans that are not consolidated into Direct Consolidation Loans may not assert a BDR claim.

In general, two separate BDR standards may be applied to eligible student loans under the Direct Loan program regulations. For eligible loans made prior to July 1, 2017, a borrower may assert as a defense to

---

[48] 34 C.F.R. §685.222(i).

[49] HEA §455(h).

[50] Other non-DL program loans that are potentially eligible for discharge under a BDR claim if they are first consolidated into a Direct Consolidation Loan include Health Professions Student Loans, Loans for Disadvantaged students made under Title VII-A-II of the Public Health Service Act, Health Education Assistance Loans, and Nursing Loans made under part E of the Public Health Service Act. 34 C.F.R. §685.212(k)(2).

[51] To assert a successful BDR claim, FFEL borrowers must satisfy the general pre-July 1, 2017, BDR standards and must also prove additional components, such as showing that the FFEL lender offered payment or other benefits to the IHE for referring borrowers to the specific FFEL lender. These standards apply to FFEL program loans held by private sector and state-based entities and those owned by ED. 34 C.F.R. §682.209(g) and U.S. Department of Education, "Notice of Interpretation," 60 Federal Register 37768-37770, July 21, 1995.

The Closure of Institutions of Higher Education 105

repayment an IHE's acts or omissions that "would give rise to a cause of action against the school under applicable State law," and the IHE's acts or omissions must relate to the making of the loan for enrollment at the IHE or the provision of educational services for which the loan was provided[52] (hereinafter, "pre-July 1, 2017, standard"). For eligible loans made on or after July 1, 2017, a borrower may assert as a defense to repayment one of the following, as it relates to the making of a borrower's loan for enrollment at the IHE or the provision of the educational services for which the loan was made (hereinafter, "post-July 1, 2017, standard"):[53]

- A substantial misrepresentation by an IHE that the borrower "reasonably relied on to the borrower's detriment when the borrower decided to attend, or to continue attending, the school" or decided to take out certain loans;[54]
- A nondefault, contested state or federal court judgment against an IHE; or
- A breach of contract by an IHE,[55] where an IHE failed to perform obligations under the terms of a contract with a student, such as the provision of specific programs or services.

As indicated above, the BDR standard applied in a borrower's case may depend to a large extent on the date on which a borrower's loans were disbursed.

---

[52] 34 C.F.R. §685.206(c).

[53] 34 C.F.R. §685.222(b)-(d).

[54] A substantial misrepresentation is "[a]ny false, erroneous, or misleading statement an [IHE] or one of its representatives...makes directly or indirectly to a student, prospective student or any member of the public, or to an accrediting agency, to a State agency, or to the Secretary" on which "the person to whom it was made could reasonably be expected to rely, or has reasonably relied, to that person's detriment." An IHE is deemed to have made a substantial misrepresentation when it (or its representatives) makes a "substantial misrepresentation about the nature of its educational programs, its financial charges, or the employability of its graduates." 34 C.F.R. §668.71(b) and (c).

[55] A contract between an IHE and a borrower could include, for instance, an enrollment agreement, a school catalog, or a student handbook. Department of Education, "Student Assistance General Provisions, Federal Perkins Loan Program, Federal Family Education Loan Program, William D. Ford Federal Direct Loan Program, and Teacher Education Assistance for College and Higher Education Grant Program," 81 *Federal Register* 39341, June 16, 2016.

Table 1. Borrower Defense to Repayment Standard Used in a BDR Proceeding. By loan type and disbursement date

Loan Type & Disbursement Date	BDR Standard Applied	
	Pre-July 1, 2017	Post-July 1, 2017
DL Program Subsidized and Unsubsidized Loans		
Disbursed pre-July 1, 2017	✓	
Disbursed on or post-July 1, 2017		✓
FFEL Program Subsidized, Unsubsidized, and Consolidation Loans[a]		
Disbursement date inapplicable[b]	✓	
DL Program Consolidation Loans Underlying DL Program Subsidized & Unsubsidized Loans		
Underlying loan disbursed pre-July 1, 2017	✓	
Underlying loan disbursed on or post-July 1, 2017		✓
Underlying Eligible Non-DL Program Loans[c]		
Direct Consolidation Loan disbursed pre-July 1, 2017	✓	
Direct Consolidation Loan disbursed on or post-July 1, 2017		✓

Source: CRS analysis of Department of Education, "Student Assistance General Provisions, Federal Perkins Loan Program, Federal Family Education Loan Program, William D. Ford Direct Loan Program, and Teacher Education Assistance for College and Higher Education Grant Program," 81 Federal Register 75926, November 1, 2016, and 34 C.F.R. §682.209(g).

[a] FFEL program borrowers must satisfy the general pre-July 1, 2017, BDR standards and must prove additional components, such as showing that the FFEL lender offered payment or other benefits to the IHE for referring borrowers to the specific FFEL lender. 34 C.F.R. §682.209(g).

[b] The SAFRA Act (P.L. 111-152, Title II, Part A) terminated the authority to make new FFEL program loans after June 30, 2010.

[c] Eligible non-DL program loans include FFEL program loans, Perkins Loan program loans, Health Professions Student Loans, Loans for Disadvantaged students made under Title VII-A-II of the Public Health Service Act, Health Education Assistance Loans, and Nursing Loans made under part E of the Public Health Service Act.

The Closure of Institutions of Higher Education   107

However, other considerations that relate to the type of federal student loan made also play a role in determining which BDR standard may apply in a borrower's case. In general, for DL program loans not paid off through a Direct Consolidation Loan, the BDR standard used would depend on the date on which a borrower's loans were disbursed. For FFEL program loans not paid off through a Direct Consolidation Loan, the pre-July 1, 2017, standard would apply. For DL program loans paid off through a Direct Consolidation Loan, the BDR standard used would depend on the date on which the underlying Direct Loan was disbursed. For eligible non-DL program loans paid off through a Direct Consolidation Loan, the BDR standard used would depend on the date on which the Direct Consolidation Loan was made.[56] Direct Consolidation Loans comprising underlying loans disbursed both before and after July 1, 2017, would necessarily have been disbursed after July 1, 2017. Thus, in this scenario, the post-July 1, 2017, standard would apply to any eligible non-DL program loans paid off through the Direct Consolidation Loan and either the pre- or post-July 1, 2017, standard would apply to any Direct Loans paid off through the Direct Consolidation Loan, depending on the date the underlying Direct Loan was disbursed. *Table 1* depicts the BDR standard that would be applied in a BDR proceeding based on type of federal student loan at issue and the date on which the loan was disbursed.

BDR Procedures

Regulations establish two separate processes through which a BDR claim may be asserted on a borrower's DL program loans: an individual claim process and a group claim process.[57] This section of the report describes the 2016 regulations' BDR procedures for DL program loans (including Direct Consolidation Loans that repaid eligible non-DL program loans for which a borrower asserts a BDR claim) under which BDR claims

---

[56] 34 C.F.R. §685.222.

[57] Prior to the current regulations going into effect on October 16, 2018, regulations did not specify formal BDR procedures. Therefore, ED had established informal procedures through which borrowers were able to seek BDR relief. Because the current regulations' implementation date was delayed from July 1, 2017, to October 16, 2018, ED has not yet fully implemented the procedures specified in the 2016 regulations.

108   *Alexandra Hegji*

may be more likely to be asserted, as DL program borrowers account for approximately 80% of all borrowers with outstanding Title IV loans.[58] The procedures described herein would not apply to ED-owned FFEL program loans or to FFEL programs loans held by private and state-based entities that are not consolidated into Direct Consolidation Loans.[59] For such ED-owned FFEL program loans, ED would review and adjudicate any BDR claims.[60] For such FFEL program loans not owned by ED, BDR claims procedures may vary by loan holder.[61]

To assert a BDR claim as an individual,[62] a borrower must submit a BDR application,[63] which among other items requires the borrower to provide evidence that supports his or her BDR claim. Upon receipt of the application and while the BDR claim is evaluated, ED places any nondefaulted Direct Loans into forbearance[64] and ceases collections on

---

[58] Office of Federal Student Aid, Data Center, "Federal Student Aid Portfolio Summary," FY2018 Q4.

[59] Under the FFEL program, loans were originated and serviced by private sector and state-based lenders and were funded with nonfederal capital. ED guaranteed lenders against loss (e.g., through borrower default or discharge due to death or permanent disability). Although FFEL program loans were last disbursed in 2010, many remain outstanding. In some instances, private or state-based lenders continue to service FFEL program loans. In other instances, ED has purchased FFEL program loans from the lenders and is now the owner of the loans. In these cases, the loans are serviced by ED-contracted student loan servicers.

[60] Upon submitting a BDR claim on an ED-owned FFEL program loan that is not consolidated into a Direct Consolidation Loan, the borrower is to be offered the opportunity to place the loan in forbearance while the claim is being reviewed. CRS email communication with U.S. Department of Education personnel on December 10, 2018.

[61] Borrowers of such loans must contact the holder of their FFEL program loans for information on the BDR process. Upon submitting a BDR claim on an FFEL program loan not owned by ED, the borrower is offered to opportunity to request that his or her loan be placed in forbearance while the claim is being reviewed. U.S. Department of Education, Application for Borrower Defense to Loan Repayment, OMB No. 1845-0146, Exp. Date December 31, 2019.

[62] 34 C.F.R. §685.222(e). In January 2017, ED promulgated regulations that updated its general hearing procedures for actions to establish liability against an IHE and establishing procedural rules governing recovery proceedings under the 2016 BDR regulations. These procedural requirements are beyond the scope of this report. See Department of Education, "Student Assistance General Provisions," 82 *Federal Register* 6253, January 19, 2017.

[63] See U.S. Department of Education, "Application for Borrower Defense to Loan Repayment," OMB No. 1845-0146, Exp. December 31, 2019. This form was approved prior to implementation of the current regulations.

[64] During forbearance, interest continues to accrue on both subsidized and unsubsidized loans. A borrower may opt out of forbearance and continue making payments on his or her loan.

The Closure of Institutions of Higher Education   109

defaulted loans.[65] If a borrower with a FFEL program loan files a BDR claim with ED, ED notifies the lender or loan holder, as appropriate.[66] The lender places the loan in forbearance in yearly increments,[67] and the loan holder ceases collection on any defaulted loans while a borrower's BDR claim is being evaluated.[68] If ED determines that the borrower would be eligible for relief if he or she consolidated the FFEL program loan into a Direct Consolidation Loan, the borrower would then be able to consolidate the loan into a Direct Consolidation Loan[69] and receive BDR relief.[70] If ED determines that the borrower would not qualify for BDR, then the loan is removed from forbearance or collections resume, as appropriate.[71]

To determine whether an individual qualifies for BDR relief, the Secretary designates an ED official to review the borrower's application and resolves the claim through a fact-finding process. As part of that process, ED notifies the IHE against which the BDR claim is asserted and reviews any evidence submitted by the borrower and other relevant information, such as ED records and any submissions from the IHE. After the fact-finding process, the ED official issues a written decision on the claim. If the claim is approved in full or in part, ED notifies the borrower of the relief provided. If the claim is denied in full or in part, ED notifies the borrower of the reason for the denial, along with other

---

[65] A borrower may continue making payments under a rehabilitation agreement or other repayment agreement on the defaulted loan.

[66] The regulations are silent regarding whether lenders of Perkins Loans are required to place Perkins Loans into forbearance or to cease collections on Perkins Loans should a Perkins Loan borrower file a BDR claim with ED. ED has indicated it is not its current practice to request or require Perkins Loan holders or servicers to place borrowers into forbearance or to cease collections on a Perkins Loan for purposes of BDR. CRS email communication with U.S. Department of Education personnel on November 6, 2018.

[67] A borrower may opt out of forbearance and continue making payments on his or her loan. 34 C.F.R. §682.211(i)(7).

[68] Regulations specify that upon receipt of a BDR application, ED will notify the borrower of the option to continue making payments under a rehabilitation agreement or other repayment agreement on a defaulted loan. It appears this might apply in the instance in which a borrower of a FFEL program loan first submits a BDR application to ED, prior to loan consolidation. 34 C.F.R. §685.222(e)(2)(ii)(C).

[69] If borrowers choose to not consolidate their FFEL program loans into a Direct Consolidation Loan, they may still pursue a BDR claim under the FFEL program BDR standards and procedures.

[70] The loan would remain in forbearance until the loan is consolidated. 34 C.F.R. §682.211(i)(7).

[71] 34 C.F.R. §§682.211(i)(7), 682.410(b)(6)(iii).

relevant information.[72] The decision made by the ED official is "final as to the merits of the claim and any relief that may be granted on the claim."[73] However, if the borrower's claim is denied in full or in part, the borrower may request that ED reconsider his or her claim upon the identification of new evidence. In addition, ED may reopen a BDR application at any time to consider evidence that was not considered in the previous decision.

Regulations also establish a group process for BDR claims.[74] Under these procedures, upon consideration of factors such as a common set of facts and claims or fiscal impact, the Secretary may initiate a process to determine whether a group of borrowers has a BDR claim. ED may identify members for a group BDR claim by either consolidating applications filed by individuals in the above-described process that have common facts and claims or by determining that there are common facts and claims that apply to borrowers who have not filed individual applications. Loans of borrowers who have filed individual claims that are consolidated into a group BDR claim remain in forbearance or suspended collections as described above, and loans of identified group members who have not filed individual claims are placed in forbearance or suspended collections as described above. ED notifies identified group members of the group proceeding and informs them that they may opt out of the group proceeding.[75] ED also notifies the school against which the group BDR claim is asserted.

For the fact-finding portion of a group BDR claim, one set of procedures applies to a BDR claim relating to loans made to attend a school that has closed[76] and from which there is no financial protection or other entity that ED may recover losses from associated with the BDR claims.[77] Another set of fact-finding procedures applies to BDR claims relating to

---

[72] 34 C.F.R. §685.222(e).

[73] 34 C.F.R. §685.222(e)(5).

[74] 34 C.F.R. §685.222(f).

[75] It is unclear how a borrower who has successfully asserted an individual BDR claim may be affected by any subsequent group proceeding.

[76] This standard would apply regardless of whether the borrower(s) were enrolled at the IHE at the time it closed.

[77] Financial protections from which ED may recover losses associated with BDR claims include, for example, letters of credit. Other entities from which ED may recover such losses include, for examples, affiliates of a closed IHE.

loans made to attend a school that has closed and for which there are financial protections or other entities from which ED may recover losses associated with BDR claims, or that is open. If the claim relates to loans made to attend a school that has closed and for which there is no financial protections or entities against ED may recover, a hearing official considers any evidence and arguments presented by ED on behalf of the group,[78] along with any additional information such as ED records or responses from the school that the ED official considers necessary. After the fact-finding process, the ED official issues a written decision on the claim. As with the individual claims process, if the group claim is approved in full or in part, ED notifies the borrowers of the relief provided. If the claim is denied in full or in part, ED notifies the borrowers of the reason for the denial, along with other relevant information. The decision made by the ED official is "final as to the merits of the group borrower defense and any relief that may be granted on the group claim."[79] However, if relief for the group has been denied in full or in part, an individual borrower may file a claim for individual relief as previously described. In addition, ED may reopen a BDR application at any time to consider evidence that was not considered in the previous decision.[80]

Group BDR procedures for a claim that relates to loans made to attend a closed school for which there are financial protections or entities from which ED may recover losses or to loans made to attend an open school are substantially similar to those procedures for group BDR claims for closed schools without financial protections described above.[81] However, in addition to the above-described procedures, the IHE against which the claim is brought is given the opportunity to present evidence and arguments during the fact-finding process. In addition, the school or the ED official who presented the group's BDR claims may appeal the decision of the hearing official within 30 days after the decision is issued and received by the school and the ED official. Should an appeal be made,

---

[78] The ED official may also present evidence and arguments, as necessary, on behalf of individual group members. 34 C.F.R. §685.222(g)(1).

[79] 34 C.F.R. §685.222(g)(2).

[80] 34 C.F.R. §685.222(g)(4).

[81] 34 C.F.R. §685.222(f).

the hearing official's decision does not take effect pending the appeal. The Secretary issues a final decision on the appealed claim. If relief for the group has been denied in full or in part, and after a final decision has been made (either following an appeal by the school or the ED official or after 30 days from the hearing official's decision have passed), an individual borrower may file a claim for individual relief as previously described. Additionally, ED may reopen a BDR application at any time to consider evidence that was not considered in the previous decision.

Finally, to obtain relief a borrower must cooperate with ED in the relevant individual or group BDR proceeding. If a borrower fails to cooperate with ED, the relief may be revoked.[82]

Relief Provided

Regulations specify the relief that may be afforded to a borrower who, as an individual or as part of a group, successfully asserts a BDR.[83] This section of the report focuses on BDR relief available to borrowers with DL program loans, including Direct Consolidation Loans that repaid eligible non-DL program loans. However, it should be noted that borrowers of FFEL program loans that have not been consolidated into Direct Consolidation Loans are eligible to have all or part of their loan discharged, and may be eligible to be reimbursed for payments previously paid toward or collected on the loans if certain conditions are met.[84] Borrowers of Perkins Loans are ineligible for BDR relief unless they first consolidate their loans into a Direct Consolidation Loan.

For Direct Loans, if a borrower defense is approved, ED (either the ED official in an individual BDR claim or the hearing official in the group

---

[82] 34 C.F.R. §685.222(j).

[83] 34 C.F.R. §685.222(i).

[84] In general, FFEL program loans (both those owned and not owned by ED) may be discharged if a borrower satisfies the general pre-July 1, 2017, BDR standards and proves additional components, such as showing that the FFEL lender offered payment or other benefits to the IHE for referring borrowers to the specific FFEL lender. 34 C.F.R. §682.209(g). Payments made on FFEL program loans may also be reimbursable. To assert a BDR claim, a FFEL program loan borrower who decided not to consolidate his or her loan into a Direct Consolidation Loan can assert a BDR claim against any lender holding the loan, including ED in the instance of ED-owned loans, and may directly pursue reimbursement from the holder. 34 CFR §382.209(g).

The Closure of Institutions of Higher Education 113

BDR claim) determines the appropriate amount of relief to award the borrower. Relief provided can include a discharge of all or part of the loan amounts owed to ED on the loan at issue. A borrower may also be eligible to have all or part of amounts previously paid toward or collected on his or her loan reimbursed by ED. Payments made or collections on Direct Loans, including Direct Consolidation Loans that repaid eligible non-DL program loans, are reimbursable by ED if the borrower asserted the BDR claim within the applicable statute of limitations[85] and the payments were made directly to ED[86] Reimbursements are to equal the amount by which the payments or collections on the loans (or portion of the loan in the case of Direct Consolidation Loans to which a BDR claim applied to some, but not all, of the underlying loans) exceed the amount of the loan that was not discharged.[87]

To calculate the amount of relief to be provided, ED takes into account a variety of factors, depending on the basis on which the BDR claim was brought.

- *Substantial misrepresentation*: ED is to factor the borrower's cost of attendance to attend the IHE, the value of the education the borrower received, the value of the education that a reasonable borrower in the borrower's circumstances would have received, the value of the education the borrower should have expected given the information provided to the borrower by the school, and/or any other relevant factors.
- *Court judgment against the THE:* If the judgment provides specific financial relief, ED will provide the unsatisfied amount of relief. If the judgment does not provide specific financial relief, ED "will

---

[85] There is no statute of limitation under which a borrower must assert a BDR claim for purposes of having the outstanding balance of his or her loan discharged. However, in certain circumstances, a borrower must assert a BDR claim within specified statutes of limitation for purposes of receiving reimbursement for previous payments made or collected on a loan. The applicable statute of limitation that applies for reimbursement purposes depends on the particular defense (i.e., substantial misrepresentation, breach of contract, or court judgment against an IHE) the borrower asserts. 34 C.F.R. §§685.212(k)(1)(ii), 685.212(k)(2)(iii).

[86] Thus, payments made on non-DL program loans prior to consolidation are not reimbursable by ED.

[87] 34 C.F.R. §§685.212(k)(1)(ii),685.212(k)(2)(iii).

114   *Alexandra Hegji*

rely on the holding of the case and applicable law to monetize the judgment."[88]

- *Breach of contract by the THE*: ED is to determine relief "based on the common law of contracts"[89] and other reasonable considerations.[90]

In addition to monetary relief, other relief, as appropriate, may be provided to a borrower. Such relief may include, but is not limited to, determining that the borrower is not in default on his or her loan and is eligible to receive additional Title IV assistance and updating reports to consumer reporting agencies so that they may delete any adverse credit history associated with the loan.[91]

Teacher Education Assistance for College and Higher Education Grants (TEACH Grants)

TEACH Grant recipients whose TEACH Grants have converted into a Direct Loan for failure to complete TEACH Grant service requirements may seek relief under either a closed school discharge or a successful BDR. Program regulations specify that for individuals who do not complete the program's teaching service requirements, the TEACH Grant converts into a DL and the individual "is eligible for all of the benefits of the Direct Loan Program."[92] Thus, so long as an individual meets all applicable closed school discharge or BDR criteria, they may be provided relief from repaying a TEACH Grant that has converted into a DL.[93]

---

[88] 34 C.F.R. §685.222(i)(2)(ii).

[89] 34 C.F.R. §685.222(i)(2)(iii).

[90] ED may consider information derived from a sample of borrowers when determining relief for a group of borrowers. For all borrowers asserting a BDR claim, ED may also rely on conceptual examples of relief provided in the regulations. 34 C.F.R. §685.222(i)(4). See 34 C.F.R. Part 685, Subpart B, Appendix A.

[91] 34 C.F.R. §685.222(i)(7).

[92] 34 C.F.R. §686.43(b)(2).

[93] TEACH Grant regulations do not provide for a discharge of an individual's duty to meet TEACH Grant service requirements due to a school closure or BDR. However, an individual may request that his or her TEACH Grant be converted into a DL because he or she has decided not to fulfill the service requirements or "for any other reason." 34 C.F.R. §686.43(a). Thus, it appears an individual could request his or her TEACH Grant be converted into a DL and then seek relief from DL repayment under a closed school

Private Education Loans

In some instances, students who attended a closed school may have borrowed private education loans to help finance their postsecondary education at the closed school. Private education loans are nonfederal loans made to a student to help finance the cost of their postsecondary education. Unlike federal student loans, which have statutorily prescribed terms and conditions that are typically uniform in nature, private education loan terms and conditions are primarily governed by market conditions that may vary greatly, depending on a variety of factors such as the lender, the borrower's creditworthiness, and the market.[94] Thus, the extent to which a private education loan borrower may be provided relief from the requirement to repay their loans may largely depend on the individual private education loan's terms and conditions.[95]

Relief for Pell Grant Recipients[96]

Pell Grant recipients who attended an IHE that closed may have some portion of their Pell eligibility restored. All Pell Grant recipients are subject to a cumulative lifetime eligibility cap on Pell Grant aid equal to 12 full-time semesters (or the equivalent). The HEA exempts from a student's lifetime eligibility cap the period of attendance at an IHE at which a

---

discharge or a BDR, while also not being required to meet TEACH Grant service requirements.

[94] For additional information on private education loans, see Department of Education, "Federal Versus Private Loans," https://studentaid.ed.gov/sa/types/loans/federal-vs-private, accessed November 2, 2018.

[95] In some instances, a private education loan lender or a third-party may agree to provide some debt relief to private education loan borrowers. For instance, a third-party agreed to provide approximately $480 million in debt relief to former Corinthian Colleges students who borrowed private education loans to attend Corinthian Colleges. Consumer Financial Protection Bureau, "Special Bulletin for Current and Former Students Enrolled at Corinthian-Owned Schools," February 3, 2015, http://files.consumerfinance.gov/f/201502_cfpb_bulletin_current-and-former-studentsenrolled-at-corinthian-owned-schools.pdf.

[96] This section of the report was authored by Cassandria Dortch, CRS Specialist in Education Policy. For additional background information, see CRS Report R45205, Harry W. Colmery Veterans Educational Assistance Act of 2017 (P.L. 115-48).

116   *Alexandra Hegji*

student was unable to complete a course of study because the IHE closed.[97] ED uses its information technology systems to adjust Pell eligibility for those students who attended a closed school and were not reported as having "graduated" from that school.[98] Following an adjustment, ED notifies students of the adjustment.

GI Bill Educational Assistance Benefits[99]

GI Bill entitlement may be restored following a school closure. However, a school closure may result in some GI Bill participants receiving an overpayment of benefits that they would become responsible for repaying.

Restoration of Entitlements

Prior to 2015, GI Bill entitlement was not restored for benefits received at an educational institution that later closed.

The Harry W. Colmery Veterans Educational Assistance Act of 2017 (P.L. 115-48) authorizes the restoration of GI Bill entitlement for individuals affected by school closures. Generally, GI Bill recipients are entitled to benefits equal to 36 months of full-time enrollment (or the equivalent for part-time educational assistance) under one GI Bill. In the case of the Survivors' and Dependents' Educational Assistance Program (DEA; 38 U.S.C., Chapter 35), recipients who first enrolled in a program of education before August 1, 2018, have 45 months (or the equivalent for part-time educational assistance) of entitlement. Entitlement is restored for

---

[97] HEA §437(c)(3).

[98] ED began restoring Pell Grant lifetime eligibility in March 2017. Previously, ED had determined it did not have the statutory authority to restore Pell Grant lifetime eligibility limits in the event of a school closure; however, on October 28, 2016, ED determined it does, in fact, have the authority to do so. Department of Education, "U.S. Department of Education Announces Final Regulations to Protect Students and Taxpayers from Predatory Institutions," press release, October 28, 2016, http://www.ed.gov/news/press-releases/us-department-education-announces-final-regulationsprotect-students-and-taxpayers-predatory-institutions?utm_name=.

[99] This section of the report was authored by Cassandria Dortch, CRS Specialist in Education Policy.

an incomplete course or program for which the individual is unable to receive credit or lost training time as a result of an educational institution closing. P.L. 115-48 applies to school closures occurring after January 1, 2015.[100]

In addition to restoring such entitlement, P.L. 115-48 permits the VA to continue paying a Post-9/11 GI Bill housing allowance through the end of the academic term following such closure but no longer than 120 days. Entitlement is not charged for the interim housing allowance. The extension of benefits following such closure is only applicable to the Post-9/11 GI Bill.[101]

Finally, P.L. 115-48 requires that the Department of Veterans Affairs (VA) notify affected individuals of imminent and actual school closures and notify them how such closure will affect their GI Bill entitlement. GI Bill participants must apply for benefit restoration and the housing allowance extension.

Overpayment of Benefits

Under general GI Bill regulations, if there are mitigating circumstances, a GI Bill participant who withdraws from all courses may remain eligible for benefits for the portion of the course completed. However, if there are no mitigating circumstances, the individual may be required to repay all benefits received for pursuit of the course. Mitigating circumstances are circumstances beyond the individual's control that prevent the individual from continuously pursuing a program of education. A school closing is considered to be a mitigating circumstance.[102]

Some GI Bill benefits, such as advance payments and the Post-9/11 GI Bill tuition and fees payment, Yellow Ribbon payment, and books and

---

[100] The amount of entitlement restored for closures occurring from January 1, 2015, through August 16, 2017, is based on the entire period of the individual's enrollment in the closed school. The restoration of entitlement went into effect November 14, 2017.

[101] Eligibility for interim housing allowance payments began August 16, 2017. The interim housing allowance payments were payable effective August 1, 2018. The later effective date gave the VA the opportunity to adapt its administrative processes and systems to make payments.

[102] The Department of Veterans Affairs (VA) automatically grants mitigating circumstances for up to six credits the first time a student reduces or terminates and mitigating circumstances must be considered. This automatic grant is called the 6-Credit Hour Exclusion.

supplies stipend, may be paid as a lump sum before or at the beginning of an academic term. An overpayment may occur for a prorated portion of those upfront payments if an individual is unable to complete the academic term without mitigating circumstances.[103]

Under Post-9/11 GI Bill regulations, the VA may determine the ending date of educational assistance based on the facts found if an eligible individual's educational assistance must be discontinued for any reason not described in regulations.[104] A school that permanently closes may qualify as a reason not described in regulations.[105]

Additional Student Aid Eligibility

For students who wish to continue their education at another IHE, another financial consideration related to an IHE's closure is the extent to which the students' eligibility for various financial aid sources may be affected by their previous use of those benefits at the closed institution. In addition to the duration of eligibility limits generally placed on Pell Grants and GI educational benefits discussed in the previous section, other federal student aid eligibility criteria that could affect future receipt of additional Title IV student loans include borrowing limits and eligibility limitations for receipt of Direct Subsidized Loans.

Loan Limits

Generally, annual and aggregate borrowing limits apply to Title IV student loans. Annual loan limits prescribe the maximum principal amount that may be borrowed in an academic year, and aggregate limits apply to

---

[103] The VA has indicated that students may be subject to debt for the closure of ITT Tech if the students received benefits (books and supplies) for a term they are unable to complete. U.S. Department of Veterans Affairs, "More Information Concerning ITT Tech's Closure," September 13, 2016, available at http://www.benefits.va.gov/gibill/, as of October 14, 2016.

[104] 38 C.F.R. §21.9635(bb).

[105] The VA has indicated that "no debts will be created against students because of the [Corinthian College] closure" unless the student dropped classes prior to the closure. U.S. Department of Veterans Affairs, "Corinthian College Students—What You Should Know," April 30, 2015, available at http://www.benefits.va.gov/gibill/as of December 14, 2015.

The Closure of Institutions of Higher Education 119

the total amount of outstanding Title IV loans that borrowers may accrue.[106] Borrowing limits for DL program loans[107] vary by borrower academic standing (e.g., grade or credential level), loan type (e.g., Subsidized or Unsubsidized Direct Loan), and dependency status.[108] For borrowers who receive a closed school discharge or whose loans have been discharged under a successful BDR claim, any discharged loans do not count against their annual and aggregate loan limits.[109]

Eligibility for Direct Subsidized Loans

In general, for borrowers of Direct Subsidized Loans, the federal government pays the interest that accrues on the loan while the borrower is enrolled in school on at least a half-time basis, during a six-month grace period thereafter, and during periods of authorized deferment. Individuals who are new borrowers on or after July 1, 2013, may only receive Direct Subsidized Loans for a period of time equal to 150% of the published length of the borrower's academic program (e.g., a borrower enrolled in a four-year degree program may receive six years' worth of Direct Subsidized Loans).[110] However, for borrowers who receive a closed school loan discharge or who successfully assert a BDR claim, the discharged loan will not count against the borrower's Subsidized Loan usage period.[111]

State Tuition Recovery Funds (STRF)

In addition to available debt relief, some states operate state tuition recovery funds (STRFs), which may reimburse students for charges paid to closed IHEs that are not covered by other sources. For example, a student

---

[106] No aggregate limits are placed on PLUS Loans.

[107] Borrowing limits also applied to FFEL and Perkins Loans; however, the authority to award new FFEL program loans was terminated in FY2010 and the authority to award new Perkins Loans expired on September 30, 2017.

[108] For additional information on loan limits, see CRS Report R40122, *Federal Student Loans Made Under the Federal Family Education Loan Program and the William D. Ford Federal Direct Loan Program: Terms and Conditions for Borrowers*.

[109] HEA §§425(a)(2), 437(c)(3), 455(a)(1). See also, U.S. Department of Education, Office of Federal Student Aid, "Frequently Asked Questions About the Closure of ITT Technical Institutes," https://studentaid.ed.gov/sa/about/announcements/itt/faq, accessed November 2, 2018.

[110] HEA §455(q).

[111] HEA §437(c)(3) and 34 C.F.R. §685.200(f)(3) and (4).

120 *Alexandra Hegji*

may have his or her Direct Loan discharged due to school closure, and an STRF may provide relief to cover expenses such as cash payments made directly to a closed IHE for tuition payments or to provide relief on private student loans borrowed to attend an IHE. The availability of and eligibility for such funds vary by state; not all states operate STRFs.[112]

Income Tax Consequences[113]

Borrowers whose student loans are discharged due to school closure will be subject to federal and state income taxes on the discharged loans unless they qualify for an exception. Students who received funds from an STRF might similarly be subject to tax on any funds received, although the tax treatment of such funds is unclear. Additionally, there could be tax consequences for individuals who had previously claimed certain federal education tax benefits. This section examines the potential federal and state tax consequences that may arise for these borrowers and students.

Federal Tax Treatment of Cancelled Debt

Under the Internal Revenue Code (IRC), borrowers whose debt is forgiven must generally include the amount of the canceled debt in income when determining their federal income tax liability.[114] In other words, they are subject to tax on the amount of the discharged loan. There are, however, various exceptions to this rule under which a borrower may exclude from income all or part of the forgiven debt.[115]

The HEA contains several exceptions providing for certain student loan discharges. These exceptions apply to borrowers of FFELs, Direct

---

[112] For additional information, see National Consumer Law Center, Student Loan Borrower Assistance Project, "State Programs," http://www.studentloanborrowerassistance.org/loan-cancellation/state-programs/, accessed October 29, 2018.

[113] This section was written by Margot Crandall-Hollick, CRS Specialist in Public Finance, and Brian T. Yeh, CRS Legislative Attorney.

[114] 26 U.S.C. §61(a)(12); Treas. Reg. §1.61-12. *See also* United States v. Kirby Lumber Co., 284 U.S. 1, 3 (1931) (treating discharged indebtedness as income at a time when the IRC did not yet address its tax treatment).

[115] See, for example, 26 U.S.C. §108 (allowing taxpayers to exclude canceled debt under certain conditions).

Loans, and Perkins Loans who borrowed such loans to attend any IHE and whose loans are discharged due to school closure.[116] Under the HEA exceptions, these borrowers will not be subject to federal income taxes on the discharged amounts so long as the student borrowers (or students on whose behalf a parent borrowed) meet the general criteria regarding the discharge of debt tied to closed schools described earlier in this chapter.[117]

The HEA does not address the tax treatment of (1) federal student loans discharged due to a successful borrower defense to repayment or (2) private education loans that are discharged under most circumstances.[118] As such, in these cases, the borrowers will be taxed on the amount of the discharged loan unless they qualify for an exception found outside of the HEA. Federal tax law provides several exceptions that may be relevant to borrowers whose loans are discharged. For example, IRC Section 108 excludes forgiven debt if the taxpayer is insolvent.[119] Thus, borrowers whose liabilities exceed the fair market value of their assets immediately prior to discharge will not be taxed on the discharged student loan.[120] Another example of an exception that might be relevant is the disputed debt doctrine. Under this doctrine, a discharged loan is not considered income for federal tax purposes if the loan was based on fraud or misrepresentation by the lender.[121] Guidance issued by the Internal Revenue Service (IRS) in 2015 and 2017 illustrates how the doctrine might be applied in the student loan context. The 2015 guidance provides that former students of Corinthian Colleges, Inc. (CCI) whose federal student loans are discharged under a defense against repayment claim will not be taxed on the

---

[116] HEA §§437(c)(4), 464(g)(4), and 455(a)(1).

[117] HEA §§437(c)(4), 464(g)(4), and 455(a)(1). *See also* Rev. Proc. 2015-57, 2015-51 I.R.B. 863 (providing that former students of Corinthian Colleges, Inc. whose federal student loans are discharged under the closed school discharge procedure will not be taxed on the amounts, citing to these statutes).

[118] Private education loans discharged after December 31, 2017, and before January 1, 2026, due to the death or total and permanent disability of the student may be excluded from gross income for purposes of federal income taxation. See 26 U.S.C. §108(f)(5).

[119] 26 U.S.C. §108(a)(1)(B).

[120] Ibid. §108(a)(3).

[121] See, for example, Preslar v. Comm'r, 167 F.3d 1323, 1329 (10th Cir. 1999); Zarin v. Comm'r, 916 F.2d 110, 115 (3rd Cir. 1990).

discharged amounts because many would likely qualify under the disputed debt doctrine due to the school's fraudulent behavior.[122] In 2017, the IRS extended this same relief to former students of schools owned by American Career Institutes, Inc. (ACI).[123] In addition, in 2018 the IRS issued guidance explaining that it would provide similar tax treatment regarding the discharge of *private* student loans taken out by borrowers who attended schools owned by CCI or ACI, where the loans are discharged due to legal settlements of cases brought by federal and state governmental agencies alleging that CCI, ACI, and certain private lenders engaged in unlawful business practices.[124]

In order to exclude a discharged loan from income, borrowers must determine that they qualify for an exception based on their individual circumstances and be able to show that the determination is correct if the IRS contests it. If the IRS disagrees and assesses tax based on the amount of the discharged loan, the taxpayer may challenge the assessment in federal court.[125]

Federal Tax Treatment of State Tuition Recovery Funds

Students who receive funds from STRFs might also face federal tax consequences, although the tax treatment is less clear. As a general rule, any amount received by a taxpayer is includible in gross income, and potentially subject to taxation, unless specifically excluded by law.[126] It is not clear how this principle applies in the context of STRF payments, as there do not appear to be court decisions or IRS guidance addressing the issue. There are several theories under which students could arguably

---

[122] Rev. Proc. 2015-57, 2015-51 I.R.B. 863.

[123] Rev. Proc. 2017-24, 2017-07 I.R.B. 916.

[124] Rev. Proc. 2018-39, 2018-34 I.R.B. 319.

[125] The borrower may file suit in the U.S. Tax Court prior to paying the disputed amount or in the U.S. Tax Court or appropriate federal district court after paying such amount. See 26 U.S.C. §§6213(a), 7421; 28 U.S.C. §1340. See also 26 U.S.C. §6201(d) (providing that if an information return filed by a third party serves as the basis for the IRS's determination that a taxpayer owes tax, the IRS then has the burden of producing reasonable and probative information concerning the alleged deficiency). This provision may be relevant for student borrowers because their discharged loans should be reported by the lender to the IRS on an information return. Ibid §6050P.

[126] Ibid. §61(a).

exclude the payments from income, depending on their circumstances and the specifics of the state's plan. For example, the payment might be treated as a nontaxable reimbursement of tuition, scholarship, or state benefit.[127] If the payment is excluded from the student's income, the student may be required to account for previously claimed federal education tax benefits, as discussed below.

Federal Higher Education Tax Benefits

Along with the potential taxation of discharged student loans and amounts received from STRFs, a school's closure or the discharge of a borrower's student loan may have consequences related to higher education tax benefits. While there are a variety of federal tax benefits that help offset some of the costs of a higher education, four are relevant for purposes of this chapter for reasons discussed below.[128] These four benefits include the following:

- *The student loan interest deduction*, under which qualifying taxpayers may annually deduct up to $2,500 of student loan interest for the entire duration of repayment.[129]
- *The tuition and fees deduction*, which allows taxpayers to reduce their income subject to tax for tuition and fees paid annually, up to $4,000, depending on their income level.[130] As of the date of this chapter, the tuition and fees deduction cannot be claimed on 2018 or subsequent tax returns.

---

[127] See, for example, Comm'r v. Glenshaw Glass Co. 348 U.S. 426, 431 (1955) (interpreting "gross income" to mean "*accessions to wealth*, clearly realized, and over which the taxpayers have complete dominion") (emphasis added); 26 U.S.C. §117 (excluding qualifying scholarships from income); Rev. Rul. 2003-12, 2003-1 C.B. 283 (discussing the general welfare exclusion, which has been developed by the IRS through a series of administrative rulings and excludes qualifying governmental benefits from income).

[128] For a summary of all higher education tax benefits that a student may be eligible for, including benefits for student debt and for saving for higher education, see CRS Report R41967, *Higher Education Tax Benefits: Brief Overview and Budgetary Effects*.

[129] 26 U.S.C. §221.

[130] Ibid §222. The ultimate tax savings from the tuition and fees deduction depends on the taxpayer's marginal tax rate. For example, if the taxpayer's top tax rate is 10%, deducting $4,000 will reduce tax liability by $400; however, if the taxpayer's top tax rate is 25%, the same deduction will reduce tax liability by $1,000.

124 *Alexandra Hegji*

- *The Lifetime Learning Credit (LLC)*, under which qualifying taxpayers may annually reduce their tax liability for tuition and fees paid, up to $2,000.[131] The LLC is a nonrefundable credit, meaning any amount of the credit in excess of income tax liability is effectively forfeited by the taxpayer.
- *The American Opportunity Tax Credit (AOTC)*, under which qualifying taxpayers can reduce tax liability by $2,500 per student annually (depending on eligible expenses and the taxpayer income level).[132] The AOTC can be claimed for tuition and fees and books, supplies, and equipment, but not room and board.[133] Additionally, the AOTC is a refundable credit, which means taxpayers with little to no tax liability can receive up to $1,000 of the AOTC as a refund check.[134]

Tuition and fees paid with the proceeds of a loan can count toward claiming these tax benefits, but any aid that is tax-free, such as a Pell Grant, must generally reduce the amount of expenses against which the benefits may be claimed.[135] As a general rule, either the parent or the student who pays the qualifying education expenses will claim the tax benefit, depending on whether the student is the parent's dependent for tax purposes.[136] Taxpayers can generally only claim one tax benefit per student annually.[137]

Availability of Benefits for Students Whose School Has Closed

Students who continue to pursue higher education after a school closure are eligible for these education tax benefits, pursuant to the requirements applicable to all taxpayers. However, in some instances, a

---

[131] Ibid §25A(c).

[132] Ibid. §25A(i). For a detailed overview of the AOTC, see CRS Report R42561, *The American Opportunity Tax Credit: Overview, Analysis, and Policy Options.*

[133] 26 U.S.C. §25A(i)(3).

[134] Ibid. §25A(i)(5).

[135] Ibid. §§25A(g)(2), 221(d)(2), 222(c)(2)(B).

[136] Ibid. §§25A(g)(3) & (5), 221(c), 222(c)(3); Treas. Reg. §1.25A-5(a). See also Treas. Reg. §1.25A-5(b) (treating expenses paid by a third party, such as grandparents or noncustodial parents, as paid by the student under certain circumstances).

[137] See, for example, 26 U.S.C. §§25A(c), 221(e)(1), 222(c)(1) & (2).

The Closure of Institutions of Higher Education 125

taxpayer who claims the AOTC may be ineligible for the credit in future years due to statutory restrictions on the period of education for which students may claim the credit. Specifically, the AOTC can only be claimed for expenses incurred during the first four years of a postsecondary education, irrespective of whether those first four years lead to a postsecondary credential.[138] Therefore, for example, it appears that if a student attended a school for three years and that school closed, the maximum remaining time the student could claim the AOTC is one additional year. There is seemingly no IRS guidance or case law addressing how this requirement is applied in the context of students whose schools have closed, including students who may have to pay back previously claimed credits (discussed below).

The other three benefits contain no limits on the period of education in which students may claim them.

Federal Tax Treatment of Previously Claimed Education Tax Benefits

Taxpayers may be required to account for previously claimed education tax benefits if they subsequently qualify to exclude discharged student loans or STRF payments. The borrowers who might be affected are those who

- claimed the LLC or AOTC for expenses that were paid with the proceeds from a student loan that was subsequently discharged,
- deducted expenses for tuition and fees that were paid with the proceeds from a student loan that was subsequently discharged,
- deducted interest on a student loan that was subsequently discharged, or
- claimed a tax credit (i.e., the LLC or AOTC) or a deduction (for tuition and fees or student loan interest) for expenses that were reimbursed by an STRF payment.[139]

---

[138] Ibid. §25A(b)(2)(A) & (C), (i)(2).

[139] Note that these tax consequences might also apply to any taxpayers who claimed the Hope Scholarship Credit, which was replaced by the AOTC beginning in 2009. See American

In order to prevent these borrowers from getting the double benefit of both (1) a credit or deduction and (2) the exclusion of the discharged loan or STRF payment, such borrowers may be required to pay back the value of the credit or deduction.[140] However, there may be circumstances in which the IRS will not require a taxpayer to account for previously claimed tax benefits. For example, in its 2015, 2017, and 2018 guidance addressing former students of CCI and ACI, the IRS announced that it would not require these borrowers to account for previously claimed education tax benefits.[141] The IRS did not explain its reasoning in reaching this determination,[142] and it is not clear the extent to which the agency may provide similar benefits to other borrowers.

State Income Tax Consequences

A school closure or the discharge of a student loan may also result in state income tax consequences. Most states use the IRC's definition of income as the starting point for computing state income tax liability.[143] As such, to the extent that the borrower must pay federal income tax on the discharged debt or account for previously claimed federal education tax benefits, he or she may be taxed at the state level as well. Similarly, to the extent that the borrower qualifies to exclude the amounts from federal income taxation, such treatment may also apply at the state level. However, while most state tax codes follow the IRC, states are not required to adopt the federal definition of income and, thus, some states may provide for different tax treatment.

Recovery and Reinvestment Act of 2009, P.L. 111-5, §1004, 123 Stat. 115, 313 (2009). The Hope credit is codified at 26 U.S.C. §25A(b).

[140] See Hillsboro Nat'l Bank v. Comm'r, 460 U.S. 370, 377-80 (1983) (discussing the origin of the judicially developed tax benefit rule, which prevents taxpayers from receiving double tax benefits on the same income or transaction); 26 U.S.C. §111 (partially codifying the tax benefit rule); Treas. Reg. §1.25A-5(f)(3), (4) (requiring the education tax credits be recaptured if the taxpayer receives a refund of the expenses).

[141] Rev. Proc. 2015-57, 2015-51 I.R.B. 863; Rev. Proc. 2017-24, 2017-07 I.R.B. 916; Rev. Proc. 2018-39. 2018-34 I.R.B. 319.

[142] Ibid.

[143] See *Personal Income Tax Quick Answer Charts: Starting Point for Personal Income Tax*, State Tax Guide (CCH) ¶700-003 (Nov. 30, 2016) (showing that most states use the federal definition of gross income, adjusted gross income, or taxable income as the basis for computing state individual income tax liability).

The Closure of Institutions of Higher Education

Furthermore, states with their own education tax benefits or tuition recovery funds may have laws or policies specifically addressing the state tax treatment of the benefits and funds.

In: Key Congressional Reports on Education   ISBN: 978-1-53615-731-4
Editor: Georgia Turner   © 2019 Nova Science Publishers, Inc.

Chapter 4

SCHOOL MEALS PROGRAMS AND OTHER USDA CHILD NUTRITION PROGRAMS: A PRIMER (UPDATED)[*]

Kara Clifford Billings and Randy Alison Aussenberg

SUMMARY

The "child nutrition programs" refer to the U.S. Department of Agriculture's Food and Nutrition Service (USDA-FNS) programs that provide food for children in school or institutional settings. The best known programs, which serve the largest number of children, are the school meals programs: the National School Lunch Program (NSLP) and the School Breakfast Program (SBP). The child nutrition programs also include the Child and Adult Care Food Program (CACFP), which provides meals and snacks in day care and after school settings; the Summer Food Service Program (SFSP), which provides food during the summer months; the Special Milk Program (SMP), which supports milk for schools that do not participate in NSLP or SBP; and the Fresh Fruit

---

[*] This is an edited, reformatted and augmented version of Congressional Research Service, Publication No. R43783, dated February 11, 2019.

and Vegetable Program (FFVP), which funds fruit and vegetable snacks in select elementary schools.

Funding: The vast majority of the child nutrition programs account is considered mandatory spending, with trace amounts of discretionary funding for certain related activities. Referred to as open-ended, "appropriated entitlements," funding is provided through the annual appropriations process; however, the level of *spending* is controlled by benefit and eligibility criteria in federal law and dependent on the resulting levels of participation. Federal cash funding (in the form of per-meal reimbursements) and USDA commodity food support is guaranteed to schools and other providers based on the number of meals or snacks served and participant category (e.g., free meals for poor children get higher subsidies).

Participation: The child nutrition programs serve children of varying ages and in different institutional settings. The NSLP and SBP have the broadest reach, serving qualifying children of all ages in school settings. Other child nutrition programs serve more-narrow populations. CACFP, for example, provides meals and snacks to children in early childhood and after-school settings among other venues. Programs generally provide some subsidy for all food served but a larger federal reimbursement for food served to children from low-income households.

Administration: Responsibility for child nutrition programs is divided between the federal government, states, and localities. The state agency and type of local provider differs by program. In the NSLP and SBP, schools and school districts ("school food authorities") administer the program. Meanwhile, SFSP (and sometimes CACFP) uses a model in which sponsor organizations handle administrative responsibilities for a number of sites that serve meals.

Reauthorization: The underlying laws covering the child nutrition programs were last reauthorized in the Healthy, Hunger-Free Kids Act of 2010 (HHFKA, P.L. 111-296, enacted December 13, 2010). This law made significant changes to child nutrition programs, including increasing federal financing for school lunches, expanding access to community eligibility and direct certification options for schools, and expanding eligibility options for home child care providers. The law also required an update to school meal nutrition guidelines as well as new guidelines for food served outside the meal programs (e.g., snacks sold in vending machines and cafeteria a la carte lines).

Current Issues: The 114th Congress began but did not complete a 2016 child nutrition reauthorization, and there was no significant legislative activity with regard to reauthorization in the 115th Congress. However, the vast majority of operations and activities continue with funding provided by appropriations laws.

INTRODUCTION AND BACKGROUND

The federal child nutrition programs provide assistance to schools and other institutions in the form of cash, commodity food, and administrative support (such as technical assistance and administrative funding) based on the provision of meals and snacks to children.[1] In general, these programs were created (and amended over time) to both improve children's nutrition and provide support to the agriculture economy.

Today, the child nutrition programs refer primarily to the following meal, snack, and milk reimbursement programs (these and other acronyms are listed in Appendix A):[2]

- National School Lunch Program (NSLP) (Richard B. Russell National School Lunch Act (42 U.S.C. 1751 et seq.));
- School Breakfast Program (SBP) (Child Nutrition Act, Section 4 (42 U.S.C. 1773));
- Child and Adult Care Food Program (CACFP) (Richard B. Russell National School Lunch Act, Section 17 (42 U.S.C. 1766));
- Summer Food Service Program (SFSP) (Richard B. Russell National School Lunch Act, Section 13 (42 U.S.C. 1761)); and
- Special Milk Program (SMP) (Child Nutrition Act, Section 3 (42 U.S.C. 1772)).

The programs provide financial support and/or foods to the institutions that prepare meals and snacks served outside of the home (unlike other food assistance programs such as the Supplemental Nutrition Assistance

---

[1] As discussed later in the report, the Child and Adult Care Food Program (CACFP) also supports food in adult day care facilities, but the child nutrition programs overwhelmingly serve children.

[2] Some lists also include the Fresh Fruit and Vegetable Program (FFVP) (Richard B. Russell National School Lunch Act, Section 19 (42 U.S.C. 1769a)), a newer program that is financed in a much different way than the programs listed. FFVP is discussed further later in the report ("Fresh Fruit and Vegetable Program"). WIC (the Special Supplemental Nutrition Program for Women, Infants, and Children) is also typically reauthorized with the child nutrition programs. WIC is not one of the child nutrition programs and is not discussed in this report.

Program (SNAP, formerly the Food Stamp Program) where benefits are used to purchase food for home consumption). Though exact eligibility rules and pricing vary by program, in general the amount of federal reimbursement is greater for meals served to qualifying low-income individuals or at qualifying institutions, although most programs provide some subsidy for all food served. Participating children receive subsidized meals and snacks, which may be free or at reduced price. Forthcoming sections discuss how program-specific eligibility rules and funding operate.

This chapter describes how each program operates under current law, focusing on eligibility rules, participation, and funding. This introductory section describes some of the background and principles that generally apply to all of the programs; subsequent sections go into further detail on the workings of each.

Unless stated otherwise, participation and funding data come from USDA-FNS's "Keydata Reports."[3]

Authorization and Reauthorization

The child nutrition programs are most often dated back to the 1946 enactment of the National School Lunch Act, which created the National School Lunch Program, albeit in a different form than it operates today.[4] Most of the child nutrition programs do *not* date back to 1946; they were added and amended in the decades to follow as policymakers expanded child nutrition programs' institutional settings and meals provided:

---

[3] This CRS report uses the May 2018 report, which contains data through March 2018. Keydata Reports available at http://www.fns.usda.gov/data-and-statistics.

[4] P.L. 79-396. There were, however, a number of smaller, more temporary precursor school food programs prior to 1946; see Gordon W. Gunderson, *National School Lunch Program: Background and Development*, 1971, http://www.fns.usda.gov/nslp/history. The 1946 law supported school lunch programs by giving formula grant funding to states based on factors such as per capita income, rather than the current-day open-ended entitlements based largely on eligibility and participation rules.

School Meals Programs and Other USDA Child Nutrition ... 133

- The Special Milk Program was created in 1954, regularly extended, and made permanent in 1970.[5]
- The School Breakfast Program was piloted in 1966, regularly extended, and eventually made permanent in 1975.[6]
- A program for child care settings and summer programs was piloted in 1968, with separate programs authorized in 1975 and then made permanent in 1978.[7] These are now the Child and Adult Care Food Program[8] and Summer Food Service Program.
- The Fresh Fruit and Vegetable Program began as a pilot in 2002, was made permanent in 2004, and was expanded nationwide in 2008.[9]

The programs are now authorized under three major federal statutes: the Richard B. Russell National School Lunch Act (originally enacted as the National School Lunch Act in 1946), the Child Nutrition Act (originally enacted in 1966), and Section 32 of the act of August 24, 1935 (7 U.S.C. 612c).[10] Congressional jurisdiction over the underlying three laws has typically been exercised by the Senate Agriculture, Nutrition, and Forestry Committee; the House Education and the Workforce Committee; and, to a limited extent (relating to commodity food assistance and Section 32 issues), the House Agriculture Committee.

Congress periodically reviews and reauthorizes expiring authorities under these laws. The child nutrition programs were most recently reauthorized in 2010 through the Healthy, Hunger-Free Kids Act of 2010 (HHFKA, P.L. 111-296); some of the authorities created or extended in

---

[5] P.L. 83-690 and P.L. 91-295. Milk purchases and donations for schools did exist prior to the 1954 law.

[6] Gordon W. Gunderson, *National School Lunch Program: Background and Development*, 1971, http://www.fns.usda.gov/nslp/history.

[7] P.L. 90-302, P.L. 94-105, P.L. 95-627. Institute of Medicine, *Child and Adult Care Food Program: Aligning Dietary Guidance for All*, 2011, p. 30, https://www.nap.edu/catalog/12959/child-and-adult-care-food-program-aligning-dietaryguidance-for.

[8] Adult day care was added in 1987 (Older Americans Act Amendments of 1987; P.L. 100-175).

[9] P.L. 107-171; P.L. 108-265; P.L. 110-246.

[10] In 1999, P.L. 106-78 renamed the National School Lunch Act in Senator Richard B. Russell's honor.

134 Kara Clifford Billings and Randy Alison Aussenberg

that law expired on September 30, 2015.[11] WIC (the Special Supplemental Nutrition Program for Women, Infants, and Children) is also typically reauthorized with the child nutrition programs. WIC is *not* one of the child nutrition programs and is not discussed in this chapter.[12]

The 114th Congress began but did not complete a 2016 child nutrition reauthorization. There was no significant legislative activity with regard to reauthorization in the 115th Congress.

Program Administration: Federal, State, and Local

The U.S. Department of Agriculture's Food and Nutrition Service (USDA-FNS) administers the programs at the federal level. The programs are operated by a wide variety of local public and private providers and the degree of direct state involvement differs by program and state.[13] At the state level, education, health, social services, and agriculture departments all have roles; at a minimum, they are responsible for approving and overseeing local providers such as schools, summer program sponsors, and child care centers and day care homes, as well as making sure they receive the federal support they are due. At the local level, program benefits are provided to millions of children (e.g., there were 30.0 million in the National School Lunch Program, the largest of the programs, in FY2017), through some 100,000 public and private schools and residential child care institutions, nearly 170,000 child care centers and family day care homes, and just over 50,000 summer program sites.

All programs are available in the 50 states and the District of Columbia. Virtually all operate in Puerto Rico, Guam, and the Virgin

---

[11] Reimbursements for NSLP, SBP, CACFP, SMP, and certain related USDA activities are permanently authorized. SFSP, WIC, and WIC Farmers Market Nutrition Program, State Administrative Expenses (discussed in "Related Programs, Initiatives, and Support Activities"), and certain related USDA activities have a September 30, 2015 expiration.

[12] See CRS Report R44115, *A Primer on WIC: The Special Supplemental Nutrition Program for Women, Infants, and Children*.

[13] In the past, the federal government (via USDA-FNS) has, for certain states, taken the place of state agencies (e.g., where a state has chosen not to operate a specific program or where there is a state prohibition on aiding private schools).

School Meals Programs and Other USDA Child Nutrition ... 135

Islands (and, in differing versions, in the Northern Marianas and American Samoa).[14]

Funding Overview

This section summarizes the nature and extent to which the programs' funding is mandatory and discretionary, including a discussion of appropriated entitlement status. Table 3 lists child nutrition program and related expenditures.

Open-Ended, Appropriated Entitlement Funding

Most spending for child nutrition programs is provided in annual appropriations acts to fulfill the legal financial obligation established by the authorizing laws. That is, the level of spending for such programs, referred to as appropriated mandatory spending, is not controlled through the annual appropriations process, but instead is derived from the benefit and eligibility criteria specified in the authorizing laws. The appropriated mandatory funding is treated as mandatory spending. Further, if Congress does not appropriate the funds necessary to fund the program, eligible entities may have legal recourse.[15] Congress typically considers the Administration's forecast for program needs in its appropriations decisions. For the majority of funding discussed in this chapter, the formula that controls the funding is not capped and fluctuates based on the reimbursement rates and the number of meals/snacks served in the programs.

---

[14] For more information on child nutrition programs in the Northern Marianas and American Samoa, see U.S. Department of the Interior, Office of Insular Affairs, Region IX Federal Regional Council, Outer Pacific Committee, *FY 2016 Report on Federal Financial Assistance to the U.S. Pacific and Caribbean Islands*, May 1, 2017, p. 10, https://www.doi.gov/sites/doi.gov/files/uploads/fy16-report-on-federal-financial-assistance-to-the-insular-areas.pdf.

[15] GAO Budget Glossary, p. 13: http://www.gao.gov/products/GAO-05-734SP.

> **Reimbursable Meals**
>
> A "reimbursable meal" (or snack in the case of some programs) is a phrase used by USDA, state, and other child nutrition policy and program operators to indicate a meal (or snack) that meets federal requirements and thereby qualifies for meal reimbursement.[16]
>
> In general, a meal or snack that is reimbursable means that it is
>
> - served to the correctly eligible person and/or at the eligible institution, and
> - in compliance with federal nutrition requirements for the meal or snack.[17]
>
> In the school meals programs (with some variation in other programs), the highest reimbursement is paid for meals served free to eligible children, a slightly lower reimbursement is paid for meals served at a reduced price to eligible children, and a much smaller reimbursement is also paid for meals served to children who are either ineligible for assistance or not certified. For this last group, the children pay the full price as advertised but meals are still technically subsidized.

Cash Reimbursements and Commodity Foods

In the meal service programs, such as the National School Lunch Program, School Breakfast Program, summer programs, and assistance for child care centers and day care homes, federal aid is provided in the form of statutorily set subsidies (reimbursements) paid for each meal/snack served that meets federal nutrition guidelines.

---

[16] See, for example, definition of "reimbursement" at 7 C.F.R. 210.2.

[17] The authorizing statutes for all four of the main child nutrition programs include nutritional requirements for the meals and snacks served; these are sometimes referred to as "nutrition standards," "nutrition guidelines," or "meal patterns." In most respects, the details of the requirements are specified in USDA-FNS regulations. The nutrition guidelines differ by program, largely in consideration of the age groups fed, meals/snacks authorized, and perhaps the settings in which meals are served. See program regulations for nutritional requirements: NSLP, 7 C.F.R. 210.10; SBP, 7 C.F.R. 220.8; CACFP, 7 C.F.R. 226.20; SFSP, 7 C.F.R. 225.16.

School Meals Programs and Other USDA Child Nutrition ...   137

Although all (including full-price) meals/snacks served by participating providers are subsidized, those served free or at a reduced price to lower-income children are supported at higher rates. All federal meal/snack subsidy rates are indexed annually (each July) for inflation, as are the income eligibility thresholds for free and reduced-price meals/snacks.[18] Subsequent sections discuss how a specific program's eligibility and reimbursements work.

Most subsidies are cash payments to schools or other providers, but a smaller portion of aid is provided in the form of USDA-purchased commodity foods.[19] Laws for three child nutrition programs (NSLP, CACFP, and SFSP) require the provision of commodity foods (or in some cases allow cash in lieu of commodity foods).[20]

Meal and snack service entails nonfood costs. Federal child nutrition per meal/snack subsidies may be used to cover local providers' administrative and operating costs. However, the separate direct federal payments for administrative/operating costs ("State Administrative Expenses," discussed in the "Related Programs, Initiatives, and Support Activities" section) are limited.

Other Federal Funding

In addition to the open-ended, appropriated entitlement funds summarized above, the child nutrition programs' funding also includes certain other mandatory funding[21] and a limited amount of discretionary funding.

---

[18] Per-meal subsidies paid to providers (e.g., schools, child care centers) are indexed annually based on the CPI-U Food Away from Home Component. For family child care homes, the annual indexing is based on the CPI-U Food at Home Component.

[19] USDA commodity foods are foods purchased by the USDA for distribution to USDA nutrition programs. These programs distribute "entitlement commodities" (an amount of USDA foods to which grantees are entitled by law) as well as "bonus commodities" (USDA food purchases based on requests from the agricultural producer community). For more information, see CRS Report R42353, *Domestic Food Assistance: Summary of Programs.*

[20] See USDA-FNS Food Distribution Division resources for more information on USDA Foods and child nutrition programs, http://www.fns.usda.gov/fdd/schoolscn-usda-foods-programs.

[21] These costs are made up of Food Safety Education, Coordinated Review, Computer Support, Training and Technical Assistance, studies, payment accuracy, and Farm to School Team. See p. 32-12 of FY2019 USDA-FNS Congressional Budget Justification, available at https://www.obpa.usda.gov/32fns2019notes.pdf.

Some of the activities discussed in "Related Programs, Initiatives, and Support Activities," such as Team Nutrition, are provided for with discretionary funding.

Aside from the annually appropriated funding, the child nutrition programs are also supported by certain permanent appropriations and transfers. Notably, funding for the Fresh Fruit and Vegetable Program is funded by a transfer from USDA's Section 32 program, a permanent appropriation of 30% of the previous year's customs receipts.

State, Local, and Participant Funds

Federal subsidies do not necessarily cover the full cost of the meals and snacks offered by providers. States and localities help cover program costs, as do children's families by paying charges for nonfree or reduced-price meals/snacks. There is a nonfederal cost-sharing requirement for the school meals programs (discussed below), and some states supplement school funding through additional state per-meal reimbursements or other prescribed financing arrangements.[22]

Child Nutrition Programs at a Glance

Subsequent sections of this chapter delve into the details of how each of the child nutrition programs support the service of meals and snacks in institutional settings; first, it is useful to take a broader perspective of primary program elements. Table 1 is a top-level look at the different programs that displays distinguishing characteristics (what meals are provided, in what settings, to what ages) and recent program spending.

---

[22] The School Nutrition Association, a trade association representing school meal operators and industry, tracks state policies and funding on the organization website at https://schoolnutrition.org/LegislationPolicy/ StateLegislationPolicyReports/.

School Meals Programs and Other USDA Child Nutrition ... 139

Table 1. Child Nutrition Programs at a Glance

Program	Authorizing Statute (Year First Authorized)	Distinguishing Characteristics	FY2017 Expenditures	FY2017 Average Daily Participation	Maximum Daily Snack/Meals[a]
National School Lunch Program	Richard B. Russell National School Lunch Act (1946)	• Lunches at school • Typically served in schools, to pre-K-12 students, during the school day and year • Possible to provide summer food and afterschool snacks.	$13.6 billion	30.0 million children	One meal and snack per child
School Breakfast Program	Child Nutrition Act (1966)	• Breakfasts at school (also for pre-K-12) • Typically served in schools, to pre-K-12 students, during the school day and year	$4.3 billion	14.7 million children	Generally one breakfast per child, with some flexibility
Child and Adult Care Food Program (child care centers, day care homes, adult day care centers)	Richard B. Russell National School Lunch Act (1968)	• Meals and snacks in early childhood and adult day care settings • Rules and funding differ based on type of institution	$3.5 billion (includes at risk after school spending, described below)	4.4 million children; 132,000 adults	Two meals and one snack, or one meal and two snacks per participant
Child and Adult Care Food Program (At Risk After-School snacks and meals)b	Richard B. Russell National School Lunch Act (1994)	• Supper and snacks for school-age children after school	(Not available; included in CACFP total above)	1.7 million children (included in CACFP children above)	One meal and one snack per child
Summer Food Service Program	Richard B. Russell National School Lunch Act (1968)	• Meals and snacks provided during summer months • Sites vary and include schools, community centers, camps, parks, and others • Eligibility rules vary for "open" and "closed" sites	$485 million	2.7 million children[c]	Lunch and breakfast or lunch and one snack per child Exception: maximum of three meals for camps or programs that serve primarily migrant children

Table 1. (Continued)

Program	Authorizing Statute (Year First Authorized)	Distinguishing Characteristics	FY2017 Expenditures	FY2017 Average Daily Participation	Maximum Daily Snack/Meals[a]
Special Milk Program	Child Nutrition Act (1954)	• Subsidizes milk, not meals or snacks • Institutions eligible must not participate in NSLP or SBP	$8 million	191,000 half pints served (average daily)d	Not specified
Fresh Fruit and Vegetable Program	Richard B. Russell National School Lunch Act (2002)	• Provides free fresh fruit and vegetable snacks to elementary school students	$184e million	Not available	Not applicable

Source: Except where noted, participation and funding data from USDA-FNS Key data May 2018 report, which contains data through March 2018. Participation data are estimated by USDA-FNS based on meals served.

a. These maximums are provided in the authorizing law for CACFP and SFSP, but specified only in regulations (7 C.F.R. 210.10(a), 220.9(a)) for NSLP and SBP.

b. At-risk after-school snacks and meals are part of CACFP law and CACFP funding, but differ in their rules and the age of children served.

c. Based only on July 2017 participation data.

d. Data from p. 32-58 of FY2019 USDA-FNS Congressional Budget Justification.

e. Obligations data displayed on p. 32-14 of FY2019 USDA-FNS Congressional Budget Justification.

SCHOOL MEALS PROGRAMS

This section discusses the school meals programs: the National School Lunch Program (NSLP) and the School Breakfast Program (SBP). Principles and concepts common to both programs are discussed first; subsections then discuss features and data unique to the NSLP and SBP, respectively.

General Characteristics

The federal school meals programs provide federal support in the form of cash assistance and USDA commodity foods; both are provided according to statutory formulas based on the number of reimbursable meals served in schools. The subsidized meals are served by both public and private nonprofit elementary and secondary schools and residential child care institutions (RCCIs)[23] that opt to enroll and guarantee to offer free or reduced-price meals to eligible low-income children. Both cash and commodity support to participating schools are calculated based on the number and price of meals served (e.g., lunch or breakfast, free or full price), but once the aid is received by the school it is used to support the overall school meal service budget, as determined by the school. This chapter focuses on the federal reimbursements and funding, but it should be noted that some states have provided state financing through additional state-specific funding.[24]

Federal law does not require schools to participate in the school meals programs. However, some states have mandated that schools provide lunch and/or breakfast, and some of these states require that their schools do so through NSLP and/or SBP.[25] The program is open to public and private schools.

A reimbursable meal requires compliance with federal school nutrition standards, which have changed throughout the history of the program based on nutritional science and children's nutritional needs. Food items not served as a complete meal meeting nutrition standards (e.g., a la carte offerings) are not reimbursable meals, and therefore are not eligible for federal per-meal, per-snack reimbursements. Following rulemaking to implement provisions in the Healthy, Hunger-Free Kids Act of 2010 (P.L.

---

[23] This CRS report refers to "schools," but it should be understood that—for NSLP and SBP—it means both schools and RCCIs. NSLP regulations, 7 C.F.R. 210.2, define RCCIs as follows: "The term 'residential child care institutions' includes, but is not limited to: homes for the mentally, emotionally or physically impaired, and unmarried mothers and their infants; group homes; halfway houses; orphanages; temporary shelters for abused children and for runaway children; long-term care facilities for chronically ill children; and juvenile detention centers. A long-term care facility is a hospital, skilled nursing facility, intermediate care facility, or distinct part thereof, which is intended for the care of children confined for 30 days or more."

[24] See School Nutrition Association, *State School Meal Mandates and Reimbursements Report: School Year 2017 2018*, https://schoolnutrition.org/uploadedFiles/Legislation_and_Policy/State_and_Local_Legislation_and_Regulations/2017-18-State-School-Meal-Mandates-and-Reimbursements.pdf.

[25] Ibid.

111-296), USDA updated the nutrition standards for reimbursable meals in January 2012 (see "Nutrition Standards" for more information). Schools serving meals that meet the updated nutrition standards are eligible for an increased reimbursement of 6 cents per lunch.

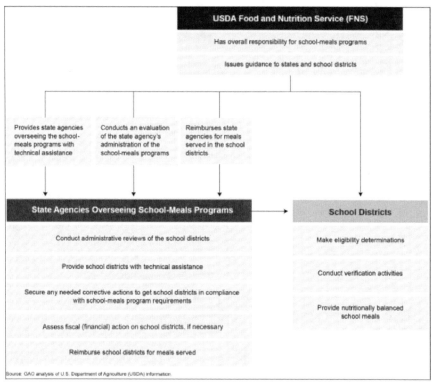

Source: Government Accountability Office (GAO), GAO-14-262, p. 47.

Figure 1. Federal, State, and Local Administration of School Meal Programs.

USDA-FNS administers the school meals programs federally, and state agencies (typically state departments of education) oversee and transmit reimbursements through agreements with school food authorities (SFAs) (typically local educational agencies (LEAs); usually these are school districts). Figure 1 provides an overview of the roles and relationships between these levels of government.

School Meals Programs and Other USDA Child Nutrition ... 143

There is a cost-sharing requirement for the programs, which amounts to a contribution of approximately $200 million from the states.[26] There also are states that choose to supplement federal reimbursements with their own state reimbursements.[27]

School Meals Eligibility Rules

The school meals programs and related funding do not serve only low-income children. *All* students can receive a meal at a NSLP- or SBP-participating school, but how much the child pays for the meal and/or how much of a federal reimbursement the state receives will depend largely on whether the child qualifies for a "free," "reduced-price," or "paid" (i.e., advertised price) meal. Both NSLP and SBP use the same household income eligibility criteria and categorical eligibility rules. States and schools receive the largest reimbursements for free meals, smaller reimbursements for reduced-price meals, and the smallest (but still some federal financial support) for the full-price meals.

There are three pathways through which a child can become certified to receive a free or reduced-price meal:

1. Household income eligibility for free and reduced-price meals (information typically collected via household application),
2. Categorical (or automatic) eligibility for free meals (information collected via household application or a direct certification process), and

---

[26] Section 7(a)(1) of Richard B. Russell National School Lunch Act, codified at 42 U.S.C. 1756(a)(1). Section 7(f) of Child Nutrition Act, codified at 42 U.S.C. 1776(f).

[27] See School Nutrition Association, *State School Meal Mandates and Reimbursements Report: School Year 2017 2018*, https://schoolnutrition.org/uploadedFiles/Legislation_and_Policy/State_and_Local_Legislation_and_Regulations/2017-18-State-School-Meal-Mandates-and-Reimbursements.pdf.

144 *Kara Clifford Billings and Randy Alison Aussenberg*

3. School-wide free meals under the Community Eligibility Provision (CEP), an option for eligible schools that is based on the share of students identified as eligible for free meals.[28]

Each of these pathways is discussed in more detail below.

Income Eligibility

The income eligibility thresholds (shown in Table 2) are based on multipliers of the federal poverty guidelines. As the poverty guidelines are updated every year, so are the eligibility thresholds for NSLP and SBP.

- Free Meals: Children receive free meals if they have household income at or below 130% of the federal poverty guidelines; these meals receive the highest subsidy rate. (Reimbursements are approximately $3.30 per lunch served, less for breakfast).
- Reduced-Price Meals: Children may receive reduced-price meals (charges of no more than 40 cents for a lunch or 30 cents for a breakfast) if their household income is above 130% and less than or equal to 185% of the federal poverty guidelines; these meals receive a subsidy rate that is 40 cents (NSLP) or 30 cents (SBP) below the free meal rate. (Reimbursements are approximately $2.90 per lunch served).
- Paid Meals: A comparatively small per-meal reimbursement is provided for full-price or paid meals served to children whose families do not apply for assistance or whose family income does not qualify them for free or reduced-price meals.[29] The paid meal

---

[28] CEP is not the only way schools may provide universal free meal service, but it is unique in that it does not require the collection of applications.

[29] The subsidy for paid meals is provided under the authority of Section 4 of the Richard B. Russell National School Lunch Act. Section 4 establishes two different payment levels: one for schools in which *less than 60%* of the school population is participating in free or reduced-price lunch and one for schools in which *60% or more* of the school population is receiving free or reduced price lunch. See https://www.federalregister.gov/documents/2018/07/19/2018-15465/national-school-lunch-special-milk-and-school-breakfast-programs-national-average-paymentsmaximum for these reimbursement rates. USDA also establishes a "maximum [reimbursement] rate" intended to ensure that states distribute federal funding to all participating school food authorities relatively equally.

School Meals Programs and Other USDA Child Nutrition ... 145

price is set by the school but must comply with federal regulations.[30] (Reimbursements are approximately 30 cents per lunch served).

The above reimbursement rates are approximate; exact current-year federal reimbursement rates for NSLP and SBP are listed in Table B.1 and Table B.3, respectively.

Households complete paper or online applications that collect relevant income and household size data, so that the school district can determine if children in the household are eligible for free meals, reduced-price meals, or neither.

Though these income guidelines primarily influence funding and administration of NSLP and SBP, they also affect the eligibility rules for the SFSP, CACFP, and SMP (described further in subsequent sections).

Table 2. Income Eligibility Guidelines for a Family of Four for NSLP and SBP for 48 states and DC, school year 20 1 8-20 1 9

Meal Type	Income Eligibility Threshold (% of the Federal Poverty Level)	Annual Income for a Family of Four
Free	<130%	<$32,630
Reduced-Price	130-185%	$32,630 - $46,435

Source: USDA, Food and Nutrition Service, "Child Nutrition Programs: Income Eligibility Guidelines," 83 Federal Register 20788, May 8, 2018.

Note: This school year is defined as July 1, 2018, through June 30, 2019. For other years, household sizes, Alaska, and Hawaii, see USDA-FNS website: http://www.fns.usda.gov/school-meals/income-eligibility-guidelines.

Categorical Eligibility

In addition to the eligibility thresholds listed above, the school meals programs also convey eligibility for free meals based on household participation in certain other need-tested programs or children's specified vulnerabilities (e.g., foster children). Per Section 12 of the National School

---

[30] The 2010 reauthorization established a policy intended to assure that paid meal revenues were covering the costs of producing a meal. See FNS paid lunch equity guidance for SY2018-2019, https://www.fns.usda.gov/school-meals/paidlunch-equity-guidance-school-year-2018-19.

Lunch Act, "a child shall be considered automatically eligible for a free lunch and breakfast ... without further application or eligibility determination, if the child is"[31]

- in a household receiving benefits through
  - o SNAP (Supplemental Nutrition Assistance Program);
  - o FDPIR (Food Distribution Program on Indian Reservations, a program that operates in lieu of SNAP on some Indian reservations) benefits; or
  - o TANF (Temporary Assistance for Needy Families) cash assistance;
- enrolled in Head Start;
- in foster care;
- a migrant;
- a runaway; or
- homeless.[32]

For meals served to students certified in the above categories, the state/school receive a reimbursement at the free meal amount and children receive a free meal. (See Table B.1 and Table B.3 for school year 2018-2019 rates).

---

[31] See Section 9(b)(12)(A) of the Russell National School Lunch Act, codified at 42 U.S.C. 1758(b)(12)(A), for the more specific definitions of these categories.

[32] SNAP, FDPIR, and TANF have income limits, but the other qualifications, as defined, in the statute, are not limited by income. In addition to the above list, following specific demonstration authority in HHFKA as well as under FNS's standing pilot authority, some states are currently directly certifying children based on Medicaid data. According to USDA-FNS, 19 states are operating direct certification with Medicaid in SY2018-2019. Four of the states (Illinois, Kentucky, New York, Pennsylvania) use Medicaid to directly certify for free meals only. Fifteen states (California, Connecticut, Florida, Indiana, Iowa, Massachusetts, Michigan, Nebraska, Nevada, Texas, Utah, Virginia, Washington, West Virginia, Wisconsin), operating under an expanded direct certification demonstration project to test direct certification with Medicaid for reduced-price meals (up to 185% of poverty), are using this process for free and reduced-price meals. Both options are discussed in USDA-FNS, Request for Applications to Participate in Demonstration Projects to Evaluate Direct Certification with Medicaid, January 27, 2016, http://www.fns.usda.gov/sites/default/files/cn/SP23-2016a.pdf.

School Meals Programs and Other USDA Child Nutrition ... 147

Some school districts collect information for these categorical eligibility rules via paper application. Others conduct a process called direct certification—a proactive process where government agencies typically cross-check their program rolls and certify a household's children for free school meals without the household having to complete a school meals application.

Prior to 2004, states had the option to conduct direct certification of SNAP (then, the Food Stamp Program), TANF, and FDPIR participants. In the 2004 child nutrition reauthorization (P.L. 108 265), states were required under federal law to conduct direct certification for SNAP participants, with nationwide implementation taking effect in school year 2008-2009. Conducting direct certification for TANF and FDPIR remains at the state's discretion.

The Healthy, Hunger-Free Kids Act of 2010 (HHFKA; P.L. 111-296) made further policy changes to expand direct certification (discussed further in the next section). One of those changes was the initiation of a demonstration project to look at expanding categorical eligibility and direct certification to some Medicaid households. The law also funded performance incentive grants for high-performing states and authorized correcting action planning for low-performing states in direct certification activities.[33]

Under SNAP direct certification rules generally, schools enter into agreements with SNAP agencies to certify children in SNAP households as eligible for free school meals without requiring a separate application from the family. Direct certification systems match student enrollment lists against SNAP agency records, eliminating the need for action by the child's parents or guardians. Direct certification allows schools to make use of SNAP's more in-depth eligibility certification process; this can reduce errors that may occur in school lunch application eligibility procedures that are otherwise used.[34] From a program access perspective,

---

[33] See CRS Report R41354, *Child Nutrition and WIC Reauthorization: P.L. 111-296*, for further discussion of these and related policies.

[34] See, for example, U.S. Government Accountability Office, *School-Meals Programs: USDA Has Enhanced Controls, but Additional Verification Could Help Ensure Legitimate*

direct certification also reduces the number of applications a household must complete.

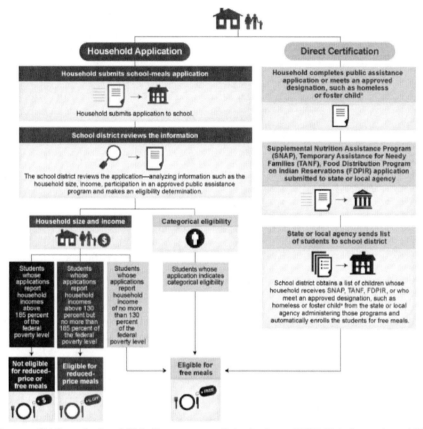

Source: GAO analysis of U.S. Department of Agriculture (USDA) information. ART Explosion (images).
Source: Figure and figure notes (below) from Government Accountability Office (GAO), GAO-14-262, p. 13.
Note: Students who meet an approved designation—(1) homeless, runaway, or migrant; (2) foster child; or (3) enrolled in a federally funded Head Start Program—are categorically eligible for free school meals.

Figure 2. Overview of Certification for Free and Reduced-Price School Meals Household Application and Direct Certification Pathways.

Program Access, GAO-14-262, May 2014, pp. 16-19, http://www.gao.gov/products/GAO-14-262.

School Meals Programs and Other USDA Child Nutrition ... 149

Figure 2, created by GAO and published in a May 2014 report, provides an overview of how school districts certify students for free and reduced-price meals under the income-based and category-based rules, via applications and direct certification.[35] A USDA-FNS study of school year 2014-2015 estimates that 11.1 million students receiving free meals were directly certified— 68% of all categorically eligible students receiving free meals.[36]

Community Eligibility Provision (CEP)

HHFKA also authorized the school meals Community Eligibility Provision (CEP), an option in NSLP and SBP law that allows eligible schools and school districts to offer *free meals to all enrolled students* based on the percentage of their students who are identified as automatically eligible from nonhousehold application sources (primarily direct certification through other programs).[37]

Based on the statutory parameters, USDA-FNS piloted CEP in various states over three school years and it expanded nationwide in school year 2014-2015. Eligible LEAs have until June 30 of each year to notify USDA-FNS if they will participate in CEP.[38] According to a database maintained by the Food Research and Action Center, just over 20,700 schools in more than 3,500 school districts (LEAs) participated in CEP in

---

[35] U.S. Government Accountability Office, *School-Meals Programs: USDA Has Enhanced Controls, but Additional Verification Could Help Ensure Legitimate Program Access*, GAO-14-262, May 2014, http://www.gao.gov/products/ GAO-14-262.

[36] Quinn Moore, Kevin Conway, and Brandon Kyler, et al., *Direct Certification in the National School Lunch Program: State Implementation Progress, School Year 2014-2015, Report to Congress* Mathematica Policy Research for USDA-FNS, CN-15-DC, October 2016, p. 24, https://www.fns.usda.gov/direct-certification-national-school-lunchprogram-report-congress-state-implementation-progress-0

[37] Explanation here draws in part from Madeleine Levin and Zoe Neuberger, *Improving Direct Certification Will Help More Low-Income Children Receive School Meals*, Center on Budget and Policy Priorities & Food Research and Action Center, July 25, 2014, p. 3. Aside from CEP, schools may also provide universal free meal service through the "Provision 2" and "Provision 3" options. CEP is unique in that no school meal applications are required. For information on other options, see USDA-FNS website, http://www.fns.usda.gov/school-meals/provisions-1-2-and-3.

[38] USDA Food and Nutrition Service, "National School Lunch Program and School Breakfast Program: Eliminating Applications through Community Eligibility as Required by the Healthy, Hunger-Free Kids Act of 2010," 81 *Federal Register* 50194, July 29, 2016.

150 *Kara Clifford Billings and Randy Alison Aussenberg*

SY2016-2017, an increase of approximately 2,500 schools compared to SY2015-2016.[39]

For a school (or school district, or group of schools within a district) to provide free meals to all children

- the school(s) must be eligible for CEP based on the share (40% or greater) of enrolled children that can be identified as categorically (or automatically) eligible for free meals, and
- the school must *opt-in* to CEP.

Though CEP schools serve free meals to all students, they are not reimbursed at the "free meal" rate for every meal. Instead, the law provides a funding formula: the percentage of students identified as automatically eligible (the "identified student percentage" or ISP) is multiplied by a factor of 1.6 to estimate the proportion of students who would be eligible for free or reduced-price meals had they been certified via application.[40] The result is the percentage of meals served that will be reimbursed at the free meal rate, with the remainder reimbursed at the far lower paid meal rate. For example, if a CEP school identifies that 40% of students are eligible for free meals, then 64% of the meals served will be reimbursed at the free meal rate and 36% at the paid meal rate.[41] Schools that identify 62.5% or more students as eligible for free meals receive the free meal reimbursement for all meals served.

Some of the considerations that may impact a school's decision to participate in CEP include whether the new funding formula would be beneficial for their school meal budget; an interest in reducing paperwork for families and schools; and an interest in providing more free meals,

---

[39] FRAC, "Community Eligibility," available at http://frac.org/community-eligibility.

[40] USDA-FNS, "National School Lunch Program and School Breakfast Program: Eliminating Applications Through Community Eligibility as Required by the Healthy, Hunger-Free Kids Act of 2010," 81 *Federal Register* 50194, July 29, 2016, p. 50201.

[41] Though, to the children of community eligibility schools, all meals are free, the USDA-FNS school meals expenditure data used throughout this report count these meals served in a more nuanced fashion. The percentage derived through this calculation is used to record those meals that are "free" and those meals that are "paid" (i.e., using the example from above, USDA-FNS data would reflect 64% of the meals served in the school as a "free" expenditure and meal served, and 36% as "paid").

School Meals Programs and Other USDA Child Nutrition ... 151

including meals to students who have not participated in the program before.

Nutrition Standards

School Meals

The Healthy, Hunger-Free Kids Act of 2010 (HHFKA; P.L. 111-296) set in motion changes to the nutrition standards for school meals, requiring USDA to update the standards within a certain timeframe.[42] The law required that the revised standards be based on recommendations from the Institute of Medicine (IOM) (now the Health and Medicine Division) at the National Academy of Sciences. The law also provided increased federal subsidies (6 cents per lunch) for schools meeting the new requirements and funding for technical assistance related to implementation.

USDA published the final regulations in January 2012.[43] The final rule sought to align school meal patterns with the 2010 Dietary Guidelines for Americans, and, generally consistent with IOM's recommendations, increased the amount of fruits, vegetables, whole grains, and low-fat or fat-free milk in school meals. The regulations also included calorie maximums and sodium limits to phase in over time, among other requirements.

The nutrition standards largely took effect in SY2012-2013 for lunches and in SY2013-2014 for breakfasts. A few other requirements were

---

[42] The 2010 law added a deadline, but it was the 2004 reauthorization (P.L. 108-265) that required USDA to update the standards based on National Academy of Sciences recommendations. The Institute of Medicine's (IOM's) report, issued in 2010, had made a number of recommendations around such topics as imposing calorie limits, increasing fruit and vegetables, and reducing sodium intake. IOM, *School Meals: Building Blocks for Healthy Children*, Washington, DC, 2010.

[43] See 7 C.F.R. 210.10 or USDA-FNS, "Nutrition Standards in the National School Lunch and School Breakfast Programs," 77 *Federal Register* 17, January 26, 2012, available at https://www.federalregister.gov/documents/2012/01/ 26/2012-1010/nutrition-standards-in-the-national-school-lunch-and-school-breakfast-programs. For related resources, see USDA-FNS website at http://www.fns.usda.gov/school-meals/nutrition-standards-school-meals.

scheduled to phase in over multiple school years.[44] Some schools experienced difficulty implementing the new guidelines, and Congress and USDA have made changes to the 2012 final rule's whole grain, sodium, and milk requirements.[45] For SY2019-2020 and onwards, schools are operating under a final rule published December 12, 2018.[46]

Competitive Foods

The HHFKA also gave USDA the authority to regulate other foods in the school nutrition environment. Sometimes called "competitive foods," these include foods and drinks sold in a la carte lines, vending machines, snack bars and concession stands, and fundraisers.

Relying on recommendations made by a 2007 IOM report, USDA-FNS promulgated a proposed rule and then an interim final rule in June 2013, which went into effect for SY2014-2015.[47] The interim final rule created nutrition guidelines for all non-meal foods and beverages that are sold *during the school day* (defined as midnight until 30 minutes after dismissal). The final rule, published on July 29, 2016, maintained the interim final rules with minor modifications.[48] Under the final standards, these foods must meet whole-grain requirements; have certain primary ingredients; and meet calorie, sodium, and fat limits, among other

---

[44] For the original implementation schedule based on the January 2012 final rule, see USDA-FNS Implementation Timeline, http://www.fns.usda.gov/sites/default/files/implementation_timeline.pdf.

[45] For more information, see CRS Report R45486, *Child Nutrition Programs: Current Issues.*

[46] USDA-FNS, "Child Nutrition Programs: Flexibilities for Milk, Whole Grains, and Sodium Requirements: Final Rule," 83 *Federal Register* 63775, December 12, 2018, available at https://www.federalregister.gov/documents/2018/12/12/2018-26762/child-nutrition-programs-flexibilities-for-milk-whole-grains-and-sodium-requirements.

[47] IOM, *Nutrition Standards for Foods in Schools: Leading the Way toward Healthier Youth,* 2007, https://www.nap.edu/catalog/11899/nutrition-standards-for-foods-in-schools-leading-the-way-toward; USDA-FNS, "Interim Rule: NSLP and SBP Nutrition Standards for All Foods Sold in Schools as Required by the Healthy, Hunger-Free Kids Act of 2010," 78 *Federal Register* 79567, December 31, 2013, available at https://www.federalregister.gov/documents/2013/12/31/2013-31350/national-school-lunch-program-and-school-breakfast-program-nutrition-standards-for-all-foods-sold-in.

[48] USDA-FNS, "National School Lunch Program and School Breakfast Program: Nutrition Standards for All Foods Sold in School as Required by the Healthy, Hunger-Free Kids Act of 2010; Final Rule," 81 *Federal Register* 50131, July 29, 2016. The final rule and related resources are available at the USDA-FNS website, https://www.fns.usda.gov/ school-meals/tools-schools-focusing-smart-snacks.

requirements. Schools are limited to a list of no- and low-calorie beverages they may sell (with larger portion sizes and caffeine allowed in high schools).

There are no limits on fundraisers selling foods that meet the interim final rule's guidelines. Fundraisers outside of the school day are not subject to the guidelines. HHFKA and the interim final rule provide states with discretion to exempt infrequent fundraisers selling foods or beverages that do not meet the nutrition standards.

The rule does not limit foods brought from home, only foods sold at school during the school day. The federal standards are minimum standards; states and school districts are permitted to issue more stringent policies.

National School Lunch Program (NSLP)

In FY2017, NSLP subsidized 4.9 billion lunches to children in close to 96,000 schools and 3,200 residential child care institutions (RCCIs). Average daily participation was 30.0 million students (58% of children enrolled in participating schools and RCCIs). Of the participating students, 66.7% (20.0 million) received free lunches and 6.5% (2.0 million) received reduced-price lunches. The remainder were served full-price meals, though schools still receive a reimbursement for these meals. Figure 3 shows FY2017 participation data.

FY2017 federal school lunch costs totaled approximately $13.6 billion (see Table 3 for the various components of this total). The vast majority of this funding is for per-meal reimbursements for free and reduced-price lunches.

The HHFKA also provided an additional 6-cent per-lunch reimbursement to schools that provide meals that meet the updated nutritional guidelines requirements.[49] This bonus is not provided for

---

[49] In January 2014, USDA-FNS issued a final rule implementing the 6-cent reimbursement: USDA-FNS, "Certification of Compliance With Meal Requirements for the National School Lunch Program Under the Healthy, Hunger-Free Kids Act of 2010," 79 *Federal*

breakfast, but funds may be used to support schools' breakfast programs. NSLP lunch reimbursement rates are listed in Table B.1.

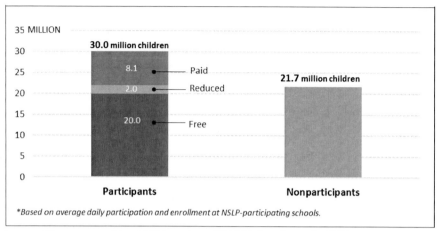

Source: Figure created by CRS based on FY2017 data from the USDA-FNS Key data May 2018 report.

Notes: Numbers may not add due to rounding. To reflect participation for the actual school year (September through May), these estimates are based on nine-month averages of October through May plus September, rather than averages of the 12 months of the fiscal year (October through September). Participation data are estimated by USDA-FNS based on average daily meals served. Children in schools participating in the Community Eligibility Provision (CEP) are counted in the free and paid meal categories.

Figure 3. National School Lunch Program, FY2017 Participation among children at NSLP-participating schools.

In addition to federal *cash* subsidies, schools participating in NSLP receive USDA-acquired *commodity foods*. Schools are entitled to a specific, inflation-indexed value of USDA commodity foods for each lunch they serve. Also, schools may receive donations of bonus commodities acquired by USDA in support of the farm economy.[50] In FY2017, the value

---

Register 326, January 3, 2014. Note: 6-cent increase authorized is also annually indexed for inflation.

[50] USDA commodity foods are foods purchased by the USDA for distribution to USDA nutrition programs. These programs distribute "entitlement commodities" (an amount of USDA foods to which grantees are entitled by law) as well as "bonus commodities" (USDA food

of federal commodity food aid to schools totaled nearly $1.4 billion. The per-meal rate for commodity food assistance is included in Table B.4.

While the vast majority of NSLP funding is for lunches served during the school day, NSLP may also be used to support snack service during the school year and to serve meals during the summer. These features are discussed in subsequent sections, "Summer Meals" and "After-School Meals and Snacks: CACFP, NSLP Options." Reimbursement rates for snacks are listed in Table B.2.

School Breakfast Program (SBP)

The School Breakfast Program (SBP) provides per-meal cash subsidies for breakfasts served in schools. Participating schools receive subsidies based on their status as a severe need or nonsevere need institution. Schools can qualify as a severe need school if 40% or more of their lunches are served free or at reduced prices. See Table B.3 for SBP reimbursement rates.

Figure 4 displays SBP participation data for FY2017. In that year, SBP subsidized over 2.4 billion breakfasts in over 88,000 schools and nearly 3,200 RCCIs. Average daily participation was 14.7 million children (30.1% of the students enrolled in participating schools and RCCIs). The majority of meals served through SBP are free or reduced-price. Of the participating students, 79.1% (11.6 million) received free meals and 5.7% (835,000) purchased reduced-price meals. Federal school breakfast costs for the fiscal year totaled approximately $4.3 billion (see Table 3 for the various components of this total).

Significantly fewer schools and students participate in SBP than in NSLP. Participation in SBP tends to be lower for several reasons, including the traditionally required early arrival by students in order to receive a meal and eat before school starts. Some schools offer (and anti-hunger groups have encouraged) models of breakfast service that can result

---

purchases based on requests from the agricultural producer community). For more information see CRS Report R42353, *Domestic Food Assistance: Summary of Programs.*

in greater SBP participation, such as Breakfast in the Classroom, where meals are delivered in the classroom; "grab and go" carts, where students receive a bagged breakfast that they bring to class, or serving breakfast later in the day in middle and high schools.[51]

Unlike NSLP, commodity food assistance is not a formal part of SBP funding; however, commodities provided through NSLP may be used for school breakfasts as well.

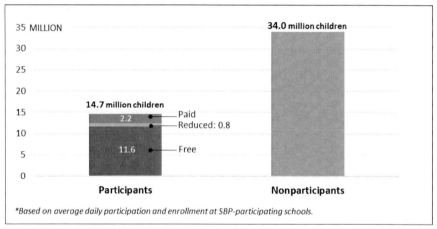

Source: Figure created by CRS based on FY2017 data from the USDA-FNS Key data May 2018 report.

Notes: Numbers may not add due to rounding. To reflect participation for the actual school year (September through May), these estimates are based on nine-month averages of October through May plus September, rather than averages of the 12 months of the fiscal year (October through September). Participation data are estimated by USDA-FNS based on average daily meals served. Children in schools participating in the Community Eligibility Provision (CEP) are counted in the free and paid meal categories.

Figure 4. School Breakfast Program, FY2017 Participation among children at SBP-participating schools.

---

[51] See Food Research and Action Center (FRAC), "School Breakfast Expansion Strategies," http://www.frac.org/ programs/school-breakfast-program/school-breakfast-expansion-strategies (accessed July 9, 2018).

OTHER CHILD NUTRITION PROGRAMS

In addition to the school meals programs discussed above, other federal child nutrition programs provide federal subsidies and commodity food assistance for schools and other institutions that offer meals and snacks to children in early childhood, summer, and after-school settings. This assistance is provided to (1) schools and other governmental institutions, (2) private for-profit and nonprofit child care centers, (3) family/group day care homes, and (4) nongovernmental institutions/organizations that offer outside-of-school programs for children. (Although this chapter focuses on the programs that serve children, one child nutrition program (CACFP) also serves day care centers for chronically impaired adults and elderly persons under the same general per meal/snack subsidy terms.) The programs in the sections to follow serve comparatively fewer children and spend comparatively fewer federal funds than the school meal programs.

Child and Adult Care Food Program (CACFP)

CACFP subsidizes meals and snacks served in early childhood, day care, and after-school settings. CACFP provides subsidies for meals and snacks served at participating nonresidential child care centers, family day care homes, and (to a lesser extent) adult day care centers.[52] The program also provides assistance for meals served at after-school programs. CACFP reimbursements are available for meals and snacks served to children age 12 or under, migrant children age 15 or under, children with disabilities of any age, and, in the case of adult care centers, chronically impaired and elderly adults. Children in early childhood settings are the overwhelming majority of those served by the program.

---

[52] CACFP also supports meals in homeless/emergency shelters. See http://www.fns.usda.gov/cacfp/emergency-shelters for further information.

CACFP provides federal reimbursements for breakfasts, lunches, suppers, and snacks served in participating centers (facilities or institutions) or day care homes (private homes). The eligibility and funding rules for CACFP meals and snacks depend first on whether the participating institution is a center or a day care home (the next two sections discuss the rules specific to centers and day care homes). According to FY2017 CACFP data, child care centers have an average daily attendance of about 56 children per center, day care homes have an average daily attendance of approximately 7 children per home, and adult day care centers typically care for an average of 48 chronically ill or elderly adults per center.[53]

Providers must demonstrate that they comply with government-established standards for other child care programs. Like in school meals, federal assistance is made up overwhelmingly of *cash* reimbursements calculated based on the number of meals/snacks served and federal per-meal/snack reimbursements rates, but a far smaller share of federal aid (4.3% in FY2017) is in the form of federal USDA commodity *foods* (or cash in lieu of foods). Federal CACFP reimbursements flow to individual providers either directly from the administering state agency (this is the case with many child/adult care centers able to handle their own CACFP administrative functions) or through "sponsors" who oversee and provide administrative support for a number of local providers (this is the case with some child/adult care centers and with all day care homes).[54]

In FY2017, total CACFP spending was over $3.5 billion, including cash reimbursement, commodity food assistance, and costs for sponsor audits. (See Table 3 for a further breakdown of CACFP costs.) This total also includes the after-school meals and snacks provided through CACFP's "at-risk after-school" pathway; this aspect of the program is discussed later in "After-School Meals and Snacks: CACFP, NSLP Options."

---

[53] USDA-FNS' administrative data on the CACFP are the source of these attendance numbers.

[54] In many cases, sponsor organizations that provide administrative support to multiple providers also are paid federal reimbursements for their costs. Day care homes must have a sponsoring organization, while child care centers may have a sponsor but are not required to do so.

CACFP Nutrition Standards

As with school foods, the HHFKA required USDA to update CACFP's meal patterns. USDA's final rule revised the meal patterns for both meals served in child care centers and day care homes, as well as preschool meals served through the NSLP and SBP, effective October 1, 2017.[55] For infants (under 12 months of age), the new meal patterns eliminated juice, supported breastfeeding, and set guidelines for the introduction of solid foods, among other changes. For children ages one and older, the new meal patterns increased whole grains, fruits and vegetables, and low-fat and fat-free milk; limited sugar in cereals and yogurts; and prohibited frying, among other requirements.

Table 3. FY2016 and FY2017 Federal Expenditures on Child Nutrition Programs, in millions of dollars

Program or Program Component	FY2016	FY2017	Change from FY2016 to FY2017	
National School Lunch Program	$13,569	$13,643	+$74	+1%
free meal reimbursements	$9,593	$9,620	+$27	0%
reduced-price meal reimbursements	$808	$783	-$25	-3%
paid meal reimbursements	$1,478	$1,480	+$2	0%
additional funding to schools with more than 60% free or reduced price participation	$76	$74	-$2	-3%
performance-based meal reimbursements	$302	$293	-$9	-3%
commodity food assistance[a]	$1,311	$1,393	+$82	+6%
School Breakfast Program	$4,213	$4,252	+$39	+1%
free meal reimbursements	$3,868	$3,912	+$44	+1%
reduced-price meal reimbursements	$239	$235	-$4	-2%
paid meal reimbursements	$106	$106	$0	0%
Child and Adult Care Food Program	$3,520	$3,537	+$17	0%
meal reimbursements at child care centers	$2,307	$2,363	+$56	+2%
meal reimbursements at child care homes	$764	$721	-$42	-6%
meal reimbursements at adult day care centers	$149	$156	+$7	+5%
commodity food assistance[a]	$155	$153	-$2	-1%

---

[55] USDA-FNS, "Child and Adult Care Food Program: Meal Pattern Revisions Related to the Healthy, Hunger-Free Kids Act of 2010; Final Rule," 81 *Federal Register* 24348 et seq., April 25, 2016, https://www.federalregister.gov/ documents/2016/04/25/2016-09412/child-and-adult-care-food-program-meal-pattern-revisions-related-to-the-healthyhunger-free-kids-act.

Table 3. (Continued)

Program or Program Component	FY2016	FY2017	Change from FY2016 to FY2017	
administrative costs for child care sponsors	$146	$145	-$1	-1%
Summer Food Service Program	$478	$485	+$7	+1%
meal reimbursements	$419	$424	+$5	+1%
commodity food assistance[a]	$2	$2	$0	0%
sponsor and inspection costs	$58	$60	+$2	+3%
Special Milk Program	$9	$8	-$1	-11%
Fresh Fruit and Vegetable Program[b]	$167	$184	+$17	+10%
State Administrative Expenses	$260	$279	+$19	+7%
Mandatory Other Program Costs[c]	$59	$83	+$24	+41%
Discretionary Activities[d]	$69	$63	-$6	-9%
TOTAL OF FUNDS DISPLAYED[e]	$22,344	$22,534	+$192	+1%

Source: Program expenditures data (outlays) from USDA-FNS Key data Reports (dated March 2017 and March 2018), except where noted below.

Notes: Expenditures displayed here will vary from displays in CRS appropriations reports and in some cases the USDA-FNS annual budget justification. Since the majority of program funding is for open-ended entitlements, expenditure data capture spending better than the total of appropriations. This table includes some functions that are funded through permanent appropriations or transfers (i.e., funding not provided in appropriations laws). Due to rounding to the nearest million, percentage increases or decreases may be exaggerated or understated.

a. Amounts included in this table for commodity food assistance include only entitlement commodities for each program, not bonus commodities.

b. Obligations data displayed on p. 32-14 of FY2019 USDA-FNS Congressional Budget Justification.

c. Obligations data displayed on p. 32-12 of FY2019 USDA-FNS Congressional Budget Justification. These costs are made up of Food Safety Education, Coordinated Review, Computer Support, Training and Technical Assistance, studies, payment accuracy, and Farm to School Team.

d. Obligations data displayed on p. 32-12 of FY2019 USDA-FNS Congressional Budget Justification. These costs include Team Nutrition, the Summer EBT demonstration, and School Meal Equipment Grants.

e. This table summarizes the vast majority of child nutrition programs' federal spending but does not capture all federal costs.

CACFP at Centers Participation

Child care centers in CACFP can be (1) public or private nonprofit centers, (2) Head Start centers, (3) for-profit proprietary centers (if they meet certain requirements as to the proportion of low-income children they enroll), and (4) shelters for homeless families. Adult day care centers include public or private nonprofit centers and for-profit proprietary centers (if they meet minimum requirements related to serving low-income

School Meals Programs and Other USDA Child Nutrition ...   161

disabled and elderly adults).[57] In FY2017, over 65,000 child care centers with an average daily attendance of over 3.6 million children participated in CACFP. Over 2,700 adult care centers served nearly 132,000 adults through CACFP.

Eligibility and Administration

Participating centers may receive daily reimbursements for up to either two meals and one snack or one meal and two snacks for each participant, so long as the meals and snacks meet federal nutrition standards.

The eligibility rules for CACFP centers largely track those of NSLP: children in households at or below 130% of the current poverty line qualify for free meals/snacks while those between 130% and 185% of poverty qualify for reduced-price meals/snacks (see Table 2). In addition, participation in the same categorical eligibility programs as NSLP as well as foster child status convey eligibility for free meals in CACFP.[58] Like school meals, eligibility is determined through paper applications or direct certification processes.

Like school meals, all meals and snacks served in the centers are federally subsidized to some degree, even those that are paid. Different reimbursement amounts are provided for breakfasts, lunches/suppers, and snacks, and reimbursement rates are set in law and indexed for inflation annually. The largest subsidies are paid for meals and snacks served to participants with family income below 130% of the federal poverty income guidelines (the income limit for free school meals), and the smallest to those who have not met a means test. See Table B.5 for current CACFP center reimbursement rates.

Unlike school meals, CACFP institutions are less likely to collect per-meal payments. Although federal assistance for day care centers differentiates by household income, centers have discretion on their pricing

---

[57] Participating adult care programs "should be structured, comprehensive and provide health and social support services to enrolled participants. Centers that simply provide social or rehabilitative services to adults do not qualify to participate in CACFP." http://www.fns.usda.gov/cacfp/facts-about-adult-component-cacfp.

[58] See also summary of CACFP eligibility rules at USDA-FNS website, http://www.fns.usda.gov/cacfp/why-cacfpimportant.

of meals. Centers may adjust their regular fees (tuition) to account for federal payments, but CACFP itself does not regulate these fees. In addition, centers can charge families separately for meals/snacks, so long as there are no charges for children meeting free-meal/snack income tests and limited charges for those meeting reduced-price income tests.

Independent centers are those without sponsors handling administrative responsibilities. These centers must pay for administrative costs associated with CACFP out of nonfederal funds or a portion of their meal subsidy payments. For centers with sponsors, the sponsors may retain a proportion of the meal reimbursement payments they receive on behalf of their centers to cover such costs.

CACFP for Day Care Homes

Participation

CACFP-supported day care *homes* serve a smaller number of children than CACFP-supported *centers*, both in terms of the total number of children served and the average number of children per facility. Roughly 17% of children in CACFP (approximately 757,000 in FY2017 average daily attendance) are served through day care homes. In FY2017, approximately 103,000 homes (with just over 700 sponsors) received CACFP support.

Eligibility and Reimbursement

As with centers, payments to day care homes are provided for up to either two meals and one snack or one meal and two snacks a day for each child. Unlike centers, day care homes must participate under the auspices of a public or, more often, private nonprofit sponsor that typically has 100 or more homes under its supervision. CACFP day care home sponsors receive monthly administrative payments based on the number of homes for which they are responsible.[59]

---

[59] As an example of the role that sponsors and homes play in CACFP, in Allentown, Pennsylvania, the Lehigh Valley Children's Centers (LVCC) serves as a sponsor for child care homes in the area. They offer a variety of administrative services to family child care

School Meals Programs and Other USDA Child Nutrition ... 163

Federal reimbursements for family day care homes differ by the home's status as "Tier I" or "Tier II." Unlike centers, day care homes receive cash reimbursements (but not commodity foods) that generally are not based on the child participants' household income. Instead, there are two distinct, annually indexed reimbursement rates that are based on area or operator eligibility criteria

- Tier I homes are located in low-income areas (defined as areas in which at least 50% of school-age and enrolled children qualify for free or reduced-price meals) or operated by low-income providers whose household income meets the free or reduced-price income standards.[60] They receive higher subsidies for each meal/snack they serve.
- Tier II (lower) rates are by default those for homes that do not qualify for Tier I rates; however, Tier II providers may seek the higher Tier I subsidy rates for individual low-income children for whom financial information is collected and verified. (See Table B.6 for current Tier I and Tier II reimbursement rates).

Additionally, HHFKA introduced a number of additional ways (as compared to prior law) by which family day care homes can qualify as low-income and get Tier I rates for the entire home or for individual children.[61]

---

homes that are registered with the state. In their brochure, they state that it is LVCC's responsibility to "monitor meals and reimburse [homes] for meals served," and it is homes' responsibility "to plan nutritional menus that meet meal requirements, maintain and submit daily attendance records and monthly meal counts." See http://www.lvcconline.org/images/pdf/CACFP-Brochure.pdf.

[60] 7 C.F.R. §226.2.

[61] Previously, child care homes could only use data from the elementary school level to establish the area as low-income. The new law allows these homes to use data from the middle and high school level as well to establish need and qualify as a "Tier I" home. Also, P.L. 111-296 included policies to streamline application processes and eliminate some paperwork. As part of this process, the annual application process has been eliminated and sponsors and child care centers will only have to submit paperwork the first time they apply, with amendments submitted as necessary. Finally, P.L. 111-296 increased CACFP sponsoring organizations' and providers' flexibility over administrative funds, including the option to carry over up to 10% of administrative funds from one fiscal year to the next. USDA-FNS has begun to implement these changes. See, for example, USDA Food and Nutrition

As with centers, there is no requirement that meals/snacks specifically identified as free or reduced-price be offered; however, unlike centers, federal rules prohibit any separate meal charges.

Summer Meals

Current law SFSP and the NSLP/SBP Seamless Summer Option provide meals in congregate settings nationwide; the related Summer Electronic Benefits Transfer (SEBTC or Summer EBT) demonstration project is an alternative to congregate settings.

Summer Food Service Program (SFSP)

SFSP supports meals for children during the summer months. The program provides assistance to local public institutions and private nonprofit service institutions running summer youth/recreation programs, summer feeding projects, and camps. Assistance is primarily in the form of cash reimbursements for each meal or snack served; however, federally donated commodity foods are also offered. Participating service institutions are often entities that provide ongoing year-round service to the community including schools, local governments, camps, colleges and universities in the National Youth Sports program, and private nonprofit organizations like churches.

Similar to the CACFP model, sponsors are institutions that manage the food preparation, financial, and administrative responsibilities of SFSP. Sites are the places where food is served and eaten. At times, a sponsor may also be a site. State agencies authorize sponsors, monitor and inspect sponsors and sites, and implement USDA policy. Unlike CACFP, sponsors are required for an institution's participation in SFSP as a site.

Service, "Child and Adult Care Food Program: Amendments Related to the Healthy, Hunger-Free Kids Act of 2010," 77 *Federal Register* 21018-21038, April 9, 2012; USDA-FNS Memorandum, *Child Nutrition Reauthorization 2010: Area Eligibility for Family Day Care Homes*, Memo Code: CACFP 05-2011-Revised, January 10, 2011, https://www.fns.usda.gov/cacfp-05-2011-revisedchild-nutrition-reauthorization-2010-area-eligibility-family-day-care-homes.

Participation

In FY2017, nearly 5,500 sponsors with 50,000 food service sites participated in the SFSP and served an average of approximately 2.7 million children daily (according to July data).[62]

Participation of sites and children in SFSP has increased in recent years. Program costs for FY2017 totaled over $485 million, including cash assistance, commodity foods, administrative cost assistance, and health inspection costs.

Eligibility and Administration

There are several options for eligibility and meal/snack service for SFSP sponsors (and their sites)

- Open sites provide summer food to all children in the community. These sites are certified based on *area* eligibility measures, where 50% or more of area children have family income that would make them eligible for free or reduced-price school meals (see Table 2).
- Closed or Enrolled sites provide summer meals/snacks free to all children enrolled at the site. The eligibility test for these sites is that 50% or more of the *children enrolled* in the sponsor's program must be eligible for free or reduced-price school meals based on household income. Closed/enrolled sites may also become eligible based on area eligibility measures noted above.
- Summer camps (that are not enrolled sites) receive subsidies only for those children with household eligibility for free or reduced-price school meals.
- Other programs specified in law, such as the National Youth Sports Program and centers for homeless or migrant children.

---

[62] According to a May 2018 GAO report, estimates of participation in SFSP may not be reliable because they have been calculated inconsistently across states and years. See U.S. Government Accountability Office, *Actions Needed to Improve Participation Estimates and Address Program Challenges,* GAO-18-369, May 2018, https://www.gao.gov/products/GAO-18-369.

Summer sponsors get operating cost (food, storage, labor) subsidies for all meals/snacks they serve—up to one meal and one snack, or two meals per child per day.[63] In addition, sponsors receive payments for administrative costs, and states are provided with subsidies for administrative costs and health and meal-quality inspections. See Table B.7 for current SFSP reimbursement rates. Actual payments vary slightly (e.g., by about 5 cents for lunches) depending on the location of the site (e.g., rural vs. urban) and whether meals are prepared on-site or by a vendor.

School Meals' Seamless Summer Option[64]

Although SFSP is the child nutrition program most associated with providing meals during summer months, it is not the only program option for providing these meals and snacks. The Seamless Summer Option, run through NSLP or SBP programs, is also a means through which food can be provided to students during summer months. Much like SFSP, Seamless Summer operates in summer *sites* (summer camps, sports programs, churches, private nonprofit organizations, etc.) and for a similar duration of time. Unlike SFSP, *schools are the only eligible sponsors*, although schools may operate the program at other sites. Reimbursement rates for Seamless Summer meals are the same as current NSLP/SBP rates.

Summer EBT for Children Demonstration

Beginning in summer 2011 and (as of the date of this chapter) each summer since, USDA-FNS has operated Summer Electronic Benefit Transfer for Children (SEBTC or "Summer EBT") demonstration projects in a limited number of states and Indian Tribal Organizations (ITOs). These Summer EBT projects provide electronic food benefits over summer months to households with children eligible for free or reduced-price school meals. Depending on the site and year, either $30 or $60 per month

---

[63] With state agency approval, camps and migrant sites (sites that predominantly serve children of migrant workers) may be reimbursed for serving three meals or two meals and one snack per child daily.

[64] For further discussion, see the USDA-FNS website: http://www.fns.usda.gov/school-meals/opportunity-schools.

School Meals Programs and Other USDA Child Nutrition ... 167

is provided, through a WIC or SNAP EBT card model. In the demonstration projects, these benefits were provided as a supplement to the Summer Food Service Program (SFSP) meals available in congregate settings.

Summer EBT and other alternatives to congregate meals through SFSP were first authorized and funded by the FY2010 appropriations law (P.L. 111-80).[65] Although a number of alternatives were tested and evaluated, findings from Summer EBT were among the most promising, and Congress provided subsequent funding.[66] Summer EBT evaluations showed significant impacts on reducing child food insecurity and improving nutritional intake.[67] Summer EBT was funded by P.L. 111-80 in the summers from 2011 to 2014. Projects have continued to operate and were annually funded by FY2015-FY2018 appropriations; most recently, the FY2018 appropriations law (P.L. 115-141) provided $28 million. According to USDA-FNS, in summer 2016 Summer EBT served over 209,000 children in nine states and two tribal nations—an increase from the 11,400 children served when the demonstration began in summer 2011.[68]

Special Milk Program (SMP)

Schools (and institutions like summer camps and child care facilities) that are not already participating in the other child nutrition programs can

---

[65] For more information, see CRS Report R45486, *Child Nutrition Programs: Current Issues.*

[66] This CRS report discusses Summer EBT, not the other tested programs ("Enhanced Summer Food Service Program (eSFSP)). For information on eSFSP, see USDA-FNS' "Enhanced Summer Food Service Program" web page, https://www.fns.usda.gov/ops/enhanced-summer-food-service-program-esfsp.

[67] Collins et al., *Summer Electronic Benefits Transfer for Children (SEBTC) Demonstration: Evaluation Findings for the Full Implementation Year.* Prepared by Abt Associates, Mathematica Policy Research, and Maximus (Alexandria, VA: USDA, Food and Nutrition Service, 2013), p. 105. This improvement is based on the entire evaluation population. Improvements in VLFS-C did vary significantly between Summer EBT sites.

[68] *FY2019 USDA Budget Explanatory Notes for Committee on Appropriations* for USDA-FNS, p. 32-40, https://www.obpa.usda.gov/32fns2019notes.pdf.

participate in the Special Milk Program. Schools may also administer SMP for their part-day sessions for kindergartners or pre-kindergartners.

Under SMP, participating institutions provide milk to children for free and/or at a subsidized paid price, depending on how the enrolled institution opts to administer the program (see Table B.8 for current Special Milk reimbursement rates for each of these options)

- An institution that *only sells milk* will receive the same per-half pint federal reimbursement for each milk sold (approximately 20 cents).
- An institution that *sells milk and provides free milk* to eligible children (income eligibility is the same as free school meals, see Table 2), receives a reimbursement for the milk sold (approximately 20 cents) and a higher reimbursement for the free milks.
- An institution that *does not sell milk* provides milk free to all children and receives the same reimbursement for all milk (approximately 20 cents). This option is sometimes called nonpricing.

In FY2017, over 41 million half-pints were subsidized, 9.5% of which were served free. Federal expenditures for this program were approximately $8.3 million in FY2017.

Fresh Fruit and Vegetable Program (FFVP)

States receive formula grants through the Fresh Fruit and Vegetable Program, under which state-selected schools receive funds to purchase and distribute *fresh* fruit and vegetable snacks to all children in attendance (regardless of family income). Money is distributed by a formula under which about half the funding is distributed equally to each state and the remainder is allocated by state population. States select participating schools (with an emphasis on those with a higher proportion of low-

School Meals Programs and Other USDA Child Nutrition ... 169

income children) and set annual per-student grant amounts (between $50 and $75).

Funding is set by law at $150 million for school year 2011-2012 and inflation-indexed for every year after. In FY2017, states used approximately $184 million in FFVP funds.[69] FFVP is funded by a mandatory transfer of funds from USDA's Section 32 program—a permanent appropriation of 30% of the previous year's customs receipts.[70] This transfer is required by FFVP's authorizing laws (Section 19 of the Richard B. Russell National School Lunch Act and Section 4304 of P.L. 110-246). Up until FY2018's law, annual appropriations laws delayed a portion of the funds to the next fiscal year.

After a pilot period, the Child Nutrition and WIC Reauthorization Act of 2004 (P.L. 108-265) permanently authorized and funded FFVP for a limited number of states and Indian reservations.[71] In recent years, FFVP has been amended by omnibus farm bill laws rather than through child nutrition reauthorizations. The 2008 farm bill (P.L. 110-246) expanded FFVP's mandatory funding, specifically providing funds through Section 32, and enabled all states to participate in the program. The 2014 farm bill (P.L. 113-79) essentially made no changes to this program but did include, and fund at $5 million in FY2014, a pilot project that requires USDA to test offering frozen, dried, and canned fruits and vegetables and publish an evaluation of the pilot. Four states (Alaska, Delaware, Kansas, and Maine) participated in the pilot in SY2014-2015 and the evaluation was published

---

[69] *FY2019 USDA Budget Explanatory Notes for Committee on Appropriations* for USDA-FNS, p. 32-14, https://www.obpa.usda.gov/32fns2019notes.pdf.

[70] For more information, see CRS Report RL34081, *Farm and Food Support Under USDA's Section 32 Program.*

[71] Permanent funding is made possible through the Section 32 account. See CRS Report RL34081, *Farm and Food Support Under USDA's Section 32 Program*, coordinated by Jim Monke.

170   *Kara Clifford Billings and Randy Alison Aussenberg*

in 2017.[72] Other proposals to expand fruits and vegetables offered in FFVP have been introduced in both the 114th and 115th Congress.[73]

OTHER TOPICS

After-School Meals and Snacks: CACFP, NSLP Options

Two of the child nutrition programs discussed in previous sections, the National School Lunch Program (NSLP) and Child and Adult Care Food Program (CACFP), provide federal support for snacks and meals served during after-school programs.[74]

NSLP provides reimbursements for after-school snacks; however, this option is open only to schools that already participate in NSLP. These schools may operate after-school snack-only programs during the school year, and can do so in two ways: (1) if low-income area eligibility criteria are met, provide free snacks in lower-income areas; or (2) if area eligibility criteria are not met, offer free, reduced-price, or fully paid-for snacks, based on household income eligibility (like lunches in NSLP). The vast majority of snacks provided through this program are through the first option. Through this program, approximately 206 million snacks were served in FY2017 (a daily average of nearly 1.3 million). This compares with nearly 4.9 billion *lunches* served (a daily average of 27.8 million).

CACFP provides assistance for after-school food in two ways. First, centers and homes that participate in CACFP and provide after-school care may participate in traditional CACFP (the eligibility and administration

---

[72] Briefel et al., Evaluation of the Pilot Project for Canned, Frozen, or Dried Fruits and Vegetables in the Fresh Fruit and Vegetable Program (FFVP-CFD), Prepared by Mathematica Policy Research. Alexandria, VA: USDA, Food and Nutrition Service, January 2017, available at https://fns-prod.azureedge.net/sites/default/files/ops/FFVP-CFD.pdf.

[73] See CRS Report R44373, *Tracking the Next Child Nutrition Reauthorization: An Overview*. In the 115th Congress, see H.R. 3402, S. 2064, and House-passed H.R. 2 §4204.

[74] For further discussion of the NSLP and CACFP after-school snack program, see Joanne Guthrie, *Feeding Children After School: The Expanding Role of USDA Child Nutrition Programs*, USDA Economic Research Service, Amber Waves, March 1, 2012, https://www.ers.usda.gov/amber-waves/2012/march/feeding-children-after-school/.

School Meals Programs and Other USDA Child Nutrition ...   171

described earlier). Second, centers in areas where at least half the children in the community are eligible for free or reduced-price school meals can opt to participate in the CACFP At-Risk Afterschool program, which provides free snacks and suppers. Expansion of the At-Risk After-School meals program was a major policy change included in HHFKA. Prior to the law, 13 states were permitted to offer CACFP At-Risk After-School meals (instead of just a snack); the law allowed all CACFP state agencies to offer such meals.[75] In FY2017, the At-Risk Afterschool program served a total of approximately 242.6 million free meals and snacks to a daily average of more than 1.7 million children.[76]

Related Programs, Initiatives, and Support Activities

Federal child nutrition laws authorize and program funding supports a range of additional programs, initiatives, and activities.[77]

Through State Administrative Expenses funding, states are entitled to federal grants to help cover administrative and oversight/monitoring costs associated with child nutrition programs. The national amount each year is equal to about 2% of child nutrition reimbursements. The majority of this money is allocated to states based on their share of spending on the covered programs; about 15% is allocated under a discretionary formula granting each state additional amounts for CACFP, commodity distribution, and Administrative Review efforts. In addition, states receive payments for their role in overseeing summer programs (about 2.5% of their summer program aid). States are free to apportion their federal administrative expense payments among child nutrition initiatives (including commodity distribution activities) as they see fit, and appropriated funding is available to states for two years. State

---

[75] S.Rept. 111-178, p. 7.

[76] Data provided by USDA-FNS on July 18, 2018.

[77] This section does not list all related federal funding and support activities; those activities that are discussed are broadly summarized. For further details on these and other functions funded by the "child nutrition programs" account, see the *2019 USDA Budget Explanatory Notes for Committee on Appropriations* for USDA-FNS, pp. 32-10 through 32-26, https://www.obpa.usda.gov/32fns2019notes.pdf.

172   *Kara Clifford Billings and Randy Alison Aussenberg*

Administrative Expense spending in FY2017 totaled approximately $279 million.[78]

Team Nutrition is a USDA-FNS program that includes a variety of school meals initiatives around nutrition education and the nutritional content of the foods children eat in schools. This includes Team Nutrition Training Grants, which provide funding to state agencies for training and technical assistance, such as help implementing USDA's nutrition requirements and the Dietary Guidelines for Americans. From 2004 to 2018, Team Nutrition also included the HealthierUS Schools Challenge (HUSSC), which originated in the 2004 reauthorization of the Child Nutrition Act. HUSSC was a voluntary certification initiative designed to recognize schools that have created a healthy school environment through the promotion of nutrition and physical activity.[79]

Farm-to-school programs broadly refer to "efforts that bring regionally and locally produced foods into school cafeterias," with a focus on enhancing child nutrition.[80] The goals of these efforts include increasing fruit and vegetable consumption among students, supporting local farmers and rural communities, and providing nutrition and agriculture education to school districts and farmers. HHFKA amended existing child nutrition programs to establish mandatory funding of $5 million per year for competitive farm-to-school grants that support schools and nonprofit entities in establishing farm-to-school programs that improve a school's access to locally produced foods.[81] The FY2018 appropriations law provided an additional $5 million in discretionary funding to remain available until expended.[82] Grants may be used for training, supporting

---

[78] For the formula for administrative and oversight/monitoring costs, see Section 7 of the Child Nutrition Act of 1966 (codified at 42 U.S.C. 1776).

[79] See USDA-FNS website, http://www.fns.usda.gov/hussc/healthierus-school-challenge-smarter-lunchrooms.

[80] USDA, *The Farm to School Program—2012-2015: Four Years in Review*, p. 3. https://fns-prod.azureedge.net/sites/default/files/f2s/Farm-to-School-at-USDA—4-Years-in-Review.pdf.

[81] HHFKA, Section 243 (Access to Local Foods: Farm to School Program), amending §18 of the Richard B. Russell National School Lunch Act (42 U.S.C. 1758(j)). In addition, appropriations are authorized "such sums as are necessary for each of fiscal years 2011 through 2015."

[82] See Section 763 of P.L. 115-141.

School Meals Programs and Other USDA Child Nutrition ... 173

operations, planning, purchasing equipment, developing school gardens, developing partnerships, and implementing farm-to-school programs. USDA's Office of Community Food Systems provides additional resources on farm-to-school issues.[83]

Through an Administrative Review process (formerly referred to as Coordinated Review Effort (CRE)), USDA-FNS, in cooperation with state agencies, conducts periodic on-site NSLP school compliance and accountability evaluations to improve management and identify administrative, subsidy claim, and meal quality problems.[84] State agencies are required to conduct administrative reviews of all school food authorities (SFAs) that operate the NSLP under their jurisdiction at least once during a three-year review cycle.[85] Federal Administrative Review expenditures were approximately $9.9 million in FY2017.

USDA-FNS and state agencies conduct many other child nutrition program support activities for which dedicated funding is provided. Among other examples, there is the Institute of Child Nutrition (ICN), which provides technical assistance, instruction, and materials related to nutrition and food service management; it receives $5 million a year in mandatory funding appropriated in statute. ICN is located at the University of Mississippi. USDA-FNS provides training on food safety education. Funding is also provided for USDA-FNS to conduct studies, provide training and technical assistance, and oversee payment accuracy.

---

[83] See USDA-FNS's Office of Community Food Systems: http://www.fns.usda.gov/farmtoschool/farm-school.

[84] Text in this paragraph is adapted from the USDA-FNS, *National School Lunch Program: Coordinated Review Effort (CRE)*, FNS-640 Data Report, January 2014.

[85] HHFKA increased the frequency of administrative reviews from once every five years to once every three years. See final rule at USDA Food and Nutrition Service, "Administrative Reviews in the School Nutrition Programs," 81 *Federal Register* 50170, July 29, 2016.

APPENDIX A. ACRONYMS USED IN THIS CHAPTER

Table A.1. Acronyms

Government Agencies	
USDA	U.S. Department of Agriculture
USDA-FNS	Food and Nutrition Service
Programs	
CACFP	Child and Adult Care Food Program
FFVP	Fresh Fruit and Vegetable Program
NSLP	National School Lunch Program
SBP	School Breakfast Program
SEBTC	Summer Electronic Benefits Transfer for Children
SFSP	Summer Food Service Program
SMP	Special Milk Program
Miscellaneous	
CEP	Community Eligibility Provision
CPI-U	Consumer Price Index for All Urban Consumers
FPL	Federal Poverty Level
HHFKA	Healthy, Hunger-Free Kids Act of 2010 (P.L. 111-296)
IOM	Institute of Medicine
LEA	Local Educational Agency
RCCI	Residential Child Care Institution
SFA	School Food Authority

APPENDIX B. PER-MEAL OR PER-SNACK REIMBURSEMENT RATES FOR CHILD NUTRITION PROGRAMS[86]

This appendix lists the specific reimbursement rates discussed in the earlier sections of the report. Reimbursement rates are adjusted for inflation for each school or calendar year according to terms laid out in the

---

[86] All reimbursement rate tables in this Appendix display rates for the 48 continental U.S. states. For Alaska, Hawaii, and territories where applicable, please see the source USDA-FNS *Federal Register* notice.

School Meals Programs and Other USDA Child Nutrition ...   175

programs' authorizing laws. Each year, the new rates are announced in the *Federal Register.*[87]

Table B.I. Reimbursement Rates, NSLP: *Lunches*
Per-meal reimbursements for 48 states and DC, school year 2018-2019

Meal Type	Serve Less than 60% of Lunches as Free and Reduced-Price	Serve 60% or More of Lunches as Free or Reduced-Price	Bonus Available for School Districts Certified as Compliant with Nutrition Guidelines
Free	$3.31	$3.33	+$0.06
Reduced-price	$2.91	$2.93	+$0.06
Paid	$0.31	$0.33	+$0.06

Source: USDA-FNS, https://www.federalregister.gov/documents/2018/07/19/2018-15465/national-school-lunchspecial-milk-and-school-breakfast-programs-national-average-paymentsmaximum. For NSLP reimbursement rates for other years, Alaska, Hawaii, and/or participating territories, see USDA-FNS website: https://www.fns.usda.gov/school-meals/rates-reimbursement.

Note: For school year 2018-2019, the maximum rate for 48 states and DC is $3.48 per free meal, $3.08 per reduced-price meal, and $0.30 per paid meal (and an additional $0.06 for nutrition guidelines). The maximum rate is the maximum per-lunch rate that a state can provide a school food authority.

Table B.2. Reimbursement Rates, NSLP: *After-School Snacks*
Per-snack reimbursements for 48 states and DC,
school year 2018-2019

Snack Type	Reimbursement
Free	$0.91
Reduced-price	$0.45
Paid	$0.08

Source: USDA-FNS. For after-school snack NSLP reimbursement rates for other years, Alaska, Hawaii, and/or participating territories, see USDA-FNS website: https://www.fns.usda.gov/school-meals/rates-reimbursement.

---

[87] For more detail on how inflation adjustment is conducted, see the child nutrition program sections of CRS Report R42000, *Inflation-Indexing Elements in Federal Entitlement Programs*, coordinated by Dawn Nuschler.

Table B.3. Reimbursement Rates, SBP
Per-meal reimbursement for 48 states and DC, school year 2018-2019

Meal Type	Nonsevere Need (less than 40% free or reduced price)a	Severe Need (greater than or equal to 40% free or reduced price)[a]
Free	$1.79	$2.14
Reduced-price	$1.49	$1.84
Paid	$0.31	$0.31

Source: USDA-FNS. For NSLP reimbursement rates for other years, Alaska, Hawaii, and/or participating territories, see USDA-FNS website: https://www.fns.usda.gov/school-meals/rates-reimbursement.

a. Generally, severe need status is determined based on the percentage of meals served two school years prior to the year the currently reimbursed meal is served. For example, a school district's severe need status in school year 2018-2019 would be calculated based on meals served in school year 2016-2017.

Table B.4. Commodity Food Assistance, NSLP and CACFP (Centers)
Rate per-meal for school year 2018-2019

	For Each NSLP/CACFP Meal Served
Commodity Food Reimbursement	$0.2350

Source: USDA, Food and Nutrition Service, "Food Distribution Program: Value of Donated Foods From July 1, 2018, Through June 30, 2019," 83 Federal Register 35607, July 1, 2018.

Notes: For past years, see USDA-FNS website: http://www.fns.usda.gov/fdd/value-donated-foods-notices. SFSP has a different commodity food assistance rate, see Table B.7.

Table B.5. Reimbursement Rates, CACFP: Child Care Centers,
At-Risk After-School Programs Per-meal/snack reimbursement for 48
States and DC, school year 2018-2019

	Lunch/Supper	Breakfast	Snack
Free	$3.31	$1.79	$0.91
Reduced-price	$2.91	$1.49	$0.45
Paid	$0.31	$0.31	$0.08

Source: For historical program reimbursement rates as well as Alaska's and Hawaii's rates, see http://www.fns.usda.gov/cacfp/reimbursement-rates.

Notes: These reimbursement rates are identical to NSLP and SBP rates.

School Meals Programs and Other USDA Child Nutrition ... 177

Table B.6. Reimbursement Rates, CACFP: *Child Care Homes*
Per-meal/snack reimbursement for 48 States and DC,
school year 2018-2019

	Lunch/Supper	Breakfast	Snack
Tier I	$2.46	$1.31	$0.73
Tier II	$1.48	$0.48	$0.20

Source: For historical program reimbursement rates as well as Alaska's and Hawaii's rates, see http://www.fns.usda.gov/cacfp/reimbursement-rates.

Note: CACFP also provides administrative reimbursements to sponsoring organizations of day care homes. Based on the number of homes sponsored, funding is provided per home, per month. These rates are not displayed in this table but are included in USDA, Food and Nutrition Service, "Child and Adult Care Food Program: National Average Payment Rates, Day Care Home Food Service Payment Rates, and Administrative Reimbursement Rates for Sponsoring Organizations of Day Care Homes for the Period July 1, 2018 Through June 30, 2019," 83 Federal Register 34108, July 1, 2018.

Table B.7. Reimbursement Rates, SFSP
Per-meal/snack reimbursement for 48 states and DC
(rounded to nearest cent), calendar year 2018

	Lunch/Supper		Breakfast		Snack	
	Rural or Self-Prep	All Other Sites	Rural or Self-Prep	All Other Sites	Rural or Self-Prep	All Other Sites
Operating Component	$3.55	$3.55	$2.03	$2.03	$0.83	$0.83
Administrative Component	$0.37	$0.31	$0.20	$0.16	$0.10	$0.08
Combined (Total) Rate	$3.92	$3.86	$2.23	$2.19	$0.93	$0.91

Source: For program reimbursement rates as well as Alaska's and Hawaii's rates, see USDA, Food and Nutrition Service, "Summer Food Service Program; 2018 Reimbursement Rates," 83 Federal Register 4025, January 29, 2018.

Note: Per authorizing law, the administrative component is calculated to the nearest quarter-cent. This table rounds to the nearest cent. As the table shows, the administrative component varies slightly (e.g., by about 5 cents for lunches) depending on the location of the site (e.g., rural vs. urban) and whether meals are prepared on-site or by a vendor. For meals prepared on-site, providers receive 1.5 cents per meal in USDA commodity foods.

Table B.8. Reimbursement Rates, SMP
Per half-pint reimbursement for 48 States and DC
(rounded to nearest cent), school year 2018-2019

	All Milk Served	Paid Milk	Free Milk to Low Income Children
Schools that only sell milk	$0.21	Not applicable	Not applicable
Schools that sell and provide free milk	Not applicable	$0.21	Average cost per half-pint of milk
Schools that provide only free milk	$0.21	Not applicable	Not applicable

Source: For program reimbursement rates, see https://www.fns.usda.gov/school-meals/rates-reimbursement.

In: Key Congressional Reports on Education   ISBN: 978-1-53615-731-4
Editor: Georgia Turner   © 2019 Nova Science Publishers, Inc.

Chapter 5

INSTITUTIONAL ELIGIBILITY FOR PARTICIPATION IN TITLE IV STUDENT FINANCIAL AID PROGRAMS[*]

Alexandra Hegji

SUMMARY

Title IV of the Higher Education Act (HEA) authorizes programs that provide financial assistance to students to assist them in obtaining a postsecondary education at certain institutions of higher education (IHEs). These IHEs include public, private nonprofit, and proprietary institutions. For students attending such institutions to be able to receive Title IV assistance, an institution must meet basic criteria, including offering at least one eligible program of education (e.g., programs leading to a degree or preparing a student for gainful employment in a recognized occupation).

In addition, an IHE must satisfy the program integrity triad, under which it must be

---

[*] This is an edited, reformatted and augmented version of Congressional Research Service, Publication No. R43159, dated February 14, 2019.

- licensed or otherwise legally authorized to operate in the state in which it is physically located,
- accredited or preaccredited by an agency recognized for that purpose by the Department of Education (ED), and
- certified by ED as eligible to participate in Title IV programs.

These requirements are intended to provide a balance between consumer protection, quality assurance, and oversight and compliance in postsecondary education providers participating in Title IV student aid programs.

An IHE must also fulfill a variety of other related requirements, including those that relate to institutional recruiting practices, student policies and procedures, and the administration of the Title IV student aid programs.

Finally, additional criteria may apply to an institution depending on its control or the type of educational programs it offers. For example, proprietary institutions must meet HEA requirements that are otherwise inapplicable to public and private nonprofit institutions, including deriving at least 10% of their revenues from non-Title IV funds (also known as the 90/10 rule). While an institution is ineligible to participate in Title IV programs if more than 50% of its courses are offered by correspondence or if 50% or more of its students are enrolled in correspondence courses.

This chapter first describes the types of institutions eligible to participate in Title IV programs and discusses the program integrity triad. It then discusses additional issues related to institutional eligibility, including program participations agreements, required campus safety policies and crime reporting, and distance and correspondence education.

OVERVIEW

Title IV of the Higher Education Act (HEA; P.L. 89-329), as amended, authorizes programs that provide financial assistance to students to attend certain institutions of higher education (IHEs). In academic year (AY) 2016-2017, 6,760 institutions were classified as Title IV eligible IHEs.[1] Of

---

[1] These 6,760 institutions were eligible to participate in Title IV Federal Student Aid (FSA) programs in AY2016-2017 (July 1, 2016-June 30, 2017). U.S. Department of Education, National Center for Education Statistics, *Postsecondary Institutions and Cost of Attendance in 2016-2017; Degrees and Other Awards Conferred: 2015-16; and 12-Month Enrollment:*

these IHEs eligible to participate in Title IV programs, approximately 29.4% were public institutions, 27.8% were private nonprofit institutions, and 42.9% were proprietary (or private, for-profit) institutions. It is estimated that $122.5 billion was made available to students through Title IV federal student aid in FY2017.[2]

To be able to receive Title IV assistance, students must attend an institution that is eligible to participate in the Title IV programs. IHEs must meet a variety of requirements to participate in the Title IV programs. First, an IHE must meet basic eligibility criteria, including offering at least one eligible program of education.

In addition, an IHE must satisfy the program integrity triad, under which it must be

- legally authorized to provide a postsecondary education in the state in which it is located;
- accredited or preaccredited by an agency recognized by the Department of Education (ED) for such purposes,[3] and
- certified by ED as eligible to participate in Title IV programs.

The state authorization and accreditation components of the triad were developed independently to address the issues of quality assurance and consumer protection, and the federal government (ED specifically) generally relies on states and accrediting agencies to determine standards of educational program quality. The federal government's only direct role in determining Title IV eligibility is through the process of certification of eligibility and ensuring IHEs meet some additional Title IV requirements. Certification, as a component of the program integrity triad, focuses on an

---

2015-16, First Look (Provisional Data), NCES 2017-075rev, Table 1, https://nces.ed.gov/pubs2017/ 2017075rev.pdf and U.S.

[2] This includes federal loans, work-study, and grants. See U.S. Department of Education, Federal Student Aid, *Annual Report 2018*, Washington, DC, November 15, 2018, p. 8, https://www2.ed.gov/about/reports/annual/2018report/fsareport.pdf.

[3] ED recognizes accrediting agencies both for Title IV and non-Title IV purposes. There are some differences in criteria for ED recognition for each. ED-recognition of accrediting agencies for purposes of participation in non-Title IV programs are beyond the scope of this report.

institution's fiscal responsibility and administrative capacity to administer Title IV funds.

An IHE must fulfill a variety of other related requirements, including those that relate to institutional recruiting practices, student policies and procedures, and Title IV program administration. Finally, additional criteria may apply to an institution depending on its control or the type of educational programs it offers. For instance, proprietary institutions must derive at least 10% of their revenues from non-Title IV funds (also known as the 90/10 rule). Failure to fulfill some of these requirements does not necessarily end an IHE's participation in the Title IV programs, but may lead to additional oversight from ED and/or restrictions placed an IHE's Title IV participation.

This chapter provides a general overview of HEA provisions that affect a postsecondary institution's eligibility for participation in Title IV student aid programs. It first describes general eligibility criteria at both the institutional and programmatic level and then, in more detail, the program integrity triad. Next, it discusses several issues that are closely related to institutional eligibility: Program Participation Agreements, campus safety policies and crime reporting required under the Clery Act, the return of Title IV funds, and distance education.

ELIGIBILITY CRITERIA

To be eligible to participate in HEA Title IV student aid programs, institutions must meet several criteria. These criteria include requirements related to programs offered by the institutions, student enrollment, institutional operations, and the length of academic programs. This section discusses the definition of an eligible IHE for the purposes of Title IV participation and program eligibility requirements.

Institutional Eligibility for Participation in Title IV ...

Eligible Institutions

The HEA contains two definitions of institutions of higher education. Section 101 provides a general definition of IHE that applies to institutional eligibility for participation in HEA programs other than Title IV programs.[4] The Section 102 definition of IHE is used only to determine institutional eligibility to participate in HEA Title IV programs.

Section 101 Institutions

Section 101 of the HEA provides a general definition of IHE. This definition applies to institutional participation in non-Title IV HEA programs. Section 101 IHEs can be public or private nonprofit educational institutions. Section 101 specifies criteria both public and private nonprofit educational institutions must meet to be considered IHEs.

Public Institutions of Higher Education

Neither the HEA nor regulations specifically define a public institution of higher education. However, in general, public institutions can be described as those whose educational programs are operated by states or other government entities and are primarily supported by public funds.[5]

Private Nonprofit Institutions of Higher Education

Regulations define a nonprofit IHE as one that (1) is owned and operated by a nonprofit corporation or association, with no part of the corporation's or association's net earnings benefiting a private shareholder or individual, (2) is determined by the Internal Revenue Service to be a tax-exempt organization under Section 501(c)(3) of the Internal Revenue Code (IRC), and (3) is legally authorized to operate as a nonprofit organization by each state in which it is physically located.[6]

---

[4] The Section 101 definition is also commonly used as a reference in many other non-HEA programs.

[5] U.S. Department of Education, National Center for Education Statistics, Integrated Postsecondary Education Data System, 2018-19 Glossary, "Public institution."

[6] 34 C.F.R. §600.2. Under IRC Section 501(c)(3), an organization is exempt from federal taxation if no part of its earnings insures to the benefit of an individual or private

Section 101 Institution of Higher Education

To be considered a Section 101 IHE, public and private nonprofit educational institutions must

- admit as regular students only individuals with a high school diploma or its equivalent, individuals beyond the age of compulsory school attendance, or individuals who are dually or concurrently enrolled in both the institution and in a secondary school;
- be legally authorized to provide a postsecondary education within the state in which they are located;
- offer a bachelor's degree, provide a program of at least two-years that is acceptable for full credit toward a bachelor's degree, award a degree that is accepted for admission to a graduate or professional program, or provide a training program of at least a one-year that prepares students for gainful employment in a recognized occupation; and
- be accredited or preaccredited by an accrediting agency recognized by ED to grant accreditation or preaccreditation status[7]

Section 102 Institutions

Section 102 of the HEA defines IHE only for the purposes of Title IV participation. The Section 102 definition includes all institutions included in the Section 101 definition (i.e., public and private nonprofit IHEs) and also includes proprietary institutions, postsecondary vocational institutions, and foreign institutions that have been approved by ED.[8] Section 102 specifies that proprietary and postsecondary vocational institutions must meet many of the same Section 101 requirements that are applicable to public and private nonprofit institutions. In addition, Section 102 specifies

---

shareholder and if it is organized and operated exclusively for, among other potential items, educational purposes.

[7] HEA §101; 20 U.S.C. §1001.

[8] HEA §102(a)(2); 20 U.S.C. §1002(a)(1). Department of Education, *2017-2018 Federal Student Aid Handbook*, vol. 2, pp. 3-5, https://ifap.ed.gov/fsahandbook/attachments/1718FSAHbkActiveIndex.pdf (hereinafter *FSA Handbook*).

Institutional Eligibility for Participation in Title IV ...   185

other criteria that all types of educational institutions must meet to be considered Title IV eligible IHEs.

Proprietary Institutions of Higher Education

HEA Section 102 specifies that a proprietary IHEs is an institution that is neither a public nor a private nonprofit institution.[9] In addition to the basic Title IV eligibility criteria that all IHEs must meet (e.g., state authorization, accreditation by an ED-recognized accrediting agency), proprietary IHEs must meet additional criteria to be considered Title IV eligible. Specifically, a proprietary IHE must (1) provide an eligible program of training "to prepare students for gainful employment in a recognized occupation"[10] or (2) provide a program leading to a baccalaureate degree in liberal arts that has been continuously accredited by a regional accrediting agency since October 1, 2007, and have provided the program continuously since January 1, 2009. Additionally, it must have been legally authorized to provide (and have continuously been providing) the same or a substantially similar educational program for at least two consecutive years.[11]

Postsecondary Vocational Institutions

HEA Section 102 defines a postsecondary vocational institution as a public or private nonprofit institution that provides an eligible program of training "to prepare students for gainful employment in a recognized occupation,"[12] and has been legally authorized to provide (and has continuously been providing) the same or a substantially similar educational program for at least two consecutive years.[13] It is possible for a public or private nonprofit IHE that offers a degree program (e.g., an associate's or bachelor's degree) to also qualify as a postsecondary vocational institution by offering programs that are less than one academic

---

[9] HEA §102(b)(1)(C); 20 U.S.C. §1002(b)(1)(C).
[10] HEA §102(b)(1)(A); 20 U.S.C. §1002(b)(1)(A).
[11] HEA §102(b)(1)(E) and 34 C.F.R. § 600.5(b). See also *FSA Handbook*, vol. 2, p. 11.
[12] HEA §102(c); 20 U.S.C. §1002(c).
[13] HEA §102(b)(1)(E) and 34 C.F.R. § 600.6(b). See also *FSA Handbook*, vol. 2, p. 11.

186   *Alexandra Hegji*

year and that lead to a nondegree recognized credential such as a certificate.

Foreign Institutions

Institutional participation in Title IV student aid programs allows students from the United States to borrow through the federal Direct Loan program to attend postsecondary institutions located outside of the United States.[14] In general, a foreign institution is eligible to participate in the Direct Loan program if it is comparable to an eligible IHE (as defined in HEA Section 101) within the United States, is a public or private nonprofit institution,[15] and has been approved by ED. Foreign graduate medical schools, veterinary schools, and nursing schools are also eligible to participate in Title IV student aid programs, but must meet additional requirements. Freestanding foreign graduate medical schools, veterinary schools, and nursing schools may be proprietary institutions.[16] Additional requirements for foreign institutions to participate in Title IV student aid programs are beyond the scope of this chapter and, generally, will not be discussed hereinafter.

Section 102 Institution of Higher Education

The definitions of proprietary institutions and postsecondary vocational institutions contained in Section 102 have several overlapping components with the Section 101 definition of IHE.[17] For instance, both proprietary and postsecondary vocational institutions must (1) admit as

---

[14] Institutions can choose to participate in Title IV programs or can choose to be designated by ED as "eligibility-only." An eligibility-only designation allows an institution and its eligible students to qualify to participate in non-Title IV programs and benefits, such as the American Opportunity Tax Credit. Additionally, students attending eligibility-only institutions qualify for in-school deferment of payment on their federal student loans that they have previously borrowed.

[15] A foreign nonprofit institution is one that is owned and operated only by one or more nonprofit corporations of associations and (1) is determined to be a nonprofit educational institution by the ED-recognized tax authority of the institution's home country or (2) if there is no ED-recognized tax authority of the institution's home country, the institution demonstrates to ED that it is a nonprofit educational institution. 34 C.F.R. §600.2.

[16] HEA §102(a)(2); 20 U.S.C. §1002(a)(2). 34 C.F.R. §600.54.

[17] Eligibility requirements differ somewhat for foreign institutions; a complete description of these differences is beyond the scope of this report.

Institutional Eligibility for Participation in Title IV ... 187

regular students only those individuals with a high school diploma or its equivalent, individuals beyond the age of compulsory school attendance, or individuals who are dually or concurrently enrolled in both the institution and in a secondary school; (2) be legally authorized to provide a postsecondary education by the state in which they are located; and (3) be accredited or preaccredited by an accrediting agency recognized by ED to grant such statuses.[18]

In addition, all types of institutions (including public and private nonprofit institutions) must meet requirements related to the course of study offered at the institution and student enrollment to be considered Title IV eligible under Section 102. In general, any type of institution is considered ineligible to participate in Title IV programs if more than 25% of its enrolled students are incarcerated, or if more than 50% of the its enrolled students do not have a secondary school diploma or equivalent and the institution does not provide a two-year associate's degree or a four-year bachelor's degree. Also, in general, an institution is ineligible if more than 50% of the courses offered are correspondence courses or if 50% or more of its students are enrolled in correspondence courses. These "50% rules" are discussed in more detail in the distance education section of this chapter.[19] Finally, an institution is considered ineligible to participate in Title IV programs if the institution has filed for bankruptcy or the institution (or its owner or chief executive officer) has been convicted of or pled no contest or guilty to a crime involving the use of Title IV funds.[20]

While the above-described criteria generally apply to most types of Section 102 institutions, specific criteria apply to individual types of Section 102 institutions. The following sections provide information on Title IV eligibility criteria that apply to those additional types of IHEs not specified in Section 101, but specified in Section 102: proprietary IHEs, postsecondary vocational institutions, and foreign institutions.

Hereinafter, unless otherwise noted, the term "institution of high education (IHE)" only refers to Section 102 institutions.

---

[18] HEA §102(b) and (c).
[19] HEA §102(a)(3); 20 U.S.C. §1002(a)(3).
[20] HEA §102(a)(4); 20 U.S.C. §1002(a)(4).

Eligible Programs

To qualify as an eligible institution for Title IV participation, an institution must offer at least one eligible program, but overall institutional eligibility does not necessarily extend to all programs offered by the institution. Not all of an institution's programs must meet program eligibility requirements for an IHE to participate in Title IV, but, in general, students enrolled solely in ineligible programs cannot receive Title IV student aid.[21] To be Title IV eligible, a program must lead to a degree (e.g., an associate's or bachelor's degree) or certificate or prepare students for gainful employment in a recognized occupation.

Before awarding Title IV aid to students, an IHE must determine that the program in which a student is participating is Title IV eligible, ensure that the program is included in its accreditation notice, and ensure that the IHE is authorized by the appropriate state to offer the program.[22]

In addition to the general criteria for all types of institutions, a program must meet specific eligibility requirements depending on whether the institution at which it is offered is a public or private nonprofit IHE, a proprietary IHE, or a postsecondary vocational IHE.[23]

Public and Private Nonprofit Institutions of Higher Education

At a public or private nonprofit IHE, the following types of programs are Title IV eligible: (1) programs that lead to an associate's, bachelor's, professional, or graduate degree; (2) transfer programs that are at least two academic years[24] in length and for which the institution does not award a

---

[21] HEA §484(a)(1); 20 U.S.C. §1091(a)(1). Students enrolled in certain preparatory or teacher certification courses, may be eligible to receive limited forms of student aid. *FSA Handbook*, vol. 2, p. 19.

[22] *FSA Handbook*, vol. 2, p. 19.

[23] In general, many of the eligible program requirements discussed herein may also apply to foreign IHEs.

[24] In general, an academic year must be at least 30 weeks of instructional time for a program measured in credit hours or via direct assessment and at least 26 weeks of instructional time for a program measured in clock hours. For both of these, an academic year must also require an undergraduate course of study to contain an amount of instructional time in which a full-time student is expected to complete at least 24 semester or trimester credit hours, 36 quarter credit hours, or 900 clock hours. HEA §481(a)(2); 20 U.S.C. §1088(a)(2).

credential but that are acceptable for full credit toward a bachelor's degree; (3) programs that lead to a certificate or other recognized nondegree credential, that prepare students for gainful employment in a recognized occupation, and that are at least one academic year in length; (4) certificate or diploma training programs that are less than one year in length, if the institution also meets the definition of a postsecondary vocational institution; and (5) programs consisting of courses required for elementary or secondary teacher certification in the state in which the student intends to teach.[25]

For all of these, an academic year must also require an undergraduate course of study to contain an amount of instructional time in which a full-time student is expected to complete at least 24 semester or trimester credit hours, 36 quarter credit hours, or 900 clock hours.

Proprietary and Postsecondary Vocational Institutions

In general, eligible programs at proprietary and postsecondary vocational institutions must meet a specified number of weeks of instruction and must provide training that prepares students for gainful employment in a recognized occupation (described below).[26] At proprietary and postsecondary vocational institutions, the following types of programs are Title IV eligible:

- undergraduate programs that provide at least 600 clock hours, 16 semester or trimester hours, or 24 quarter hours of instruction offered over a minimum of at least 15 weeks[27]; such programs may

---

34 C.F.R. §668.10(a)(3)(i). Regulations define the terms credit and clock hours. See 34 C.F.R. §600.2.

[25] These programs must be offered in credit or clock hours. 34 C.F.R. §668.8(c); *FSA Handbook*, vol. 2, p 20.

[26] As with public and private nonprofit IHEs, an academic year for programs at proprietary and postsecondary vocational IHEs must require an undergraduate course of study to contain an amount of instructional time in which a full-time student is expected to complete at least 24 semester or trimester credit hours, 36 quarter credit hours, or 900 clock hours over a period of at least 30 weeks for credit hour programs or 26 weeks for clock hour programs.

[27] Regulations define the terms clock hours, semester hours, trimester hours, and quarter hours. See 34 C.F.R. §§600.2 and 668.8

admit, as regular students, individuals who have not completed the equivalent of an associate's degree;

- programs that provide at least 300 clock hours, 8 semester hours, or 12 quarter hours of instruction offered over a minimum of 10 weeks; such programs must be graduate or professional programs or must admit as regular students only individuals who have completed the equivalent of an associate's degree;

- short-term programs that provide between 300 and 600 clock hours of instruction over a minimum of 10 weeks[28]; such programs must have been in existence for at least one year, have verified completion and placement rates of at least 70%, may not last more than 50% longer than the minimum training period required by the state or federal agency for the occupation for which the program is being offered, and must admit as regular students some individuals who have not completed the equivalent of an associate's degree; and

- programs offered by accredited proprietary IHEs that lead to a bachelor's degree in liberal arts; the school must have been continuously accredited by an ED-recognized accrediting agency since at least October 1, 2007 and must have provided the program continuously since January 1, 2009.[29]

Programs Required to Prepare Students for Gainful Employment

Most nondegree programs offered by public and private nonprofit IHEs[30] must prepare students for "gainful employment in a recognized

---

[28] Short-term programs are only eligible to participate in the Direct Loan Program. 34 C.F.R. §668.8(d)(3).

[29] 34 C.F.R. §668.8(d); *FSA Handbook*, vol. 2, p. 21.

[30] The following types of nondegree programs offered by public and private nonprofit IHEs are not subject to gainful employment requirements: (1) preparatory classwork necessary for enrollment in a Title IV eligible program; (2) approved comprehensive transition and postsecondary programs for students with intellectual disabilities; (3) transfer programs that are at least two academic years in length and for which the school does not award a credential but that are designed to be acceptable for full credit toward a bachelor's degree; and (4) teacher certification programs for which the institution does not award a credential. *FSA Handbook*, vol. 2, p. 23.

occupation."[31] Gainful employment requirements also apply to almost all programs offered by proprietary and postsecondary vocational institutions, regardless of whether they lead to a degree.[32]

Status of Gainful Employment Regulations

In response to concerns about the quality of programs that prepare students for gainful employment and the level of student debt assumed by individuals who attend these programs, ED issued final rules on gainful employment on October 31, 2014.[33] The regulations require that educational programs subject to gainful employment requirements offered by IHEs meet minimum performance standards to be considered offering education that prepares students for gainful employment in a recognized occupation. They also require IHEs to disclose specified information about each of its gainful employment programs to enrolled or prospective students. Finally, the gainful employment rules require IHEs to report information to ED necessary to calculate the debt-to-earnings ratios.

Although the gainful employment regulations became effective July 1, 2015, various aspects of them have not yet been fully implemented or have been delayed in implementation. For example, ED delayed until July 1, 2019, some portions of the rule relating to certain disclosure requirements.[34] Additionally, to enable ED to calculate whether an IHE's programs meet the minimum performance standards (discussed below),

---

[31] HEA §§101(b)(1); 20 U.S.C. §§1001(b)(1).

[32] HEA §§ 102(b)(1)(A)(i) and 102(c)(1)(A); 20 U.S.C. §§ 1002(b)(1)(A)(i) and 1002(c)(1). The following programs offered by proprietary IHEs are not subject to gainful employment requirements: (1) programs offered by proprietary IHEs accredited by an ED-recognized regional accrediting agency that lead to a bachelor's degree in liberal arts. The school must have been continuously accredited by an ED-recognized accrediting agency since at least October 1, 2007, and must have provided the program continuously since January 1, 2009; (2) preparatory classwork necessary for enrollment in a Title IV eligible program; and (3) approved comprehensive transition and postsecondary programs for students with intellectual disabilities. *FSA Handbook*, vol. 2, p. 23.

[33] Previously, ED had issued rules on gainful employment in late 2010 and early 2011. On June 30, 2012, the day before the final regulations related to gainful employment performance metrics were to go into effect, the U.S. District Court for the District of Columbia vacated most of the gainful employment regulations. *Association of Private Colleges & Universities v. Duncan*, 2012 U.S. Dist. LEXIS 90434 (D.C. 2012). Rather than appealing the decision, ED promulgated new gainful employment rules.

[34] Department of Education, "Program Integrity: Gainful Employment," 83 *Federal Register* 28177, June 18, 2018.

regulations specify that ED obtains data from the Social Security Administration (SSA).[35] However, a memorandum of understanding relating to data sharing between ED and SSA lapsed in 2018.[36]

In August 2018, ED issued a Notice of Proposed Rulemaking that proposes to rescind the gainful employment rules in their entirety.[37] Based on HEA requirements relating to the implementation date for Title IV regulations,[38] the earliest possible date the proposed rules could go into effect is July 1, 2020.[39]

Current Gainful Employment Regulations

The gainful employment regulations establish a framework within which educational programs offered by IHEs must meet minimum performance standards to be considered offering education that prepares students for gainful employment in a recognized occupation. Under the framework, ED annually calculates two debt-to-earnings (D/E) rates for each gainful employment program offered by an IHE, the discretionary income rate and the annual earnings rate.[40] These rates measure a gainful employment program's completers' debt[41] (their annual loan payments) as a percentage of their post-completion earnings. Using these measures, institutions will be determined to be "passing," "in the zone," or "failing." Thresholds for each category are as follows:

---

[35] 34 C.F.R. §668.404(c)(1).

[36] Emily Wilkins, "Student Loan, Gainful Employment Rules Delayed, Official Says," *Bloomberg Government*, October 2, 2018, https://about.bgov.com/blog/student-loan-rules-delayed-official-says/.

[37] Department of Education, "Program Integrity: Gainful Employment," 83 *Federal Register* 40167, August 14, 2018.

[38] HEA §492(c); 20 U.S.C. §1089(c).

[39] Emily Wilkins, "Student Loan, Gainful Employment Rules Delayed, Official Says," *Bloomberg Government*, October 2, 2018, https://about.bgov.com/blog/student-loan-rules-delayed-official-says/.

[40] 34 C.F.R. Part 668, Subpart Q.

[41] To be included in a program's D/E calculation, a program completer must have received Title IV aid to enroll in the program. Program completer debt used in the D/E rates include both Title IV loans and private education loans. 34 C.F.R. §§668.402 & 668.404.

- Passing: Programs whose completers have annual loan payments[42] less than or equal to 8% of annual earnings[43] (the annual earnings rate) *or* less than or equal to 20% of discretionary income[44] (the discretionary income rate).
- In the zone: Programs whose completers have annual loan payments greater than 8% but less than or equal to 12% of annual earnings *or* greater than 20% but less than or equal to 30% of discretionary income.
- Failing: Programs whose completers have annual loan payments greater than 12% of annual earnings *and* greater than 30% of discretionary income.

Programs that are failing in two out of any three consecutive years or that are in the zone for four consecutive years will be ineligible for Title IV participation for three years.

The gainful employment rules also contain several disclosure requirements. For any year in which ED notifies an IHE that a gainful employment program could become ineligible in the next year based on its debt-to-earnings ratios (i.e., one year of failure or three years in the zone), the IHE must provide a warning to current and prospective students that the program does not meet the gainful employment standards and that if the program does not meet the gainful employment standards in the future, students would not be able to receive Title IV aid.[45]

---

[42] Annual loan payments are calculated by determining the median loan debt of a program's completers during the cohort period (two or four years, depending on number of program completers) and amortizing the median loan debt over a specified repayment period, depending on the credential offered by the program (i.e., over a 10-year repayment period for a program that leads to an undergraduate certificate, a post-baccalaureate certificate, an associate's degree, or a graduate certificate; over a 15-year repayment period for a program that leads to a bachelor's or a master's degree; or over a 20-year period for a program that leads to a doctoral or first-professional degree). 34 C.F.R. §668.404(b).

[43] Annual earnings are the greater of the mean or median annual earnings. ED obtains the earnings of gainful employment program completers during the cohort period from the Social Security Administration. 34 C.F.R. §668.404(c).

[44] Discretionary income is the difference between the greater of the mean or median annual earnings and 150% of the Federal Poverty Guidelines. 34 C.F.R. §668.404(a).

[45] Additional information required in the warning includes descriptions of the academic and financial options available to enrolled students to continue in another program at the IHE or

194 *Alexandra Hegji*

In addition, an IHE must disclose specified information about each of its gainful employment programs to enrolled and prospective students. Information to be disclosed includes the following:[46]

- the primary occupation that the program prepares students to enter;
- whether the program satisfies applicable educational prerequisites for professional licensure or certification in each state within the institution's metropolitan statistical area (MSA);
- program length and number of clock or credit hours, or equivalent, in the program;
- the program's completion rates for full-time and less-than-full-time students and the program's withdrawal rates;
- Federal Family Education Loan (FFEL) and Direct Loan program loan repayment rates for all students who entered repayment on Title IV loans and who enrolled in the program, for those who withdrew from the program, and for those who completed the program;[47]
- the program tuition, fees, and additional costs incurred by a student who completes the program within the program's published length;
- the job placement rate for the program, if otherwise required by the institution's accrediting agency or state;
- the percentage of enrolled students who received Title IV or private loans for enrollment in the program;
  - o the median loan debt and mean or median earnings of students who completed the program, of students who withdrew from the program, and of both groups combined;

---

to transfer credits to another IHE. An IHE must provide prospective students with similar information and may not enroll, register, or enter into a financial commitment with a prospective student earlier than (a) three business days after it provided the prospective student with the warning or (b) if 30 days have passed from the date the IHE first provided the warning to the prospective student, three business days after it provides the prospective student with a second warning. 34 C.F.R. §668.410(a)(6).

[46] 34 C.F.R. §668.412.

[47] For information on how the loan repayment rate is calculated, see 34 C.F.R. §668.413.

Institutional Eligibility for Participation in Title IV ... 195

o   the program cohort default rate; and
o   the annual earnings rate for the program.[48]

Institutions must also certify that each of their gainful employment programs is included in the IHE's accreditation, meets any state or federal entity accreditation requirements, and meets any state licensing and certification requirements for the state in which the IHE is located.

PROGRAM INTEGRITY TRIAD

Title IV of the HEA sets forth three requirements to ensure program integrity in postsecondary education, known as the program integrity triad. The three requirements are state authorization, accreditation by an accrediting agency recognized by ED, and eligibility and certification by ED. This triad is intended to provide a balance in the Title IV eligibility requirements. The states' role is to provide consumer protection, the accrediting agencies' role is to provide quality assurance, and the federal government's role is to provide oversight of compliance to ensure administrative and fiscal integrity of Title IV programs at IHEs.

State Authorization

The state role in the program integrity triad is to provide legal authority for an institution to operate a postsecondary educational program in the state in which it is physically located.[49]

There are two basic requirements for an IHE to be considered legally authorized by a state:

---

[48] The annual earnings rate is the percentage of a gainful employment program's annual loan payments divided by the higher of the mean or median annual earnings of the program's completers during the applicable cohort period.

[49] 34 C.F.R. §600.9.

1. the state must authorize the IHE by name to operate postsecondary educational programs, and
2. the state must have in place a process to review and address complaints concerning IHEs, including enforcing applicable state law.[50]

An IHE can be authorized by name through a state charter, statute, constitutional provision, or other action by an appropriate state agency (e.g., authorization to conduct business or operate as a nonprofit organization). Additionally, an institution must also comply with any applicable state approval or licensure requirements.[51]

The state agency responsible for the authorization of postsecondary institutions must also perform three additional functions:

- upon request, provide the Secretary with information about the process it uses to authorize institutions to operate within its borders;
- notify the Secretary if it has evidence to believe that an institution within its borders has committed fraud in the administration of Title IV programs; and
- notify the Secretary if it revokes an institution's authorization to operate.[52]

---

[50] These two requirements do not apply to (1) institutions authorized by the federal government by name to operate postsecondary educational programs and (2) institutions authorized by name by an Indian tribe to operate postsecondary educational programs, provided they are located on tribal lands and the tribal government has a process to review and address complaints concerning the IHEs and enforces applicable tribal law. Additionally, religious institutions are considered authorized to operate postsecondary educational programs within a state if they are exempt under state law from state authorization as religious institutions. *Federal Student Aid Handbook*, vol. 2, pp. 5-6.

[51] States may exempt institutions established through a state charter, statute, or constitutional provision from state approval or licensure requirements based on the IHE's having been in operation for at least 20 years or based on its accreditation by one or more ED-recognized accrediting agencies. If the IHE was authorized by the state to conduct business or operate as a nonprofit organization, the state may not exempt the IHE from state approval or licensure requirements based on years in operation, accreditation, or comparable exemptions. *Federal Student Aid Handbook*, vol. 2, p. 6.

[52] HEA §495; 20 U.S.C. §1099a.

On December 19, 2016, ED issued final regulations related to state authorization for IHEs offering postsecondary distance or correspondence education (discussed later in this chapter). The regulations would require an IHE offering postsecondary distance or correspondence education to students residing in a state in which the IHE is not physically located to meet any requirements within the student's state of residence. Under the rules, an IHE may meet this requirement if it participates in a state authorization reciprocity agreement.[53] These regulations were scheduled to become effective July 1, 2018. However, on July 3, 2018 (and effective June 29, 2018), the Secretary of Education (Secretary) issued a final rule delaying the implementation of these requirements until July 1, 2020.[54]

Accreditation

The second component of the program integrity triad is accreditation by an ED-recognized accrediting agency or association.[55] In higher education, accreditation is intended to help ensure an acceptable level of quality within IHEs. For Title IV purposes, an institution must be accredited or preaccredited by an ED-recognized accrediting agency. Each accrediting agency must meet HEA-specified standards to be recognized by ED.

Background

From its inception, accreditation has been a voluntary process. It developed with the formation of associations that distinguished between IHEs that merited the designation of college or university from those that

---

[53] A state reciprocity agreement is "an agreement between two or more states that authorizes institutions located and legally authorized in a state covered by the agreement to provide postsecondary education through distance education or correspondence courses to students residing in other states covered by the agreement." U.S. Department of Education, "Program Integrity and Improvement," 81 *Federal Register* 92262, December 19, 2016.

[54] Department of Education, "Program Integrity and Improvement," 83 *Federal Register* 31296, July 3, 2018.

[55] For additional information on accreditation and the federal government's role, see CRS Report R43826, *An Overview of Accreditation of Higher Education in the United States*, by Alexandra Hegji.

198 *Alexandra Hegji*

did not. Since then, accreditation has been used as a form of "external quality review ... to scrutinize colleges, universities and programs for quality assurance and quality improvement."[56]

In 1952, shortly after the passage of the Veterans' Readjustment Act of 1952 (the Korean GI Bill; P.L. 82-550), the federal government began formally recognizing accrediting agencies. This was done as one means to assess higher education quality and link it to determining which institutions would qualify to receive federal aid under the Korean GI Bill. Rather than creating a centralized authority to assess quality, the federal government chose to rely in part on the existing expertise of accrediting agencies.[57] Today, ED's formal recognition of accrediting agencies is important, because an IHE's Title IV eligibility is conditioned upon accreditation from an ED-recognized accreditation organization.[58]

As part of the accreditation system's development, three types of accrediting agencies have emerged:

- Regional accrediting agencies. These operate in six regions of the United States, with each agency concentrating on a specific region. Generally, these accredit entire public and private nonprofit degree-granting IHEs.
- National accrediting agencies. These operate across the United States and also accredit entire institutions. There are two types of national accrediting agencies: faith-based agencies that accredit religiously affiliated or doctrinally based institutions, which are typically private nonprofit degree-granting institutions, and career-related agencies that typically accredit proprietary, career-based, degree- and nondegree-granting institutions.

---

[56] Judith S. Eaton, *An Overview of U.S. Accreditation*, Council for Higher Education Accreditation, Washington, DC, November 2015, p. 1, http://chea.org/pdf/Overview%20of%20US%20Accreditation%202015.pdf (hereinafter CHEA, *An Overview of U.S. Accreditation*).

[57] For additional information on the history of accreditation and the federal role, see John R. Proffit, The Federal Connection for Accreditation, *The Journal of Higher Education*, 1979, http://www.jstor.org/stable/1980935?seq=1.

[58] HEA §101(a)(5); 20 U.S.C. §1001(a)(5).

Institutional Eligibility for Participation in Title IV ... 199

- Specialized or programmatic accrediting agencies. These operate throughout the United States and accredit individual educational programs (e.g., law) and single-purpose institutions (e.g., freestanding medical schools). Specific educational programs are often accredited by a specialized accrediting agency, and the institution at which the program is offered is accredited by a regional or national accrediting organization.[59]

Accreditation Process

Generally, an institution must be accredited by an ED-recognized accrediting agency that has the authority to cover all of the institution's programs.[60] Alternatively, a public or private nonprofit IHE may be preaccredited by an agency recognized by ED to grant such preaccreditation, and a public postsecondary vocational institution may be accredited by a state agency[61] that ED determines is a reliable authority. Proprietary institutions must be accredited by an ED-recognized accrediting agency.[62]

The accreditation process begins with an institution or program requesting accreditation. Institutional accreditation is cyclical, with a cycle ranging from every few years up to 10 years. Initial accreditation does not guarantee subsequent renewal of the accredited status.[63]

Typically, an institution seeking accreditation will first perform a self-assessment to determine whether its operations and performance meet the basic standards required by the relevant accrediting agency. Next, an outside group of higher education peers (e.g., faculty and administrators) and members of the public conduct an on-site visit at the institution during which the team determines whether the accrediting organization's standards are being met. Based on the results of the self-assessment and site visit, the accrediting organization determines whether accreditation

---

[59] CHEA, *An Overview of U.S. Accreditation*, p. 2.
[60] Such an agency is known as the institution's primary accrediting agency.
[61] This requirement is distinct from the state authorization requirement.
[62] *FSA Handbook*, vol. 2, p. 8.
[63] CHEA, *An Overview of U.S. Accreditation*, p. 4.

200 *Alexandra Hegji*

will be awarded, renewed, denied, or provisionally awarded to an institution.[64]

Educational programs within institutions can be accredited by programmatic accrediting agencies; however, a program is not required to be accredited by a programmatic accrediting agency for Title IV purposes. Rather, it only needs to be covered by the IHE's primary accrediting agency.[65] Frequently, programmatic accrediting agencies review a specific program within an IHE that is accredited by a regional or national accrediting agency.

An institution that has had its accreditation revoked or terminated for cause cannot be recertified as an IHE eligible to participate in Title IV programs for 24 months following the loss of accreditation, unless the accrediting agency rescinds the loss. The same rules apply if an institution voluntarily withdraws its accreditation. The Secretary can, however, continue the eligibility of a religious institution whose loss of accreditation, whether voluntary or not, is related to its religious mission and not to the HEA accreditation standards.[66] If an institution's accrediting agency loses its recognition from ED, it has up to 18 months to obtain accreditation from another ED-recognized agency.[67]

Federal Recognition of Accrediting Agencies

Although the federal government does not set specific standards for institutional or programmatic accreditation, generally, it does require that

---

[64] Ibid., pp. 4-5. Accrediting agency terms such as "award" or "deny" that are used in this report are meant to provide general descriptions of the types of actions taken by accrediting agencies, as accrediting agencies' definitions for these terms may vary.

[65] Generally, although institutions are not required to have their programs accredited by programmatic accrediting agencies, they may wish to have a program accredited for various reasons. For instance, many employers require prospective employees to be graduates of an accredited program, and licensure requirements for some occupations in certain states require programmatic accreditation. Under the gainful employment regulations, however, an institution must certify to ED that each gainful employment program it operates is programmatically accredited, if such accreditation is required by a federal government entity or by the state in which the institution is located to participate in the Title IV student aid programs. This certification requirement effectively requires programmatic accreditation for Title IV eligibility in certain instances. 34 C.F.R. §668.414(d)(1).

[66] 20 U.S.C. §1099b(j).

[67] HEA §498(h)(2); 20 U.S.C. §1099c(h)(2).

institutions be accredited or preaccredited by a recognized accrediting organization to be eligible for Title IV participation. ED's primary role in accreditation is to recognize an accrediting agency as a "reliable authority regarding the quality of education or training offered" at IHEs through the processes and conditions set forth in the HEA and federal regulations.[68]

For ED recognition, Section 496 of the HEA specifically requires that an accrediting agency be a state, regional, or national agency that demonstrates the ability to operate as an accrediting agency within the relevant state or region or nationally. Additionally, agencies must meet one of the following criteria:

- IHE membership with the agency must be voluntary, and one of the primary purposes of the agency must be accreditation of the IHEs.[69]
- The agency must be a state agency approved by the Secretary as an accrediting agency on or before October 1, 1991.
- The agency must either conduct accreditation through a voluntary membership of individuals in a profession, or it must have as its primary purpose the accreditation of programs within institutions that have already been accredited by another ED-recognized agency.

Agencies that meet the first or third criterion listed above must also be administratively and financially separate and independent of any related trade association or membership organization.[70] For an agency that meets

---

[68] HEA §496; 20 U.S.C. §1099b; 34 C.F.R. §602.1.

[69] ED also recognizes accrediting agencies for the purpose of participating in other federal programs. ED-recognition of accrediting agencies for purposes of participating in non-Title IV programs are beyond the scope of this report.

[70] Section 496 of the HEA (20 U.S.C. §1099b) sets forth four criteria for an accrediting agency to be considered "separate and independent." They are (1) members of the postsecondary education governing body of the agency cannot be elected or selected by the board or chief executive officer of any related or affiliated trade association or membership organization; (2) for every six members of the board of the agency, at least one must be a member of the public; (3) dues to the agency must be paid separately from dues to any related or associated trade association or membership organization; and (4) the agency's budget must be

202 *Alexandra Hegji*

the third criterion and that was ED-recognized on or before October 1, 1991, the Secretary may waive the requirement that the agency be administratively and financially independent of any related organization, but only if the agency can show that the existing relationship with the related organization has not compromised its independence in the accreditation process.

All types of accrediting agencies must show that they consistently apply and enforce standards that ensure that the education programs, training, or courses of study offered by an IHE are of sufficient quality to meet the stated objectives for which the programs, training, or courses are offered. The standards used by the accrediting agencies must assess student achievement in relation to the institution's mission; this may include course completion, job placement rates, and passage rates of state licensing exams. Agencies must also consider curricula, faculty, facilities, fiscal and administrative capacity, student support services, and admissions practices.

Accrediting agencies must also meet requirements that focus on the review of an institution's operating procedures, including reviewing an institution's policies and procedures for determining credit hours, the application of those policies and procedures to programs and coursework, and reviewing any newly established branch campuses.[71] They must also perform regular on-site visits that focus on the quality of education and program effectiveness.[72]

Eligibility and Certification by ED

The final component of the program integrity triad is eligibility and certification by ED. Here, ED is responsible for verifying an institution's legal authority to operate within a state and its accreditation status. ED also evaluates an institution's financial responsibility and administrative

---

developed and determined by the agency, without review or consultation from another entity or organization.

[71] 34 C.F.R. §602.24.

[72] 34 C.F.R. §602.17.

Institutional Eligibility for Participation in Title IV ... 203

capability to administer Title IV student aid programs. An institution can be certified to participate in Title IV for up to six years before applying for recertification.

Financial Responsibility

ED determines an IHE's financial responsibility based on its ability to provide the services described in its official publications, to administer the Title IV programs in which it participates, and to meet all of its financial obligations.[73] A public IHE is deemed financially responsible if its debts and liabilities are backed by the full faith and credit of the state or another government entity.[74] A proprietary or private nonprofit IHE is financially responsible if it meets specific financial ratios (e.g., equity ratio) established by ED,[75] has sufficient cash reserves to make any required refunds (including the return of Title IV funds), is meeting all of its financial obligations, and is current on its debt payments.[76]

Even if an institution meets the above requirements, ED does not consider it financially responsible if the IHE does not meet third-party financial audit requirements or if the IHE violated past performance requirements, such as failing to satisfactorily resolve any compliance issues identified in program reviews or audits.[77]

Alternatively, if an institution does not meet the above standards of financial responsibility, ED may still consider it financially responsible or give it provisional certification, under which it may operate for a time, if it qualifies under an alternative standard. These alternative standards include submitting an irrevocable letter of credit to ED that is equal to at least 50% of the Federal Student Aid (FSA) program funds that the IHE received during its most recently completed fiscal year, meeting specific monitoring

---

[73] HEA §498(c); 20 U.S.C. §1099c(c); 34 C.F.R. §668, Subpart L.

[74] An IHE is considered to have the full faith and credit backing if it notifies ED that it is designated as a public institution by the state, local, or municipal government entity; tribal authority; or other government entity that has the legal authority to make such a designation. The IHE must provide ED with a letter from an appropriate official confirming its status as a public institution. *FSA Handbook*, vol. 2, p. 89.

[75] In evaluating an IHE's financial responsibility, ED will calculate a composite score based on its equity, primary, and net income ratios. 34 C.F.R. §668.172.

[76] *FSA Handbook,* vol. 2, p. 90.

[77] *FSA Handbook*, vol. 2, pp. 89-90; 100-101.

204 *Alexandra Hegji*

requirements, or participating in the Title IV programs under provisional certification.[78]

Administrative Capability

Along with demonstrating financial responsibility, an institution must demonstrate its ability to properly administer the Title IV programs in which it participates and to provide the education it describes in public documents (e.g., marketing brochures). Administrative capability focuses on the processes, procedures, and personnel used in administering Title IV funds and indicators of student success.[79]

Administrative capability standards address numerous aspects of Title IV administration. For example, to administer Title IV programs an institution must use ED's electronic processes[80] and develop a system to identify and resolve discrepancies in Title IV information received by various institutional offices. The IHE must also refer cases of Title IV student fraud or criminal misconduct to ED's Office of Inspector General for resolution, and it must provide all enrolled and prospective students financial aid counseling. Finally, the IHE must have an adequate internal system of checks and balances that includes dividing the functions of authorizing payments and disbursing funds between two separate offices.[81]

Institutions are required to have a capable staff member to administer Title IV programs and coordinate those programs with other aid received by students.[82] This person must also have an adequate number of qualified staff to assist with aid administration. Before receiving Title IV funds, an

---

[78] *FSA Handbook*, vol. 2, pp. 96-99.

[79] HEA §498(d); 20 U.S.C. § 1099c(d); 34 C.F.R. §668.16.

[80] Some of the required electronic processes include establishment of a Student Aid Internet Gateway mailbox to transmit student data records to ED, use of the E-App to submit and update an institution's eligibility information, and use of the Default Management website to receive draft and official cohort default rate data. A list of required electronic processes can be found at *FSA Handbook*, vol. 2, p. 64.

[81] 34 C.F.R. §668.16.

[82] ED considers an individual capable for purposes of Title IV administration if the individual: (1) is certified as a financial aid administrator, if the institution's state requires such certification; (2) has successfully completed an ED-provided or ED-approved Title IV training program; or (3) has previous experience and success in administering Title IV programs. This list is not definitive; ED may consider other relevant factors. 34 C.F.R. §668.16(b)(1).

IHE must certify that neither it nor its employees have been debarred or suspended by a federal agency; similar limitations apply to lenders, loan servicers, and third-party servicers.[83]

Relating to indicators of student success, an institution must have satisfactory academic progress (SAP) standards for students receiving Title IV funds. In general, IHEs must develop SAP standards that establish a minimum grade point average (or its equivalent) for students and a maximum time frame in which students must complete their educational programs. A student who fails to meet the SAP requirements becomes ineligible to receive Title IV funds.[84] Also related to student success indicators, an institution that seeks to participate in Title IV programs for the first time may not have an undergraduate withdrawal rate for regular students that is greater than 33% during its most recently completed award year.[85]

Cohort Default Rate

An institution may be deemed administratively incapable if it has a high cohort default rate (CDR). In general, the CDR is the number of an IHE's federal loan recipients who enter repayment in a given fiscal year (the cohort fiscal year) and who default within a certain period of time after entering repayment (cohort default period; CDP), *divided by* the total number of borrowers who entered repayment in the cohort fiscal year.[86]

Since 2014, ED has used a three-year CDP in calculating an institution's CDR.[87] An IHE will be found administratively incapable if one of the following conditions is met:

---

[83] *FSA Handbook*, vol. 2, pp. 50-58.

[84] For more information about SAP and student eligibility for FSA programs, see *FSA Handbook*, vol. 1.

[85] Withdrawal occurs when students drop out of all Title IV eligible coursework during an academic term. *FSA Handbook*, vol. 2, p. 2-14.

[86] For institutions with fewer than 30 students entering repayment in a given cohort fiscal year, an "average rate" CDR is used, which is calculated by dividing the number of borrowers who entered repayment in the current cohort fiscal year and the two preceding cohort fiscal years, by the number who defaulted in the CDP for the cohort fiscal year in which they entered repayment. HEA § 434(m)(1)(A); 20 U.S.C. §1085(m)(1)(A).

[87] For instance, the 2013 cohort fiscal year includes the number of borrowers who entered repayment in 2013 and who defaulted in 2013, 2014, or 2015. In 2016, the CDR for the 2013 cohort fiscal year was used to determine whether an institution is administratively

1. an institution's CDR is greater than 40% in one year for loans made under the FFEL and Direct Loans programs;[88] an institution's CDR is 30% or greater for each of the three most recent fiscal years for loans made under the FFEL and Direct Loans programs; or
2. an institution's CDR is 15% or greater in any single year for loans made under the Federal Perkins Loan Program.

When an IHE is determined to be administratively incapable due to a high CDR, it may become ineligible to participate in the Direct Loan, Pell Grant, and/or Perkins Loan programs (but not other Title IV programs). ED may grant provisional certification for up to three years to an institution that would be deemed administratively capable except for its high cohort default rates.[89]

Provisional Certification

If an institution is seeking initial certification, ED can grant it up to one year of provisional certification. ED can also grant an institution provisional certification for up to three years if ED is determining the IHE's administrative capacity and financial responsibility for the first time, if the IHE has experienced a partial or total change in ownership, or if ED determines that the administrative or financial condition of the IHE may hinder its ability to meet its financial responsibilities. Additionally, if an accrediting agency loses its ED recognition, any institution that was accredited by that agency may continue to participate in Title IV programs for up to 18 months after ED's withdrawal of recognition.[90]

---

incapable based on that information. Prior to 2014, ED used a two-year CDP in calculating an institution's CDR.

[88] These first two CDRs are calculated for Federal Family Education Loan program Subsidized and Unsubsidized Stafford Loans and Direct Loan program Subsidized and Unsubsidized Loans. An institution may be subject to provisional certification if two of the three of its most recent CDRs are 30% or greater. 34 C.F.R. §668.16(m).

[89] 34 C.F.R. §668.16(m)(2)(i).

[90] 34 C.F.R. §668.13(c).

Program Reviews

To ensure that an institution is conforming to eligibility requirements, ED can conduct program reviews. During a program review, ED evaluates an institution's compliance with Title IV requirements and identifies actions the IHE must take to correct any problem(s). Review priority is given to those institutions with high cohort default rates; IHEs with significant fluctuations in Pell Grant awards or Direct Loan volume that are not accounted for by changes in programs offered; IHEs that are reported to have deficiencies or financial aid problems by their state or accrediting agency; IHEs with high annual dropout rates;[91] and IHEs determined by ED to pose a significant risk of failing to comply with the administrative capability or financial responsibility requirements.[92] If, during a review, ED determines that an institution is not administratively capable or financially responsible or is violating Title IV program rules, ED may grant it provisional certification, take corrective actions, or impose sanctions.

Sanctions and Corrective Actions

ED has the authority to impose a variety of sanctions and corrective actions on an institution that violates Title IV program rules, a Program Participation Agreement (discussed later in this chapter) or any other agreement made under the laws or regulations, or if it substantially misrepresents the nature of its educational programs, financial charges, or graduates' employability. Sanctions include fines, limitations, suspensions, emergency actions, and terminations. ED can also sanction third-party servicers performing tasks related to the institution's Title IV programs.

Fines, Limitations, and Suspensions

ED may impose several types of sanctions on institutions for statutory and regulatory violations, including fines, limitations, and suspensions. ED can fine an institution up to $55,907 for each statutory or regulatory

---

[91] "High annual dropout rates" is undefined.
[92] HEA §498A(a)(2); 20 U.S.C. §1099c-1(a)(2).

violation it commits, depending on the size of the IHE and the seriousness of the violation.[93]

Under a limitation, ED imposes specific conditions or restrictions on an institution related to its administration of Title IV funds. A limitation lasts for at least 12 months, and if an institution fails to abide by the limitation, ED may initiate a termination proceeding.

Finally, under a suspension, an institution is not allowed to participate in Title IV programs for up to 60 days.

Each of these sanctions may require an institution to take corrective actions as well, which may include repaying illegally used funds or making payments to eligible students from the IHE's own funds.[94]

Emergency Action

ED can take emergency action to withhold Title IV funds from an institution if it receives reliable information that an IHE is violating applicable laws or regulations, agreements, or limitations. ED must determine that the institution is misusing federal funds, that immediate action is necessary to stop misuses, and that the potential losses outweigh the importance of using established procedures for limitation, suspension, or termination. An emergency action suspends an institution's participation in Title IV programs and prohibits it from disbursing such funds. Typically, the emergency action may not last more than 30 days.[95]

Termination of Title IV Participation

The final action ED can take is the termination of an institution's participation in Title IV programs. Generally, an institution that has had its participation terminated cannot reapply to be reinstated for at least 18 months. To request reinstatement, an institution must submit a fully

---

[93] HEA Section 487(c)(3)(B) (20 U.S.C. §1094(c)(3)(B)) specifies that fines may equal up to $25,000 for each violation. However, the Inflation Adjustment Act (20 U.S.C. §2461, note) requires that each federal agency annually adjust for inflation their civil monetary penalties. The $55,907 fine for institutional Title IV violations represents ED's most recent adjustment to its civil monetary penalties. Department of Education, "Adjustment to Civil Monetary Penalties for Inflation," 83 *Federal Register* 2062, January 16, 2018.

[94] *FSA Handbook*, vol. 2, p. 212.

[95] Ibid.

completed application to ED and demonstrate that it has corrected the violation(s) for which its participation was terminated. ED may then approve, approve subject to limitations, or deny the institution's request.[96]

OTHER RELATED ISSUES

Several other requirements affect institutional eligibility for Title IV programs. Some of these requirements include institution Program Participation Agreements, which include provisions related to incentive compensation and campus crime reporting requirements; return of Title IV funds; and distance education. The failure to meet the requirements for any of these may result in the loss of Title IV eligibility or other sanctions.

Program Participation Agreements

HEA Section 487 specifies that each institution wanting to participate in Title IV student aid programs is required to have a current Program Participation Agreement (PPA). A PPA is a document in which the institution agrees to comply with the laws, regulations, and policies applicable to the Title IV programs; it applies to an IHE's branch campuses and locations that meet Title IV requirements, as well as its main campus. It also lists all of the Title IV programs in which the IHE is eligible to participate, the date on which the PPA expires, and the date on which the IHE must reapply for participation.

By signing a PPA, an institution agrees that it will act as a fiduciary responsible for properly administering Title IV funds, will not charge students a processing fee to determine a student's eligibility for such funds, and will establish and maintain administrative and fiscal procedures to ensure the proper administration of Title IV programs. The PPA reiterates many provisions required for institutional eligibility and ED certification

---

[96] Ibid.

210 *Alexandra Hegji*

discussed earlier in this chapter and contains several additional notable requirements that may affect an IHE's Title IV eligibility, which are described below. Along with the general participation requirements with which an institution must comply, a PPA may also contain institution-specific requirements.[97]

90/10 Rule

As part of their PPAs, domestic and foreign proprietary IHEs must agree to derive at least 10% of their revenue from non-Title IV funds (i.e., no more than 90% of their revenue can come from Title IV funds). This is known as the 90/10 rule. Examples of non-Title IV funds include private education loans and some military and veterans' benefits, such as benefits provided under the Post-9/11 GI Bill program. If an IHE violates the 90/10 rule in one year, it does not immediately lose its Title IV eligibility. Rather, it is placed on a provisional eligibility status for two years. If the IHE violates the 90/10 rule for two consecutive years, it loses its eligibility for at least two years.[98]

Incentive Compensation

In a PPA, an IHE must agree it will not provide any commission or incentive compensation to individuals based directly or indirectly on their success in enrolling students or the enrolled students' obtaining financial aid; however, some exceptions apply to this general rule. For instance, IHEs can provide incentive compensation to individuals for the recruitment of foreign students who are ineligible to receive Title IV funds or they can provide incentive compensation through a profit-sharing plan.[99]

---

[97] 34 C.F.R. §668.14.

[98] 20 U.S.C. §1094(a)(24) and (d)(2). Of the 1,764 IHEs reporting revenues for purposes of the 90/10 rule, between July 1, 2016, and June 30, 2017, a total of 12 had Title IV revenues that were greater than 90%, and all remained Title IV eligible because they satisfied the 90/10 rule in the previous year. Source: Letter from Diane Auer Jones, Principal Deputy Under Secretary, Delegate the Duties of Under Secretary, U.S. Department of Education, to Virginia Foxx, Chairwoman, Committee on Education and the Workforce, U.S. House of Representatives, December 10, 2018, and Office of Federal Student Aid, Data Center, 2016-2017 Award Year: Report and Summary Chart.

[99] 34 C.F.R. §668.14(22).

Institutional Eligibility for Participation in Title IV ... 211

The ban on incentive compensation only applies to the activities of securing enrollment (recruitment) and securing financial aid. Other activities are not banned, and ED draws a distinction between activities that involve directly working with individual students and policy-level determinations that affect recruitment and financial aid awards. For instance, an individual who is responsible for contacting potential student applicants or assisting students in filling out an enrollment application cannot receive incentive compensation, but an individual who conducts marketing activities, such as the broad dissemination of informational brochures or the collection of contact information, can receive incentive compensation.[100]

Clery Act Requirements

HEA Section 485(f), referred to as the Clery Act,[101] requires domestic Title IV participating IHEs (1) to report to ED campus crime statistics and (2) establish and disseminate campus safety and security policies. Both the campus crime statistics and campus safety and security policies must be compiled and disseminated to current and prospective students and employees in an IHE's annual security report (ASR).

Campus crime statistics required to be reported to ED and included in an ASR include data on the occurrence on campus[102] of a range of offenses specified in statute, including murder, burglary, robbery, domestic violence, rape, and other forms of sexual violence.

In addition to campus crime statistics, ASRs must include statements of campus safety and security policies regarding, for example,

---

[100] For a detailed list of activities covered by the incentive compensation prohibition, see *FSA Handbook*, vol. 2, pp. 59 62, Tables 1-3 and U.S. Department of Education, "Higher Education: Program Integrity Questions and Answers— Incentive Compensation," http://www2.ed.gov/policy/highered/reg/hearulemaking/2009/compensation.html.

[101] For additional information, see Department of Education, *The Handbook for Campus Safety and Security Report: 2016 Edition*, June 2016.

[102] For purposes of the Clery Act, "campus" includes campus areas, noncampus areas, and public property, if certain criteria are met. HEA §485(f)(6)(A)(ii); 20 U.S.C. §1092(f)(6)(A)(ii).

- procedures and facilities for students and others to report criminal actions or other emergencies occurring on campus and an IHE's response to such reports;
- security and access to campus facilities;
- campus law enforcement, including the law enforcement authority of campus security personnel, and the working relationship between campus security personnel and state and local law enforcement;
- programs designed to inform students and employees about the prevention of crimes; and
- the possession, use, and sale of alcoholic beverages and illegal drugs; enforcement of state underage drinking laws; enforcement of federal and state drug laws; and any drug or alcohol abuse education programs required under the HEA.[103]

An ASR must also include statements of policies specifically relating to incidence of domestic and sexual violence. For example, an ASR must include statements of policy regarding

- programs to prevent such incidents;
- procedures a victim should follow if such an incident as occurred;
- procedures an IHE will follow once such an incident has been reported and procedures for institutional disciplinary actions in cases of alleged incidents (including a statement of the standard of evidence that will be used in any school proceeding arising from the incident report); and
- possible sanctions and protective measures that an IHE may impose following a final determination in an institutional proceeding regarding such incidences.

---

[103] HEA Section 120 requires that IHEs adopt and implement a program to prevent the use of illicit drugs and the abuse of alcohol by students and employees.

Institutional Eligibility for Participation in Title IV ...   213

The Clery Act prohibits the Secretary of Education from requiring IHEs to adopt particular policies, procedures, or practices; and prohibits retaliation against anyone exercising his or her rights or responsibilities under the act.

Return of Title IV Funds

HEA Section 484B specifies that when a Title IV aid recipient withdraws from an IHE before the end of the payment or enrollment period for which funds were disbursed, Title IV funds must be returned to ED according to a statutorily prescribed schedule. In general, when a student withdraws from an IHE, an IHE first determines the portion of Title IV aid considered to be "earned" by the student while enrolled and the portion considered to be "unearned." Unearned aid must be returned to ED. Up to the 60% point of a payment or enrollment period, unearned funds must be returned on a pro rata schedule. After the 60% point of a payment or enrollment period, the total amount of funds awarded is considered to have been earned by the student and no funds are required to be returned. Whether an IHE and/or the student is required to return the funds to ED depends on a variety of circumstances, including whether Title IV funds have been applied directly to a student's institutional charges.[104] Unearned funds must be returned to their respective programs in a specified order, with loans being returned first, followed by Pell Grants, and then other Title IV aid.[105] In some instances, a student may have earned more aid than has been disbursed, and the difference is disbursed to the student after the student withdraws.[106]

---

[104] Generally, institutional charges are defined as charges for tuition and fees, institution-provided or contracted room and board, and other educational expenses that are paid directly to the institution (e.g., charges for supplies, equipment, and materials).

[105] Under certain circumstances, portions of Federal Supplemental Educational Opportunity Grants are excluded from the return of Title IV calculations. Federal Work-Study funds are not included in the calculation. *FSA Handbook*, vol. 5, p. 27.

[106] For additional information on the return of Title IV funds, including examples of how to calculate the amount of Title IV funds to be returned, see *FSA Handbook*, vol. 5.

Distance Education and Correspondence Education

Generally, distance education and correspondence education refers to educational instruction with a separation in time, place, or both between the student and instructor. It is a way in which institutions can increase student access to postsecondary education by offering alternatives to traditional on-campus instruction. Recently, due to the greater availability of new technologies, there has been substantial growth in the amount and types of courses institutions offer.

Section 103(7)(A) and (B) of the HEA and the accompanying regulations define distance education as instruction that uses "(1) the internet; (2) one-way and two-way transmissions through open broadcast, closed circuit, cable, microwave, broadband lines, fiber optics, satellite, or wireless communications devices; [or] ... (3) audio conferencing" to deliver instruction to students separated from the instructor. A course taught through a video cassette, DVD, or CD-ROM is considered a distance education course if one of the above-mentioned technologies is used to support student-instructor interaction. Regardless of the technology used, "regular and substantive interaction between the students and the instructor" must be ensured.[107]

Correspondence courses are expressly excluded from the definition of distance education.[108] A correspondence course is one for which an

---

[107] HEA §103(7); 20 U.S.C. §1003(7); 34 C.F.R. §600.2.

[108] The original HEA definition of distance education did not reference correspondence courses and courses offered via telecommunications; rather, such courses were considered subsets of distance education. Before July 1, 2010, Section 484(l)(4) of the HEA defined a telecommunications course as one offered principally through television, audio, or computer transmission, and a correspondence course was defined as a home-study course in which an IHE provided students who were separated from their instructor with instructional materials, including examinations, either by mail or electronic transmission. For correspondence courses and telecommunications courses, students completed the instructional materials and corresponding examinations and returned the examinations to the IHE for grading. Interaction between the instructor and the student was not regular and substantive, and the correspondence course was predominantly offered by an IHE via print-based media. For the purposes of Title IV aid eligibility, telecommunications programs were treated the same as traditional on-campus programs, while correspondence courses were subject to stricter requirements. With the substantial growth in the use of technology for educational instruction, the separate definition of telecommunications courses became unnecessary. Therefore in 2010, the Higher Education Opportunity Act (P.L. 110-315) eliminated the

Institutional Eligibility for Participation in Title IV ...   215

institution provides instructional materials and exams for students who do not physically attend classes at the IHE, but does not include those courses that are delivered with "regular and substantive interaction between the students and the instructor" via one of the above-described technologies.[109]

50% Rule for Correspondence Courses

In 1992, partially in response to cases of some correspondence institutions' fraudulent and abusive practices used to attract unqualified students to enroll in programs of poor or questionable quality, Congress incorporated provisions referred to as the "50% rules" into the HEA. The rules affected both the eligibility of institutions offering correspondence courses and their students' eligibility for Title IV aid. In general, under the rules, an institution is ineligible for Title IV aid if more than 50% of its courses are offered by correspondence,[110] or if 50% or more of its students are enrolled in correspondence courses.[111]

State Authorization for Correspondence and Distance Education Courses

As discussed earlier in this chapter, rules promulgated in 2016 would have required an IHE offering postsecondary distance or correspondence education in a state in which it is not physically located to meet any state authorization requirements within that state. Under the regulations, an IHE

---

separate definition for telecommunications and incorporated the various technologies referenced in that definition into the definition of distance education. Department of Education, "Federal Student Aid Programs," 71 *Federal Register* 45667, August 9, 2006.

[109] 34 C.F.R. §600.2. In certain instances, elements of a correspondence course may be combined with non-correspondence course elements. These multi-component courses may or may not be considered correspondence courses for the purposes of Title IV eligibility. For specific examples of such courses, see *FSA Handbook*, vol. 2, p. 37.

[110] HEA § 102(a)(3)(A) and (B); 20 U.S.C. §1002(a)(3)(A) and (B). This rule does not apply to "a public nonprofit technical institution or career and technical education school used exclusively or principally for the provision of career and technical education to individuals who have completed or left secondary school and who are available for study in preparation for entering the labor market." 20 U.S.C. §2302(3)(C).

[111] 34 C.F.R. 600.7(a)(1)(i) and (ii). This second limitation may be waived if an IHE offers a two-year associate's degree or four-year bachelor's degree program and it demonstrates to ED that in the award year, students who were enrolled in correspondence courses received 5% or less of the total FSA funds received by all of the IHE's students. ED, *FSA Handbook*, vol. 2, p. 103.

could meet this requirement if it participates in a state authorization reciprocity agreement. These regulations were scheduled to become effective July 1, 2018. However, on July 3, 2018 (and effective June 29, 2018), the Secretary of Education issued a final rule delaying the implementation of these requirements until July 1, 2020.[112]

Foreign IHE Eligibility

The distinction between distance education and traditional instruction is also important for the purposes of Title IV program eligibility. Distance education programs provided by domestic IHEs are eligible for Title IV participation if they have been accredited by an accrediting agency recognized by ED to evaluate distance education programs.[113] A program offered by a foreign IHE, in whole or in part, through distance education (including telecommunications) or correspondence is ineligible for Title IV participation.[114]

---

[112] Department of Education, "Program Integrity and Improvement," 83 *Federal Register* 31296, July 3, 2018.

[113] *FSA Handbook*, vol. 2, 36.

[114] 34 C.F.R. §600.51(d).

In: Key Congressional Reports on Education ISBN: 978-1-53615-731-4
Editor: Georgia Turner © 2019 Nova Science Publishers, Inc.

Chapter 6

DEPARTMENT OF EDUCATION FUNDING: KEY CONCEPTS AND FAQ[*]

Kyle D. Shohfi and Jessica Tollestrup

SUMMARY

Like most federal agencies, the Department of Education (ED) receives funds in support of its mission through various federal budget and appropriations processes. While not unique, the mechanisms by which ED receives, obligates, and expends funds can be complex. For example, ED receives both mandatory and discretionary appropriations; ED is annually provided forward funds and advance appropriations for some—but not all—discretionary programs; ED awards both formula and competitive grants; and a portion of ED's budget subsidizes student loan costs (direct loans and loan guarantees). As such, analyzing ED's budget requires an understanding of a broad range of federal budget and appropriations concepts. This chapter provides an introduction to these concepts as they are used specifically in the context of the congressional appropriations process for ED.

---

[*] This is an edited, reformatted and augmented version of Congressional Research Service Publication No. R44477, Updated February 19, 2019.

The first section of this chapter provides an introduction to key terms and concepts in the federal budget and appropriations process for ED. In addition to those mentioned above, the report includes explanations of terms and concepts such as authorizations versus appropriations; budgetary allocations, discretionary spending caps, and sequestration; transfers and reprogramming; and matching requirements.

The second section answers frequently asked questions about federal funding for ED or education in general. These are as follows:

- How much funding does ED receive annually?
- How much does the federal government spend on education?
- Where can information be found about the President's budget request and congressional appropriations for ED?
- How much ED funding is in the congressional budget resolution?
- What is the difference between the amounts in appropriations bills and report language?
- What happens to education funding if annual appropriations are not enacted before the start of the federal fiscal year?
- What happens if an ED program authorization "expires"?

The third section includes a brief description of, and links to, reports and documents that provide more information about budget and appropriations concepts.

INTRODUCTION

Federal policymakers statutorily established the U.S. Department of Education (ED) as a Cabinet-level agency in 1980.[1] Its mission is to "promote student achievement and preparation for global competitiveness by fostering educational excellence and ensuring equal access."[2]

Like most federal agencies, ED receives funds in support of its mission through various federal budget and appropriations processes. These processes are complex.

---

[1] P.L. 96-88.
[2] U.S. Department of Education, "About ED," http://www2.ed.gov/about/landing.jhtml, accessed December 28, 2018.

Department of Education Funding: Key Concepts and FAQ 219

For example, ED receives both mandatory and discretionary appropriations; ED is annually provided forward funds and advance appropriations for some—but not all—discretionary programs; ED awards both formula and competitive grants; and a portion of ED's budget subsidizes student loan costs (through both direct loans and loan guarantees).

Because of this complexity, analyzing ED's budget requires an understanding of a broad range of federal budget and appropriations concepts. This chapter provides an introduction to these concepts as they are used specifically in the context of the congressional appropriations process for ED. It was designed for readers who are new or returning to the topic of ED budget and appropriations. The first section of this chapter provides an introduction to key terms and concepts in the federal budget and appropriations process with special relevance for ED. The second section answers frequently asked questions (FAQs) about federal funding for the department, as well as closely related questions about education funding in general. The third section includes a brief description of, and links to, reports and documents that provide more information about budget and appropriations concepts.

The scope of this chapter is generally (but not exclusively) limited to concepts associated with funding provided to ED through the annual appropriations process. It does not address all possible sources of federal funding for education, training, or related activities. For example, it does not seek to address education tax credits, student loans, or education and training programs at agencies other than ED.[3] Where this chapter does address such topics, it does so in order to provide broad context for questions and key terms related to the appropriations process for ED. This chapter also addresses some frequently asked questions about education funding in general.

---

[3] Such funds are not typically included in the annual discretionary appropriations act for ED, which is the primary focus of this report. Congressional readers seeking such information are referred to the many publications on these topics at http://www.crs.gov.

KEY CONCEPTS AND TERMS

The following section provides an introduction to selected key terms and concepts used in the congressional debate about federal funding for ED.

Budget Authority, Obligation, Outlay, and Rescission

In the federal budget process, the concept of spending is broken down into three related but distinct phases—budget authority, obligation, and outlay. *Budget authority* is the authority provided by federal law to enter into financial *obligations* that will result in immediate or future expenditures (or *outlays*) involving federal government funds. For reasons that are explained below, the amounts of budget authority, obligations, and outlays in a fiscal year are rarely the same for a budget account (or activity in that account). For example, ED's Education for the Disadvantaged account[4] in FY2017 had $16.805 billion in total budget authority.[5] That is, ED had legal authority to spend up to $16.805 billion in federal funds for the purposes associated with this account (which consists primarily of grants allocated to local educational agencies).[6] During that same fiscal year, ED newly obligated (i.e., committed to spend) $16.789 billion of that

---

[4] 4 An account is a separate financial reporting unit for budget, management, and/or accounting purposes. For more information on accounts, see U.S. Government Accountability Office, *A Glossary of Terms Used in the Federal Budget Process*, GAO-05-734SP, September 1, 2005, http://www.gao.gov/products/GAO-05-734SP.

[5] 5 Consisting of $660 million in unobligated balances brought forward, $10.841 billion in advance appropriations from FY2016, and $5.303 billion in current-year (FY2017) appropriations. See Executive Office of the President, Office of Management and Budget, "Department of Education," *The Appendix: Budget of the United States Government, Fiscal Year 2019*, https://www.govinfo.gov/content/pkg/BUDGET-2019-APP/pdf/BUDGET-2019-APP-1-9.pdf.

[6] 6 This account includes programs such as Elementary and Secondary Education Act (ESEA) Title I-A Grants to Local Educational Agencies, School Improvement Grants, and Migrant Education Program grants.

available budget authority. Total outlays during FY2017 in the Education for the Disadvantaged account were $16.237 billion.[7]

Budget authority can only be provided through the enactment of law, and generally its amount, purpose, and the time period in which it may be used is specified. Budget authority may be for a broad set of purposes (e.g., improving the academic achievement of disadvantaged children) or for a particular purpose (e.g., obtaining annually updated local educational agency-level census poverty data from the Bureau of the Census). The amount of the budget authority is usually defined in specific terms (e.g., $10 billion) but sometimes is indefinite (e.g., "such sums as may be necessary"). The time element of budget authority provides a deadline as to when the funds must be obligated—one fiscal year, multiple fiscal years, or without fiscal year restriction (referred to as "no year" budget authority).

Once an agency receives its budget authority, it may take actions to obligate it legally, for example, by signing contracts or grant agreements. Over the course of a fiscal year, an agency may obligate budget authority that was first provided during that year or was provided in a prior fiscal year with a multiyear or no-year period of availability. Generally, all obligations must occur prior to the deadline associated with the budget authority. It is not until those obligations are due to be paid (i.e., become outlays) that federal funds from the Treasury are used to make the payments.

In addition to the amount of budget authority that is available to be obligated, the primary factor that affects the total amount of obligations in a fiscal year is when they are due. For example, outlays to pay salaries usually occur over the course of the year that the budget authority is made available because those payments must occur regularly (e.g., every two weeks). In contrast, outlays for a construction project may be structured to occur over several years as various stages of the project are completed. Outlays are reported in the fiscal year in which they occur, even those

---

[7] Executive Office of the President, Office of Management and Budget, "Department of Education, " *The Appendix: Budget of the United States Government, Fiscal Year 2019*, p. 333, https://www.govinfo.gov/content/pkg/BUDGET2019-APP/pdf/BUDGET-2019-APP-1-9.pdf.

outlays that result from budget authority that first became available in previous fiscal years.

Budget authority that reaches the end of its period of availability is considered to have "expired." At this point, no new obligations may be incurred, although outlays to liquidate existing obligations are generally allowable, usually up to five fiscal years after the budget authority expired. Once that liquidation period has ended, it is generally the case that no further outlays may occur and the agency is to take administrative steps to cancel any remaining budget authority.[8]

Rescissions are generally provisions of law that repeal unobligated budget authority prior to its expiration. Such provisions may be used to eliminate budget authority for purposes that are considered to be outdated or no longer desirable. Rescissions also may be used to offset increases in budget authority for higher-priority activities.

Authorizations and Appropriations

The congressional budget process generally distinguishes between two types of measures— *authorizations*, which create or modify federal government programs or activities, and *appropriations*, which fund those activities. The provisions within authorization measures may be further distinguished as either *enabling or organic* provisions (e.g., statutory language or acts that authorize certain programs, policies, or activities) or express *authorizations of appropriations* provisions (e.g., statutory language or acts that recommend a future funding level for authorized programs, policies, or activities). These distinctions between authorizations and appropriations, and between the types of authorization provisions, are important for understanding why programs with "expired" authorizations can continue to function. This section focuses on the distinction between appropriations and enabling or organic authorizations; the section titled

---

[8] 31 U.S.C. §1552(a). For a detailed discussion of these general principles, see GAO, *Principles of Appropriations Law*, 3rd Ed., pp. 5-71 to 5-75, http://www.gao.gov/assets/210/2024 37.pdf.

Department of Education Funding: Key Concepts and FAQ   223

"Authorization of Appropriations" addresses the authorization of funding levels.[9]

Authorizations and Appropriations

Authorization provisions generally come in two types: (1) Provisions that define the authority of the government to act, by establishing, altering, or terminating authorities, are referred to as "enabling" or "organic" authorizations; (2) "Authorizations of appropriations" essentially recommend a funding level for a program or agency in a given fiscal year but do not themselves provide that funding.

Appropriations provisions provide funding for federal agencies to carry out certain purposes that are usually specified in authorization acts.

Enabling or organic authorizations may be generally described as statutory provisions that define the authority of the government to act. These acts establish, alter, or terminate federal agencies, programs, policies, and activities. For example, the Economic Opportunity Act of 1964 (P.L. 88-452) contained statutory provisions that established the Federal Work-Study (FWS) program. The Higher Education Opportunity Act of 2008 (HEOA, P.L. 110- 315) contained statutory provisions that altered and continued (e.g., "reauthorized") FWS. Authorization measures may also address organizational and administrative matters, such as the number or composition of offices within a department. Authorization measures are under the jurisdiction of legislative committees, such as the House Committee on Education and Labor and the Senate Committee on Health, Education, Labor and Pensions.

Authorizations may be permanent or limited-term. Permanent authorizations remain in place until Congress and the President enact a law or laws to amend or repeal the authorization. Most ED authorizations are

---

[9] More information about the distinction between types of authorizations, and between authorizations and appropriations, is available in U.S. Government Accountability Office, "Chapter 2: The Legal Framework," *Principles of Federal Appropriations Law*, GAO-16-464SP, 4th ed., 2016 Revision, pp. 2-54 – 2-56, at http://www.gao.gov/legal/ redbook/redbook.html. See also the section entitled, "What happens if an ED program authorization "expires"?"

permanent. For example, Title I-A of the Elementary and Secondary Education Act of 1965, as amended and reauthorized by the Every Student Succeeds Act (ESSA, P.L. 114- 95), gives ED the authority to provide aid to local educational agencies (LEAs) for the education of disadvantaged children. In general, unless Congress and the President enacted legislation to repeal provisions of Title I-A, ED may distribute any budget authority it receives for such aid in accordance with the program parameters defined in such statutory language.

Limited-term authorizations end after a specified period of time, typically without requiring further legislative action. (These are sometimes called *sunset provisions*.) For example, the statute authorizing the Advisory Committee for Student Financial Assistance (ACSFA, 20 U.S.C. 1098(k)) specifies that ACSFA was authorized from the date of enactment until October 1, 2015. At that point, ACSFA was disbanded. The authorizations for some programs are intended to receive legislative action on a regular basis, as the authorities for those programs expire, while others are expected to receive legislative action as needed and not on a regular schedule.

Appropriations measures, on the other hand, are typically enacted annually and provide new budget authority for agencies, programs, policies, and activities that are already authorized and are under the jurisdiction of the House Appropriations Committee and the Senate Appropriations Committee.[10] That is, appropriations give federal agencies the authority to use a certain amount of federal funds for program purposes that are usually specified in authorization acts. For example, the Department of Defense and Labor, Health and Human Services, and Education Appropriations Act, 2019 and Continuing Appropriations Act, 2019 (P.L. 115-245) appropriated $71.4 billion in discretionary budget

---

[10] In certain instances, federal programs can receive appropriations through their authorizing acts instead of (or in addition to) the budget authority they receive through annual appropriations acts. This process is described more fully in the section on "Discretionary and Mandatory Spending (Including Appropriated Mandatory Spending)."

Department of Education Funding: Key Concepts and FAQ   225

authority to ED, of which $22.5 billion was specifically for the Pell Grant program.[11]

Budget authority that is provided in appropriations measures may be available for a single fiscal year, multiple fiscal years (or portions thereof), or an indefinite period of time. For example, P.L. 115-245 provided budget authority that was available for one year for ED's Indian Education account, a year-and-a-quarter for Special Education, and two years for Impact Aid.

In general, during a calendar year Congress may consider the following:

- 12 *regular appropriations bills* for the fiscal year that begins on October 1 (often referred to as the budget year) to provide the annual funding for the agencies, projects, and activities funded therein;[12]
- one or more *continuing resolutions* for that same fiscal year, to provide temporary funding if all 12 regular appropriations bills are not enacted by the start of the fiscal year; and
- one or more *supplemental appropriations measures* for the current fiscal year, to provide additional funding for selected activities over and above the amount provided through annual or continuing appropriations.[13]

Congress typically includes most regular annual ED appropriations in the Departments of Labor, Health and Human Services, and Education, and Related Agencies appropriations bill.

---

[11] The department also receives budget authority through other provisions of law. This amount represents only the amount it received through the annual regular appropriations process. See section on "Discretionary and Mandatory Spending (Including Appropriated Mandatory Spending)" for more information on this distinction.

[12] In some years, Congress combines two or more of these bills into what may be referred to as an "omnibus" or "consolidated" appropriations act.

[13] In general, supplemental funding may be provided to address cases where resources provided through the annual appropriations process are determined to be inadequate or not timely.

"Authorization of Appropriations"

In addition to enabling or organic authorizations that establish the authority for federal government activities and appropriations that provide the authority to actually expend federal funds on those activities, laws may include provisions that provide an explicit *authorization of appropriations*.

An authorization of appropriations (or, alternatively, appropriations authorization) is a provision of law that essentially recommends a funding level for a program or agency in a given fiscal year. Appropriations authorizations may include a range of fiscal years and a specific funding level for each fiscal year within that range (e.g., $10 million in FY2007, $12 million in FY2008, etc.); may be indefinite (e.g., "such sums as may be necessary"); or may not be provided at all. For example, Section 1002 of the Elementary and Secondary Education Act of 1965, as amended and reauthorized by the Every Student Succeeds Act (ESSA, P.L. 114-95), includes an authorization of appropriations provision effectively recommending a specific funding level ($15.9 billion) for the Title I-A program in a certain fiscal year (FY2019).

GEPA and Appropriations Authorizations at ED

The General Education Provisions Act (GEPA), as amended, contains a broad array of statutory provisions that are applicable to the majority of federal education programs administered by ED. One such provision, Section 422, effectively adds one additional fiscal year to most ED appropriations authorizations. For example, if Congress does not enact legislation extending the appropriations authorization of the Title I-A program by FY2020 (the last fiscal year for which the Elementary and Secondary Education Act (ESEA) provides an appropriations authorization for this program), then Section 422 of GEPA will authorize appropriations for the Title I-A program for one additional fiscal year (FY2021). The authorized Title IA funding level under the GEPA extension in FY2021 will be the same level as the final year authorized under ESEA.

Department of Education Funding: Key Concepts and FAQ 227

Contrary to common misconception, an authorization of appropriations does not convey actual budget authority. Further, a lapse or gap in the fiscal years covered by an authorization of appropriations (its "expiration") does not usually affect the underlying organic authorization, which provides authority to the federal government to engage in the programs or activities to which the authorization of appropriations relates.[14] If appropriations are provided for programs with an expired authorization of appropriations, federal agencies generally would have sufficient legal authority to implement and operate these programs. This is because an authorization of appropriations is "basically a directive to Congress itself, which Congress is free to follow or alter (up or down) in the subsequent appropriation act."[15]

Authorizations of appropriations, however, are significant for the purposes of congressional rules. House and Senate rules require that a purpose must have been "authorized" prior to when discretionary appropriations are provided.[16] While simply establishing an entity, program, or activity in law generally satisfies that authorization requirement, sometimes provisions are enacted that explicitly authorize future appropriations ("authorizations of appropriations"). If the period of time for which an authorization of appropriations has been provided lapses and is not renewed—for example, at the start of FY2010, if the authorization of appropriations ended in FY2009—then subsequent appropriations for those purposes are sometimes described as being

---

[14] There can be exceptions to this rule. For example, from September 30, 2015, to December 18, 2015, ED curtailed the operations of the federal Perkins Loan program. ED took this step because the department considered the authorization of appropriations provision under HEA Section 461(b)(1) to control the duration of the program. ED interpreted this section, along with the automatic one-year extension under the General Education Provisions Act (GEPA) Section 422, to mean that the Perkins Loan program was authorized through September 30, 2015. The program resumed after Congress enacted the Federal Perkins Loan Program Extension Act of 2015 (the Extension Act; P.L. 114-105), which extended ED's authorization to make new Perkins Loans to eligible students through September 30, 2017. See CRS Report R44343, *The Federal Perkins Loan Program Extension Act of 2015: In Brief.*

[15] U.S. Government Accountability Office, "Chapter 2: The Legal Framework," *Principles of Federal Appropriations Law*, GAO-16-464SP, 4th ed., 2016 Revision, p. 2-56, at http://www.gao.gov/legal/redbook/redbook.html.

[16] See the section on "Discretionary and Mandatory Spending (Including Appropriated Mandatory Spending)" for more information about discretionary appropriations.

"unauthorized" from the perspective of House and Senate rules and could be subject to a point of order during floor consideration.[17] However, such points of order are frequently waived.

Discretionary and Mandatory Spending (Including Appropriated Mandatory Spending)

There are two broad categories of budget authority in the federal budget and appropriations process: *discretionary spending* and *mandatory spending*. ED receives both kinds of spending, but there are important distinctions between them that are relevant to understanding both *how* ED receives federal funding and *how much* it receives.

Discretionary spending is budget authority that is provided and controlled by appropriations acts. This spending is for programs and activities that are authorized by law, but the amount of budget authority for those programs and activities is determined through the annual appropriations process. Even if a discretionary spending program has been authorized previously, Congress is not required to provide appropriations for it or to provide appropriations at authorized levels. For example, Section 399 of the Higher Education Act, as amended (HEA), authorized discretionary appropriations of $75 million in FY2010 for the Predominantly Black Institutions (PBIs) program authorized under HEA, Section 318. However, actual discretionary appropriations for the Section 318 PBI program in FY2010 were $10.8 million.

Mandatory spending is budget authority that is controlled by authorizing acts. Such spending includes "entitlements," which are programs that require payments to persons, state or local governments, or other entities if those entities meet specific eligibility criteria established in the authorizing law.[18] This budget authority may be provided through a

---

[17] A point of order is an objection that the pending proposal or proceeding is in violation of House or Senate rules. For further information with regard to these rules, see CRS Report R42098, *Authorization of Appropriations: Procedural and Legal Issues*, pp. 4-8.

[18] Entitlement payments are legal obligations of the federal government, and eligible beneficiaries may have legal recourse if full payment under the law is not provided.

one-step process in which the authorizing act sets the program parameters (usually eligibility criteria and a payment formula) and provides the budget authority for that program. Such funding remains available automatically each year for which it is provided, without the need for further legislative action by Congress. For example, HEA, Section 420R provides mandatory appropriations for Iraq and Afghanistan Service Grants (IASG).

Sometimes, however, the authorizing statute for an entitlement does not include language providing authority to make the payment to fulfill the legal obligation that it creates. Under this approach to mandatory spending, the budget authority is provided in appropriations measures. Such spending is referred to as *appropriated mandatory spending* or an "appropriated entitlement" and occurs through a two-step process. First, authorizing legislation becomes law that sets program parameters (through eligibility requirements and benefit levels, for example), then the appropriations process is used to provide the budget authority needed to finance the commitment.

As with mandatory spending, congressional appropriations committees have limited control over the amount of budget authority provided for appropriated mandatory spending because the amount needed is the result of previously enacted commitments in law. In other words, the authorizing statute for appropriated mandatory spending establishes a legal obligation to make payments (such as an entitlement) and the funding in annual appropriations acts is provided to fulfill that legal financial obligation. Because the cost of appropriated mandatory programs may vary from year to year, the funding that is provided through the annual appropriations process is based on a projection of costs for the relevant fiscal year.

Most ED line items included in regular annual appropriations acts are discretionary. One exception to this is the Vocational Rehabilitation State Grants program, which is appropriated mandatory spending.[19]

---

[19] For more information, see CRS Report R43855, Rehabilitation Act: Vocational Rehabilitation State Grants.

Pell Grants: A Quasi-entitlement?

The Pell Grant program is sometimes referred to as a "quasi-entitlement," because the way that it functions in practice is similar to appropriated mandatory spending. That is to say, the Pell Grant program is "appropriated," but the funds it receives through the annual appropriations process are considered to be discretionary spending because there is no legal obligation to provide them. However, Congress and the President have not frequently exercised the option to reduce award levels or cap the number of recipients—which are variables that factor into the calculation of how much funding the program requires each year—and have generally provided the amount of budget authority (through the annual appropriations process or other means) necessary to fund the formula in the authorizing statute.[20]

302(a) and 302(b) Allocations

The concepts in this section relate to how Congress decides the amount of discretionary and mandatory funding to appropriate each fiscal year, which ultimately impacts how much funding ED is provided. Generally speaking, Congress does not start by estimating the cost of every ED program and adding those amounts to reach a total. What happens instead (typically) is that the House and the Senate agree on a total for *all* federal spending through a budget resolution.[21] That amount is then divided between appropriations and authorizing committees. The appropriations committees then divide their portions among each of their subcommittees. Each subcommittee then determines funding levels for the agencies within its jurisdiction. This is called the 302(a) and 302(b) allocation process.

---

[20] For further information about the Pell Grant program, see CRS Report R45418, *Federal Pell Grant Program of the Higher Education Act: Primer.*

[21] In the absence of agreement on a budget resolution, Congress may employ alternative legislative tools to serve as a substitute for a budget resolution. These substitutes are typically referred to as "deeming resolutions," because they are deemed to serve in place of an annual budget resolution for the purposes of establishing enforceable budget levels for the upcoming fiscal year. For further information, see CRS Report R44296, *Deeming Resolutions: Budget Enforcement in the Absence of a Budget Resolution.*

Department of Education Funding: Key Concepts and FAQ   231

More specifically, the Congressional Budget and Impoundment Control Act of 1974 (CBA)[22] requires that Congress adopt a concurrent resolution on the budget each fiscal year. This budget resolution constitutes a procedural agreement between the House and the Senate that establishes overall budgetary and fiscal policy to be carried out through subsequent legislation. The spending elements of the agreement establish total new budget authority and outlay levels for each fiscal year covered by the resolution. The agreement also allocates federal spending among 20 functional categories (such as national defense; transportation; and education, training, employment, and social services), setting budget authority and outlay levels for each function.

Within each chamber, the total new budget authority and outlays for each fiscal year are also allocated among committees with jurisdiction over spending, thereby setting spending ceilings for each committee. These ceilings are referred to as the *302(a) allocations*.[23] The 302(a) allocation to each of the authorizing committees (such as the Senate Health, Education, Labor and Pensions Committee) establishes spending ceilings on the mandatory spending under each committee's jurisdiction. The 302(a) allocations to the House and the Senate appropriations committees include discretionary spending and also appropriated mandatory spending.

Once the appropriations committees receive their spending ceilings, they separately subdivide the amount among their respective subcommittees, providing spending ceilings for each subcommittee. These spending ceilings are referred to as *302(b) suballocations*.[24] For example, for FY2019 the amount of the initial 302(a) allocation to the House Appropriations Committee was $1.2 trillion for discretionary budget authority and $955 billion for appropriated mandatory budget authority. The appropriations subcommittee that is responsible for funding ED is the Labor, Health and Human Services, Education, and Related Agencies (LHHS) subcommittee. When the committee apportioned that allocation

---

[22] 2 U.S.C. §621 et seq.

[23] This refers to §302(a) of the CBA. Typically, these 302(a) allocations are provided in the joint explanatory statement that accompanies the conference report on the budget resolution.

[24] This refers to §302(b) of the CBA. These 302(b) suballocations are reported by the House and the Senate appropriations committees.

among its 12 subcommittees, the initial suballocation for the LHHS subcommittee was $177 billion for discretionary budget authority and $783 billion for appropriated mandatory budget authority.[25]

The congressional allocations are of budget authority for the upcoming fiscal year. Budget authority enacted in previous fiscal years that first becomes available for obligation in the upcoming fiscal year counts against the congressional allocations for the upcoming fiscal year. (This type of budget authority is referred to as "advance appropriations" and is discussed further in the section ""Carry Forward," Advance Appropriations, and Forward Funding.")

Fiscal Year, Award Year, and Other Units of Time

Department of Education budget, appropriations, and program-related data may be reported using a variety of different "years" or units of time. These units of time include the fiscal year, calendar year, academic or school year, and the award year. Readers are cautioned to remain alert to the unit of time when considering and comparing various funding levels reported for ED activities. To be strictly comparable, the units of time must be the same.

When the federal government accounts for the funds it has budgeted, appropriated, or spent, the unit of time it uses is the *fiscal year* (FY). The federal fiscal year is generally the 12-month period between October 1 and the following September 30. The *current year* is the fiscal year that is in progress; the prior year is the fiscal year immediately preceding the current year. *Outyears* are any future fiscal years beyond the current year. The fiscal year is the standard unit of time used in the congressional

---

[25] The 302(a) allocation for the House Appropriations Committee was entered into the *Congressional Record* by the House Budget Committee Chair pursuant to authority granted by Section 30104 of the Bipartisan Budget Act of 2018 (P.L. 115-123). See "Publication of Budgetary Material," *Congressional Record*, daily edition, vol. 164, part 76 (May 10, 2018), p. H3926. The initial LHHS 302(b) suballocation for FY2019 is in H.Rept. 115-710.

Department of Education Funding: Key Concepts and FAQ   233

appropriations process; most funding levels in appropriations bills and committee documents are reported by fiscal year.[26]

The federal fiscal year differs from the *calendar* year (January 1 to December 31), the typical *academic* or *school* year (fall to spring),[27] and the federal student aid *award* year (July 1 through the following June 30). Annual funding levels reported in ED budget and program-related documents may use one or more of these different units of time. For example, ED's FY2019 congressional budget justification includes both fiscal year and award year funding levels for the Pell Grant program. These funding levels are not strictly comparable.

"Carry Forward," Advance Appropriations, and Forward Funding

Funding for federal programs that is provided in regular appropriations acts is usually available for obligation at the start of the fiscal year and may only be obligated during that fiscal year unless otherwise specified. Budget authority also may be provided for more than one fiscal year ("multiyear") or without fiscal year limitation ("no-year"). (See section on "Authorizations and Appropriations.") In other words, in some cases, budget authority may be obligated over multiple fiscal years or may be available to be obligated indefinitely (until it is exhausted).

The concept of *carry forward* (or *carry over*) applies to budget authority that was enacted and became available in a previous fiscal year and *is still available* for obligation in the next fiscal year. (If a federal agency has not entirely obligated its multi- or no-year budget authority by the end of the fiscal year, any unexpired multiyear budget authority and all remaining no-year budget authority may continue to be available for

---

[26] Funds may also be made available for more than one year ("multiyear" funds) or without fiscal year limitation ("no year" funds). For further information on the appropriations process, see CRS Report R42388, *The Congressional Appropriations Process: An Introduction.*

[27] Schools and colleges follow their own separate fiscal years. A typical fiscal year for an elementary and secondary school is July 1 to June 30. Fiscal years at institutions of higher education tend to vary.

obligation in the next fiscal year.) Such carry forward budget authority is typically notated as "unobligated balances brought forward" in the OMB *Appendix* to the annual budget. For example, the FY2019 OMB *Appendix* reports that budgetary resources available to the Education for the Disadvantaged account in FY2017 included $660 million in unobligated balances brought forward (of $16.805 billion, total).

The concepts of *advance appropriations* and *forward funding* relate to when such funding *first becomes available* to be obligated relative to the timing of its enactment and thus differ significantly from carry forward. With advance appropriations and forward funding, the budget authority becomes available for obligation at a point in time that is delayed beyond the start of the fiscal year.

- *Advance appropriations* become available for obligation starting at least one fiscal year after the budget year.
- Forward funding becomes available beginning late in the budget year and is carried into at least one following fiscal year.

Federal accounts and programs may receive annual appropriations, advance appropriations, forward funding, or a mixed approach. The most common mixed approach used in ED appropriations combines advance appropriations and forward funding.

Figure 1 illustrates the period of availability for annual appropriations, forward funding, and advance appropriations. It also includes an illustration of the default (or typical) period of availability for annual appropriations.[28]

The period of availability for budget authority in ED's accounts does not usually follow a single rule. In a typical appropriations act, some ED accounts and programs will receive annual appropriations (e.g., Indian Education), while others will receive appropriations under a mixed approach including advance appropriations and forward funding (e.g., ESEA Title I). In general, the advance appropriations-forward funding

---

[28] For more information, see CRS Report R43482, Advance Appropriations, Forward Funding, and Advance Funding: Concepts, Practice, and Budget Process Considerations.

Department of Education Funding: Key Concepts and FAQ

combination is used for accounts that provide funds to recipients (such as elementary and secondary schools) who might experience service disruptions if they received funds aligned with the federal fiscal year and not the academic or school year. One advantage of this approach is that it allows schools to obligate funds prior to the start of the school year. It also gives schools time to plan for, and adjust to, changes in federal funding levels.

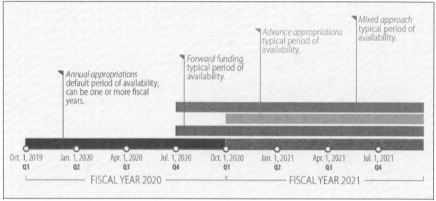

Source: Congressional Research Service (CRS).

Note: Q indicates fiscal quarter. The dark blue line represents the default period of availability for FY2020; the striped dark blue line represents the default period for the following fiscal year (FY2021).

Figure 1. Start of Period of Availability. Annual Appropriations, Forward Funding, Advance Appropriations, and Mixed Approach; Shown in FY2020 and FY2021, by Quarter.

Budget Caps and Sequestration

The Budget Control Act of 2011 (BCA, P.L. 112-25) sought to reduce the federal budget deficit through a variety of budgetary mechanisms, including the establishment of limits (or *caps*) on discretionary spending and automatic spending reductions (known as *sequestration*) for both discretionary and mandatory spending. The BCA only places limits on discretionary spending, and the purpose and triggers for budgetary reductions through sequestration differ significantly between discretionary and mandatory spending. In addition to describing how the BCA operates in light of these key distinctions, the following sections discuss the implications of the BCA for ED.[29]

BCA-Related Budget Control Mechanisms

The BCA imposed statutory limits on discretionary spending for specified fiscal years. (The BCA established no statutory limits on mandatory spending.) The BCA also established procedures to lower the discretionary limits to achieve additional savings.

The BCA requires that sequestration—a largely across-the-board reduction of funding for nonexempt programs and activities—occur under certain circumstances. These circumstances differ for discretionary and mandatory spending.

- Discretionary spending sequestration is to occur when the statutory limits on discretionary spending are breached. The role of sequestration in this context is to reduce nonexempt spending subject to the limit so that it no longer exceeds that limit.
- Mandatory spending sequestration is to occur each fiscal year to achieve specified savings. Sequestration in this context serves as a mechanism to impose across-the-board cuts to nonexempt mandatory spending. It is not triggered by spending levels in those programs or other budgetary factors.

Discretionary Spending Limits

The BCA imposes separate limits on "defense" and "nondefense" discretionary spending each fiscal year from FY2012 to FY2021. The defense category includes all discretionary spending under budget function 050 (defense).[30] The nondefense category includes discretionary spending

---

[29] For more information about the BCA, see CRS Report R42506, The Budget Control Act of 2011 as Amended: Budgetary Effects; and CRS Report R44874, The Budget Control Act: Frequently Asked Questions.

[30] For information on the budget functions, see CRS Report 98-280, *Functional Categories of the Federal Budget.*

Department of Education Funding: Key Concepts and FAQ   237

in all the other budget functions. In general, discretionary budget authority for ED is subject to the nondefense limit.

If discretionary spending is enacted in excess of the statutory limits, enforcement primarily occurs through sequestration, which is the automatic cancelation of budget authority through largely across-the-board reductions of nonexempt programs and activities.[31] The purpose of sequestration is to reduce the level of spending subject to the discretionary spending limit so that it no longer exceeds that limit. Any across-the-board reductions through sequestration affect only nonexempt spending subject to the breached limit, and they are in the amount necessary to reduce spending so that it complies with the limit.

Pursuant to procedures under the BCA, the discretionary spending limits initially established by that act are to be further lowered each fiscal year to achieve certain additional budgetary savings.[32] The amount of the revised limits for the upcoming fiscal year is calculated by OMB and reported with the President's budget submission each year.[33] The timing of this calculation, which occurs many months prior to the beginning of the fiscal year, is intended to allow time for congressional consideration of appropriations measures that comply with the revised limits. Since the enactment of the BCA, however, a series of laws have been enacted that supersede the spending limit level that otherwise would have been established by the OMB calculation. The effect of these laws in most cases has been to increase the limits above what they otherwise would have been. The most recent such law, which increased the spending limits for

---

[31] Procedures for discretionary spending sequestration are provided in the Balanced Budget and Emergency Deficit Control Act of 1985 (BBEDCA), Sections 251 and 256. Exempt programs and activities, including the Pell Grant program, are listed in BBEDCA, Section 255.

[32] The lowering of the limits was triggered when the BCA "joint committee" process did not result in the enactment of legislation to achieve a targeted level of spending reductions. For information on this process, see CRS Report R41965, *The Budget Control Act of 2011*.

[33] The procedures through which these limits are reduced are in Section 251A of the Balanced Budget and Emergency Deficit Control Act of 1985 (BBEDCA). For a description of these procedures and how they were initially carried out for the FY2014 reductions, see OMB Report to Congress on the Joint Committee Reductions for Fiscal Year 2014, pp. 11-16, https://obamawhitehouse.archives.gov/sites/default/files/omb/assets/legislative_reports/fy14 _preview_and_joint_committee_reductions_reports_05202013.pdf.

FY2018 and FY2019, was the Bipartisan Budget Act of 2018 (BBA 2018, P.L. 115-123).[34]

Mandatory Spending Sequestration

In addition to the lowered discretionary spending limits, the BCA provides for reductions to mandatory spending each fiscal year, which are also achieved through sequestration. (Some mandatory spending is exempt from these automatic reductions.) However, mandatory spending sequestration differs from discretionary spending sequestration in that it occurs automatically each fiscal year, and is not triggered by spending levels or other budgetary factors. In other words, mandatory spending sequestration in the BCA context is used as a means to automatically reduce that type of spending each fiscal year on a largely across-the-board basis.

The amount of the reduction to defense and nondefense mandatory spending is calculated by OMB and announced at the same time as the reductions to the statutory discretionary spending limits each fiscal year (with the President's budget submission). Nonexempt mandatory budget authority at ED is subject to the nondefense reduction.

The BCA and ED Funding

The BCA affects funding levels at ED in several ways. In establishing caps on total federal discretionary budget authority—caps which are the basis for the allocations of both total federal spending and the division of that amount to each of the appropriations subcommittees through the 302(a) and 302(b) processes (discussed above)—the BCA can impact total discretionary funding at ED. Further, if those caps are exceeded, ED's discretionary budget authority may be subject to sequestration. Since the BCA has been in effect, a discretionary spending sequestration has only occurred once—in FY2013.[35]

---

[34] For further information, see CRS Insight IN10861, Discretionary Spending Levels Under the Bipartisan Budget Act of 2018.

[35] For the FY2013 sequestration of nondefense discretionary spending, a total reduction of $25.798 billion or 5% of such spending was required. The circumstances that triggered discretionary spending sequestration during FY2013 were somewhat different than the circumstances that

Department of Education Funding: Key Concepts and FAQ   239

For ED programs that receive nonexempt mandatory funding, the BCA requires an annual sequester in an amount calculated by OMB. The dollar amount of the reduction for a particular ED account is based on the percentage by which nonexempt mandatory spending in the nondefense category needs to be cut to achieve the total required savings. For example, in FY2018 mandatory funds in the Rehabilitation Services and Disability Research, Higher Education, TEACH Grant Program, IASG, and Student Financial Assistance Debt Collection accounts were subject to the nondefense mandatory sequestration that was calculated based on a reduction of 6.6%.[36] For FY2019, this reduction is 6.2%.[37]

For both mandatory and discretionary spending sequestration, the dollar amount that is canceled in each account differs depending on the amount of sequesterable budgetary resources in that account. For example, for the FY2013 sequester, OMB calculated that nondefense discretionary spending would need to be reduced by 5%. The English Language Learner account, which had total sequesterable budgetary resources of $737 million, would thus be reduced by $37 million (5% of $737 million). Likewise, Impact Aid had sequesterable budgetary resources of $1.299 billion and was reduced by $65 million (5% of $1.3 billion).

Some ED programs, such as the Pell Grant program, are exempt from sequestration or follow special rules. For example, during periods when a sequestration order is in effect for mandatory spending, the BCA directs that origination fees charged on federal student loans made under the

---

could trigger sequestration in future fiscal years, but the basic principles discussed in this paragraph as to how sequestration would be carried out continue to apply. For further information with regard to the FY2013 sequestration, including the reductions to particular accounts, see OMB Report to the Congress on the Joint Committee Sequestration for Fiscal Year 2013, March 1, 2013, https://obamawhitehouse.archives.gov/sites/default/files/omb/assets/legislative_reports/fy13ombjcsequestrationreport.pdf.

[36] Executive Office of the President, Office of Management and Budget, *OMB Report to the Congress on the Joint Committee Reductions for Fiscal Year 2018*, May 23, 2017, https://www.whitehouse.gov/sites/whitehouse.gov/files/omb/sequestration_reports/2018_jc_sequestration_report_may2017_potus.pdf.

[37] Executive Office of the President, Office of Management and Budget, *OMB Report to the Congress on the Joint Committee Reductions for Fiscal Year 2019*, February 12, 2018, https://www.whitehouse.gov/wp-content/uploads/2018/02/Sequestration_Report_February_2018.pdf.

240   *Kyle D. Shohfi and Jessica Tollestrup*

William D. Ford Federal Direct Loan program must be increased by the nondefense, mandatory sequestration percentage.[38]

Readers are cautioned, when comparing or analyzing funding levels for ED accounts and programs, to assess whether such funding levels reflect pre- or post-sequestration funding levels. Administration and congressional budget and appropriations materials may use pre- or post-sequestration amounts, or both.

Transfer and Reprogramming

Both authorization and appropriations measures may also provide transfer authority. *Transfers* shift budget authority from one account or fund to another or allow agencies to make such shifts. Agencies are prohibited from making transfers between accounts without statutory authority. For example, in FY2019 the appropriations act that funded ED provided that up to 1% of any discretionary budget authority appropriated to the department could be transferred between accounts, subject to certain restrictions.[39]

Agencies may, however, generally shift budget authority from one activity or program to another within an account without additional statutory authority. This is referred to as *reprogramming*. For example, in FY2016 ED shifted $158,336 from the Strengthening Native American-serving Nontribal Institutions program that would have otherwise lapsed to the Fund for the Improvement of Postsecondary Education/First in the World (FIPSE/FITW) program using reprogramming authority.[40] The appropriations subcommittees have established notification and other oversight procedures for various agencies to follow regarding reprogramming actions. Generally, these procedures differ with each

---

[38] For more information, see CRS Report R40122, *Federal Student Loans Made Under the Federal Family Education Loan Program and the William D. Ford Federal Direct Loan Program: Terms and Conditions for Borrowers.*

[39] P.L. 115-245, Division B, Title III, §302.

[40] See Department of Education, "Fiscal Year 2018 Justifications of Appropriations Estimates to the Congress: Volume II," p. R-38, https://www2.ed.gov/about/overview/budget/budget18/justifications/r-highered.pdf.

Department of Education Funding: Key Concepts and FAQ   241

subcommittee. For instance, in FY2019 reprogramming requirements applicable to ED were carried in the appropriations act that funded the department. Those requirements included consultation with the House and the Senate appropriations committees, as well as written notification, ahead of reprogramming actions that met certain criteria.[41]

Formula and Competitive Grants

The Department of Education uses one of two processes to distribute the funds it receives for grant making. It may distribute such funds by mathematical *formula*—usually such formulas are predetermined and established in statute—or through merit-based *competitions*.

ED's Title I, Part A program, for example, is a formula grant program. It provides funding to local educational agencies (through state educational agencies) using various mathematical formulas that consider the number of school-age children in poverty, state average per-pupil expenditures, and similar variables.[42] The Innovative Approaches to Literacy program, on the other hand, is a merit-based competitive grant program. Applicants must meet certain criteria (such as whether they promote science, technology, engineering, and math education) and are awarded points based on how well they meet those criteria. Applicants with the highest weighted scores receive grants.[43]

Block and Categorical Grants

Policy debates about education funding sometimes focus on whether funds ought to be provided through *block grants* or *categorical grants*.[44]

---

[41] P.L. 115-245, Division B, Title III, §5.

[42] See CRS Report R44164, *ESEA Title I-A Formulas: In Brief.*

[43] More information about the Innovative Approaches to Literacy Program is available at https://www2.ed.gov/ programs/innovapproaches-literacy/index.html.

[44] For more information about block and categorical grants (in general), see CRS Report R40486, *Block Grants: Perspectives and Controversies.*

Block grants are general or multipurpose grants that, in the federal education context, are typically awarded to states through a formula-based process. Block grant funding may be used for a wide variety of purposes. Awardees (not federal officials) determine how to use such funds within a broad set of options. For example, the Elementary and Secondary Education Act, as amended by ESSA (P.L. 114-95), authorized a new block grant program at ED called "Student Support and Academic Enrichment Grants." Formula funding provided through this block grant could serve a variety of purposes. Such purposes include providing all students with access to a well-rounded education, improving school conditions for student learning, and improving the use of technology in order to improve the academic achievement and digital learning of all students.[45]

Categorical grants, on the other hand, are typically available for a more narrow and defined set of purposes or program activities. They may be distributed by formula or competition. ED's Carol M. White Physical Education program, which provides funds to schools and community-based organizations to initiate, expand, or enhance physical education programs, is an example of a competitively awarded categorical grant. (ESSA incorporated this program into the Student Support and Academic Enrichment block grant.)

Matching Funds or Requirements

Some federal grants include what are known as *matching* requirements. In such scenarios, federal funds or assistance are granted to awardees who are willing and able to "match" federal funds with a nonfederal contribution (such as funding from state government or private sources). This nonfederal contribution is called the "nonfederal share." Typically, matching fund requirements specify that the nonfederal share must meet or exceed a certain percentage of the federal award amount

---

[45] CRS In Focus IF10333, *The Every Student Succeeds Act (ESSA) and ESEA Reauthorization: Summary of Selected Key Issues.*

Department of Education Funding: Key Concepts and FAQ   243

(such as 20% or 50%). Depending on the grant requirements, nonfederal matching contributions may be in cash or what is known as "in-kind" (such as computer equipment or staff time), or a combination of the two. For example, the maximum federal share of compensation in the Federal Work-Study program (which provides funding to support part-time employment of needy college and university students) is 75% (with certain exceptions). Institutions participating in the Work-Study program are required to provide the remaining 25%.[46]

FREQUENTLY ASKED QUESTIONS

The following section includes frequently asked questions about the budget and appropriations process for ED (and closely related topics).

How Much Funding Does the Department of Education Receive Annually?

ED's annual budget includes two types of spending: discretionary and mandatory. In FY2019, ED received approximately $71 billion in budget authority through the annual discretionary appropriations process.[47] About three-quarters of these funds ($52 billion) were distributed to local educational agencies to provide supplementary educational and related services for disadvantaged and disabled children or to low-income postsecondary students (in the form of Pell Grants, which provide financial assistance for college).[48]

---

[46] The required match in the Federal Work-Study program can be as high as one-half of the federal share or as low as zero, depending on the type of employment. For more information, see CRS Report RL31618, *Campus-Based Student Financial Aid Programs Under the Higher Education Act.*

[47] This amount includes only funds appropriated to the department through the annual appropriations process.

[48] For more information on these programs, see CRS Report RL31618, *Campus-Based Student Financial Aid Programs Under the Higher Education Act*; and CRS Report R41833, *The*

244   *Kyle D. Shohfi and Jessica Tollestrup*

ED also has programs that receive mandatory funding directly through their authorizing statutes. These programs received about $2.5 billion in net funding in FY2019. However, most of ED's mandatory funding is for student loan subsidies. In some years, the net cost of student loan subsidies is positive (i.e., there is a cost to the government for providing the subsidy); in other years the net cost of student loan subsidies is negative (i.e., the government received fees and other receipts in excess of subsidy costs).[49] Because of this dynamic, ED's "total" budget can vary widely from year to year. (See *Table 1.*)

Table 1. Discretionary, Mandatory, and Total ED Appropriations: FY2015 to FY2019 (In thousands, rounded)

	FY2015	FY2016	FY2017	FY2018	FY2019
Discretionary	67,135,576	68,306,763	68,239,156	70,867,406	71,448,416
Mandatory (net)	20,377,890	8,772,739	47,802,686	(692,311)	2,555,285
Total	87,513,466	77,079,502	116,041,842	70,175,095	74,003,701

Source: Mandatory spending levels for all years and discretionary spending levels for FY2015-FY2017 are from U.S. Department of Education, Budget Tables, "President's Budget Request," FY2017-FY2019. Discretionary spending levels for FY2018 and FY2019 are from U.S. Department of Education, Budget Tables, "FY2019 Congressional Action," October 9, 2019, https://www2.ed.gov/about/ overview/budget/budget19/19action.pdf.

Notes: Numbers in parentheses are negative numbers. Mandatory funding levels in Table 1 represent net cost (including both gains and expenditures). Mandatory funding levels for FY2018 and FY2019 are estimates. Discretionary funding for FY2019 is current as of the date of this chapter.

How Much Does the Federal Government Spend on Education?

In short, the answer depends on what federal accounts or activities are defined as "education spending," on the point in the fiscal year when

---

Individuals with Disabilities Education Act (IDEA), Part B: Key Statutory and Regulatory Provisions.

[49] The costs of student loan and other federal credit program subsidies are calculated in accordance with the Federal Credit Reform Act of 1990 (FCRA). For a comparison of the FCRA accounting method and the alternative fair-value method, see CRS Report R44193, *Federal Credit Programs: Comparing Fair Value and the Federal Credit Reform Act (FCRA).*

budget authority is estimated, and which federal agency is reporting. Any aggregation of federal funding provided for educational purposes across agencies or accounts requires judgements about which activities should be counted (in whole or in part) and about how such activities should be grouped (e.g., higher education, K-12, etc.). Moreover, any such exercise may be limited by the granularity of information available about the use of the funds. Complicating the situation is the fact that federal funding for education overlaps with (but is not the same as) funding for ED.

The following sections explore and describe two commonly referenced ways that the federal government accounts for the funds it spends on education: by Treasury Department function code and as calculated and tracked in ED's *Digest of Education Statistics*.

Function 500

The Treasury Department classifies all federal funding according to certain numbered functions (e.g., Health (550) and Transportation (400)) and by numbered subfunctions (e.g., Health Care Services (551) and Health Research and Training (552)). The Congressional Budget Office (CBO), Office of Management and Budget (OMB), and congressional budget process also use this same taxonomy.

Federal education funding is included in function 500 (Education, Training, Employment, and Social Services). Within function 500, subfunction 501 includes elementary, secondary, and vocational education; and subfunction 502 includes higher education. While these are two of the primary areas in which federal education funding is concentrated, simply adding the totals for these two subfunctions does not capture all federal funding for education. For example, other subfunctions, such as 503 (research and general education aids) and 504 (training and employment), could be considered federal education spending as well. Additionally, subfunction 506 (social services) includes ED's Rehabilitation Services and Disability Research Account.

246   *Kyle D. Shohfi and Jessica Tollestrup*

Furthermore, only a portion of total outlays for subfunctions 501 and 502 were spent by ED, and not all ED funding is classified as function 500. For example, other agencies (such as the National Science Foundation and National Institutes of Health) provide federal funds for educational programs and activities that may be captured in the totals for subfunctions 501 and 502. In addition, some ED programs and activities are classified under other functional categories, such as the Office for Civil Rights (subfunction 751, federal law enforcement activities).

Digest of Education Statistics

ED's National Center for Education Statistics (NCES) tracks federal funding for education and related activities in the periodically updated *Digest of Education Statistics* (*Digest*). Funding data in *Digest* tables may represent appropriations or outlays. Major *Digest* federal education funding tables present data on federal support for education broken down by program, agency, state, education level, and other facets.[50]

As per Table 401.10, "Federal support and estimated federal tax expenditures for education, by category," the federal government provided $228.4 billion in direct budget authority (measured primarily as outlays, but sometimes as obligations) for education (broadly defined to include research grants to universities) in FY2017. If nonfederal funds generated by federal legislation are included, the amount was $322.6 billion.

Where Can Information Be Found About the President's Budget Request and Congressional Appropriations for the Department of Education?

The ED congressional budget justifications, which provide details about the President's budget request for the department, are published on the department's website.[51]

---

[50] These tables may be found at http://nces.ed.gov/programs/digest/current_tables.asp.
[51] Available at http://www2.ed.gov/about/overview/budget/index.html.

Department of Education Funding: Key Concepts and FAQ 247

Appropriations for many (but not all) ED accounts are typically included in annual Departments of Labor, Health and Human Services, and Education, and Related Agencies appropriations acts. The Congressional Research Service (CRS) tracks these acts—including related bills and committee reports—each year.[52]

How Much ED Funding Is in the Congressional Budget Resolution?

As discussed in the "302(a) and 302(b) Allocations" section of this chapter, the budget resolution sets procedural parameters for the consideration of mandatory and discretionary spending legislation; those parameters are enforceable by points of order. The budget resolution does not provide actual funding for ED or any other purpose.

While the procedural parameters in the budget resolution do involve underlying assumptions about levels of funding for particular purposes, there are two general reasons why the amount of funding assumed for ED (or education-related purposes) in the annual congressional budget resolution cannot be determined by CRS. First, the procedural parameters in the budget resolution allocate funding by congressional committee and not by department. Because the jurisdiction of the relevant authorizing committees and appropriations subcommittees encompasses more than ED, it is not possible to determine the assumed amount of funding for ED through those allocations. Second, although the basis of those authorizing committee and appropriations subcommittee allocations is a distribution of funding based on "functional categories," those functional categories do not neatly correspond to ED or education-related purposes. (Functional categories are discussed in the section "How much does the federal government spend on education?") As a result, absent specific information with regard to the budget resolution from the House or the Senate budget committees, it is not possible for CRS to determine amounts of funding for

---

[52] See the "Appropriations Status Table" on CRS.gov, http://www.crs.gov/AppropriationsStatus Table/Index.

248 Kyle D. Shohfi and Jessica Tollestrup

ED or education-related purposes that are assumed by the budget resolution.

What Is the Difference Between the Amounts in Appropriations Bills and Report Language?

The answer to this question centers on the force of law. Funding levels included in House and Senate appropriations *bills* are proposed until enacted. That is to say, until an appropriations bill is signed by the President (i.e., it is enacted), the funding levels included therein simply represent what each appropriations committee or subcommittee—or if the bill has passed the House or the Senate, that chamber—proposes to appropriate for the various programs and agencies included in that bill. Once Congress and the President enact an appropriations measure, the funding levels included in that *act* are statutorily established and provide a legal basis for agencies to obligate and expend that funding. Appropriations acts, therefore, carry the force of law.

Funding levels and program directives included in House and Senate appropriations *committee reports* are committee recommendations and are not usually legally binding. (In some cases, report language is enacted by reference in the appropriations act that it accompanies, giving it statutory effect.)[53] However, while report language itself generally is not law, agencies usually seek to comply with it because it represents congressional intent.

Typically, report language is used to supplement legislative text at either of two stages in the congressional appropriations process. First, as noted, reports may accompany annual appropriations bills reported by the House or the Senate appropriations committees. If these committee reports differ with respect to a particular funding level or program directive (e.g., the House Appropriations Committee report recommends setting the

---

[53] For further information about appropriations report language, see CRS Report R44124, *Appropriations Report Language: Overview of Development, Components, and Issues for Congress.*

Department of Education Funding: Key Concepts and FAQ 249

maximum discretionary portion of Pell Grants at \$5,035 and the Senate report recommends setting it at \$5,135), a *joint explanatory statement* (JES) may be used to reconcile conflicting language and also provide additional instructions. (The JES is sometimes referred to colloquially as a *conference report*, though from a technical standpoint, it is not. The JES accompanies the conference report, which contains only legislative text.)[54]

For appropriations measures that are not reported from an appropriations committee but still receive congressional consideration—or when differences are resolved through an amendment exchange and not a conference committee process—an *explanatory statement* from an appropriations committee is sometimes entered into the *Congressional Record*. This language may be regarded similarly to report language. When this text is used during the resolving differences phase of the legislative process, such statements can serve the same purposes and function as a JES.

What Happens to Education Funding If Annual Appropriations Are Not Enacted Before the Start of the Federal Fiscal Year?

It depends. First, Congress and the President may provide partial-year funding through a temporary appropriations law, often referred to as a "continuing resolution" (CR), while they negotiate agreement on annual appropriations that have yet to be enacted. CRs typically (but not always) provide appropriations at a rate based on the previous fiscal year's appropriations acts and for the same purposes as those provided in the previous fiscal year. (Adjustments in funding levels or allowable activities must be specified in the CR.) The typical effect, then, of providing federal education funding through a continuing resolution is that planned or proposed changes to federal education programs may not occur or may be

---

[54] A conference report contains the formal legislative language on which the conference committee has agreed. A JES explains the various elements of the conferees' agreement. For further information, see CRS Report 98-382, Conference Reports and Joint Explanatory Statements.

delayed.[55] In addition, while a CR is in effect, ED makes limited obligations until budget authority for the entire fiscal year is enacted.

If appropriations actually lapse, the effects of that lapse—including whether a shutdown of agency operations commences—will depend on a variety of factors. Several factors that might mitigate the effects of a lapse include

- the extent to which unexpired budget authority is available for ED to obligate during the period of the lapse (generally, such funding would be multiyear or no-year budget authority enacted in prior fiscal years, including as forward funds or advance appropriations);
- the extent to which ED staff who would regularly administer programs or funds are furloughed as a consequence of the lapse;
- the timing of the grant cycle for individual grant programs and the type of funds that are typically awarded and distributed; and
- the availability of alternative sources of funding that can be used (temporarily or on an ongoing basis) to sustain supported activities.[56]

What Happens If an ED Program Authorization "Expires"?

As discussed in the sections titled "Authorizations and Appropriations" and "Authorization of Appropriations" most of ED's enabling or organic program authorizations are permanent. Therefore, unless the program's enabling authorization specifically includes a sunset provision, or Congress and the President enact legislation repealing the enabling authorization, the program can continue so long as Congress continues to fund it through the appropriations process.

---

[55] For further information on CRs, see CRS Report R42647, Continuing Resolutions: Overview of Components and Recent Practices.

[56] For further information on funding lapses and government shutdowns, including a discussion of some of the factors listed in this report, see CRS Report RL34680, Shutdown of the Federal Government: Causes, Processes, and Effects.

Department of Education Funding: Key Concepts and FAQ 251

This remains true, in general (but not always), even if the program's authorization of appropriations has expired and the GEPA extension has lapsed. (See text box titled, "GEPA and Appropriations Authorizations at ED.") This is because an authorization of appropriations is a directive from Congress to itself and does not typically function as a sunset provision for the program or purpose to which it relates. An expired authorization of appropriations may, however, lead to a point of order during floor consideration against an appropriations measure or amendment under certain circumstances. They are, therefore, significant from the perspective of congressional procedure.

INDEX

A

academic plans, ix, 87
academic progress, 95, 205
accreditation, 8, 92, 181, 184, 185, 188, 195, 196, 197, 198, 199, 200, 201, 202
affirmative action, v, vii, viii, 1, 2, 3, 4, 5, 33, 34, 36, 38, 39, 41, 42, 43, 45, 48, 51, 52, 53, 54, 56, 59, 61, 64, 67, 68
affirmative obligation, vii, 1, 5, 11, 16, 28, 29, 32, 33, 61, 67
after school settings, xi, 129
age, 79, 82, 136, 139, 140, 157, 160, 163, 184, 187, 241
agencies, viii, ix, xiii, 2, 62, 63, 64, 66, 71, 72, 75, 92, 93, 103, 114, 122, 134, 142, 147, 164, 171, 172, 173, 181, 195, 196, 198, 199, 200, 201, 202, 217, 218, 219, 220, 223, 224, 225, 227, 230, 240, 241, 243, 245, 246, 248
appropriations, ix, xi, xii, xiii, xiv, 22, 24, 72, 85, 130, 135, 138, 159, 167, 169, 171, 172, 217, 218, 219, 220, 222, 223, 224, 225, 226, 227, 228, 229, 230, 231, 232, 233, 234, 235, 237, 238, 240, 243, 244, 246, 247, 248, 249, 250, 251

authorizations, xiv, 218, 222, 223, 224, 226, 227, 233, 250, 251
authorized programs, 222

B

benefits, ix, xi, 4, 6, 37, 40, 42, 47, 49, 50, 51, 52, 62, 71, 72, 73, 74, 75, 76, 78, 79, 80, 81, 82, 83, 84, 85, 88, 89, 91, 97, 101, 104, 106, 112, 114, 116, 117, 118, 120, 123, 124, 125, 126, 132, 134, 146, 166, 186, 210
benign, viii, 2, 4, 33, 34, 36, 38, 39, 40, 42
borrower defense to repayment (BDR), x, 88, 89, 97, 98, 103, 104, 105, 106, 107, 108, 109, 110, 111, 112, 113, 114, 119, 121
borrowers, x, xi, 88, 89, 91, 97, 99, 101, 103, 104, 106, 107, 108, 109, 110, 111, 112, 114, 115, 119, 120, 121, 122, 125, 126, 205
budget deficit, 235
budget resolution, 230, 231, 247
budgetary allocations, xiv, 218
budgetary resources, 234, 239

254 *Index*

C

cash, ix, xi, 71, 72, 120, 130, 131, 137, 140, 146, 154, 155, 158, 163, 164, 165, 203, 243

cash benefits, ix, 71, 72

checks and balances, 204

Child and Adult Care Food Program (CACFP), xi, xii, 129, 130, 131, 133, 134, 136, 137, 139, 140, 145, 155, 157, 158, 159, 160, 161, 162, 163, 164, 170, 171, 174, 176, 177

child nutrition programs, v, xi, xii, 129, 130, 131, 132, 133, 135, 136, 137, 138, 139, 145, 152, 157, 160, 167, 170, 171, 172

children, ix, xi, 10, 27, 71, 72, 78, 79, 80, 82, 129, 130, 131, 132, 134, 136, 137, 138, 139, 140, 141, 143, 144, 145, 146, 147, 150, 153, 154, 155, 156, 157, 158, 160, 161, 162, 163, 164, 165, 166, 167, 168, 170, 171, 172, 221, 224, 241, 243

claimants, ix, 72

classes, viii, x, 2, 3, 46, 48, 88, 118, 215

closed school discharge, x, 88, 98, 100, 101, 102, 114, 115, 119, 121

closed school loan discharge, x, 88, 97, 99, 100, 101, 102, 103, 119

closure, ix, x, 16, 17, 18, 87, 88, 90, 91, 92, 96, 97, 99, 101, 102, 103, 114, 116, 117, 118, 120, 121, 123, 124, 126

colleges, viii, 2, 4, 5, 7, 9, 14, 18, 25, 33, 44, 61, 63, 67, 68, 164, 198, 233

commodity, xi, 130, 131, 133, 137, 140, 154, 156, 157, 158, 159, 163, 164, 165, 171, 176, 177

communication, 23, 92, 98, 108, 109

compensation, 74, 78, 81, 209, 210, 211, 243

compliance, ix, xiii, 2, 7, 26, 63, 64, 67, 136, 141, 173, 180, 195, 203, 207

Congress, ix, xii, 39, 62, 64, 65, 66, 69, 72, 85, 130, 133, 134, 135, 149, 152, 167, 170, 215, 223, 225, 226, 227, 228, 229, 230, 231, 237, 239, 240, 248, 249, 250, 251

congressional budget, xiv, 218, 222, 233, 240, 245, 246, 247

Constitution, 6, 7, 16, 38, 39, 41

constitutional challenges, 38

constitutional law, 34, 61

consumer protection, xiii, 180, 181, 195

cost, 72, 77, 81, 83, 93, 113, 115, 138, 143, 165, 166, 178, 229, 230, 244

cost of living, 72, 77, 83

credit history, 99, 103, 114

credit transfers, x, 88, 94

D

day care, xi, 129, 131, 133, 134, 136, 139, 157, 158, 159, 160, 161, 162, 163, 177

debts, 118, 203

deduction, 123, 125, 126

denials of benefits, ix, 72

Department of Defense, 224

Department of Education (ED), vi, xiii, xiv, 5, 62, 63, 64, 66, 89, 90, 91, 93, 96, 97, 98, 99, 100, 101, 102, 103, 104, 105, 106, 107, 108, 109, 110, 111, 112, 113, 114, 115, 116, 119, 180, 181, 182, 183, 184, 185, 186, 187, 190, 191, 192, 193, 195, 196, 197, 198, 199, 200, 201, 202, 203, 204, 205, 206, 207, 208, 209, 210, 211, 213, 215, 216, 217, 218, 219, 220, 221, 222, 223, 225, 226, 227, 228, 229, 230, 231, 232, 233, 234, 236, 237, 238, 239, 240, 241, 242, 243, 244, 245, 246, 247, 250, 251

Department of Justice (DOJ), ix, 3, 4, 33, 59, 62, 63, 64, 66, 67, 72, 73, 79, 84, 85

Index

Department of Veterans Affairs, xi, 83, 88, 89, 117, 118
Direct Subsidized Loans, x, 88, 118, 119
Direct Unsubsidized Loans, x, 88
disability, ix, 72, 73, 76, 77, 78, 79, 80, 81, 82, 84, 85, 108, 121
discretionary spending caps, xiv, 218
discrimination, viii, 2, 3, 4, 5, 16, 25, 26, 28, 29, 31, 33, 35, 36, 37, 38, 39, 41, 44, 47, 59, 61, 62, 63, 64, 66, 69
distance education, 182, 187, 197, 209, 214, 216
diversity, 4, 19, 33, 42, 43, 44, 45, 46, 47, 48, 49, 50, 51, 52, 53, 55, 57, 60, 61, 68

E

earnings, 183, 191, 192, 193, 194, 195
education, vii, ix, x, xii, xiii, xiv, 1, 3, 4, 6, 8, 9, 26, 27, 28, 33, 61, 63, 67, 71, 72, 82, 83, 87, 88, 89, 90, 91, 93, 94, 95, 96, 97, 100, 113, 115, 116, 117, 118, 120, 121, 123, 124, 125, 126, 134, 142, 172, 173, 179, 180, 181, 184, 187, 191, 192, 195, 197,201, 202, 204, 212, 214, 215, 216, 218, 219, 224, 226, 231, 241, 244, 245, 246, 247, 249
education loans, x, 88, 115, 121, 192, 210
educational institutions, 183, 184, 185
educational objective, 17
educational opportunities, 9
educational policy, 4, 13, 16, 17
educational practices, 15, 16
educational programs, xiii, 62, 66, 90, 93, 94, 105, 180, 182, 183, 191, 192, 196, 199, 205, 207, 246
educational pursuits, 90, 95
educational qualifications, 6
educational services, x, 88, 97, 103, 105
elementary school, xi, 30, 130, 140, 163

eligibility criteria, xi, 118, 130, 135, 143, 163, 170, 181, 182, 185, 187, 228
emergency, ix, 71, 72, 73, 75, 77, 91, 157, 207, 208
emergency management, ix, 71, 72, 73, 75
emergency management agencies, ix, 71, 72, 75
employees, ix, 71, 72, 75, 78, 200, 205, 211, 212
employment, xiii, 24, 179, 184, 185, 188, 189, 190, 191, 192, 193, 194, 195, 200, 231, 243, 245
employment programs, 191, 194, 195
enforcement, 19, 62, 63, 64, 67, 68, 69, 74, 212, 237, 246
enrollment, xi, 14, 24, 36, 88, 105, 116, 117, 190, 191, 194, 211, 213
environment, 55, 57, 152, 172
equal protection, v, vii, viii, 1, 2, 3, 5, 6, 7, 8, 9, 10, 14, 15, 16, 19, 22, 25, 26, 28, 32, 33, 34, 35, 37, 38, 39, 41, 42, 46, 48, 49, 52, 53, 59, 61, 62, 65, 66, 67, 68
Equal Protection Clause, vii, viii, 1, 2, 5, 6, 7, 8, 15, 16, 19, 25, 26, 28, 32, 33, 35, 37, 38, 39, 42, 46, 48, 49, 52, 53, 59, 61, 62, 65, 66, 67, 68
evidence, 10, 13, 20, 21, 22, 24, 27, 28, 29, 30, 31, 37, 58, 69, 77, 108, 109, 111, 196, 212
exclusion, viii, 2, 33, 68, 69, 123, 126
executive branch, 62, 64
expenditures, 135, 159, 168, 173, 220, 241, 244, 246

F

families, 138, 144, 150, 160, 161
family income, 144, 161, 165, 168
federal agency, 190, 205, 208, 233, 245
federal aid, 22, 136, 158, 198
federal assistance, 158, 161

Index

federal court, vii, viii, 1, 2, 3, 4, 9, 21, 27, 30, 32, 41, 64, 68, 105, 122

Federal Emergency Management Agency, 75

federal funds, 5, 22, 37, 38, 63, 65, 157, 208, 220, 221, 224, 226, 242, 246

federal government, xii, xiv, 3, 5, 25, 67, 74, 81, 119, 130, 134, 181, 195, 196, 197, 198, 200, 218, 220, 222, 226, 227, 228, 232, 245, 246, 247

federal law, xi, 22, 38, 78, 130, 147, 220, 246

Federal Register, 79, 98, 102, 104, 105, 106, 108, 145, 149, 150, 151, 152, 154, 160, 163, 173, 174, 175, 176, 177, 191, 192, 197, 208, 215, 216

federal regulations, 145, 201

Federal Student Aid, 96, 99, 100, 108, 119, 180, 181, 184, 196, 203, 210, 215

federal student loans, x, 88, 91, 97, 99, 101, 115, 119, 121, 186, 239, 240

financial, x, xii, 5, 37, 62, 63, 67, 82, 88, 90, 95, 96, 105, 110, 111, 113, 118, 131, 135, 143, 163, 164, 179, 180, 193, 202, 203, 204, 206, 207, 210, 211, 220, 229, 243

financial condition, 206

financial relief, 90, 113

financial support, 131, 143

firefighters, ix, 71, 72, 74, 78

fiscal policy, 231

fiscal year, xiv, 154, 155, 156, 163, 169, 172, 203, 205, 206, 218, 220, 221, 222, 223, 225, 226, 227, 229, 230, 231, 232, 233, 234, 235, 236, 237, 238, 239, 244, 249, 250

Fisher v. University of Texa, viii, 2, 40, 43, 49

food, xi, xii, 129, 130, 131, 132, 133, 137, 139, 142, 144, 154, 155, 156, 157, 158, 159, 160, 164, 165, 166, 167, 170, 173, 175, 176

food support, xi, 130, 169

Fourteenth Amendment, vii, viii, 1, 2, 3, 5, 6, 9, 14, 35, 38, 59, 61, 64

free meals, xi, 130, 143, 144, 145, 146, 149, 150, 155, 161, 171

Fresh Fruit and Vegetable Program (FFVP), xi, 130, 131, 133, 138, 140, 159, 168, 169, 170, 174

fruit and vegetable snacks, xi, 130, 140, 168

funding, viii, ix, xi, xii, xiv, 2, 15, 19, 20, 22, 23, 32, 62, 63, 66, 72, 85, 130, 131, 132, 135, 137, 138, 139, 140, 141, 143, 144, 145, 150, 151, 153, 155, 156, 158, 159, 167, 168, 169, 171, 172, 173, 177, 218, 219, 220, 222, 223, 225, 226, 228, 229, 230, 231, 232, 233, 234, 236, 238, 239, 240, 241, 242, 244, 245, 246, 247, 248, 249, 250

funds, xi, xiii, 22, 23, 24, 39, 63, 64, 65, 72, 85, 89, 95, 96, 97, 103, 119, 120, 122, 127, 130, 135, 137, 154, 162, 163, 168, 169, 180, 182, 183, 187, 203, 204, 205, 208, 209, 210, 213, 215, 217, 218, 219, 220, 221, 230, 232, 233, 235, 239, 241, 242, 243, 245, 246, 250

G

GI Bill educational benefits, xi, 88, 97

graduate students, 95

grant programs, 250

grants, xiv, 20, 22, 62, 85, 102, 117, 147, 168, 171, 172, 181, 217, 219, 220, 241, 242, 246

guidance, 3, 25, 30, 53, 62, 66, 121, 122, 125, 126, 145

guidelines, xii, 36, 130, 136, 144, 145, 152, 153, 160, 161, 175

Index

H

health, 44, 76, 134, 160, 165, 166
high school, 25, 48, 49, 56, 79, 153, 156,
 163, 184, 187
high school diploma, 184, 187
higher education, v, vii, viii, ix, x, xii, 1, 2,
 3, 4, 5, 6, 7, 9, 10, 11, 12, 13, 18, 19, 20,
 21, 25, 26, 27, 28, 31, 32, 33, 38, 40, 41,
 42, 44, 45, 52, 60, 61, 63, 67, 68, 79, 82,
 83, 84, 87, 88, 89, 91, 98, 104, 105, 106,
 114, 123, 124, 179, 180, 183, 184, 185,
 186, 188, 197, 198, 199, 211, 214, 223,
 228, 230, 233, 239, 243, 245
Higher Education Act, x, xii, 83, 84, 88, 89,
 90, 179, 180, 228, 230, 243
higher-education assistance, ix, 71, 72
history, 18, 19, 20, 39, 41, 53, 64, 68, 99,
 104, 132, 133, 141, 198
homes, 134, 136, 137, 139, 141, 157, 158,
 159, 160, 162, 163, 170, 177
House, 133, 170, 210, 223, 224, 227, 228,
 230, 231, 232, 241, 247, 248
House of Representatives, 210
household income, 143, 144, 161, 163, 165,
 170

I

income, xi, xii, 78, 89, 91, 120, 121, 122,
 123, 124, 126, 130, 132, 137, 141, 143,
 144, 145, 146, 149, 160, 161, 162, 163,
 168, 169, 170, 192, 193, 203, 243
income tax, xi, 78, 89, 91, 120, 121, 124,
 126
individuals, 40, 59, 64, 79, 97, 110, 114,
 116, 117, 120, 132, 184, 187, 190, 191,
 201, 210, 215
inflation, 137, 154, 161, 169, 174, 175, 208
injury, 76, 77, 78, 79, 81, 82

institution of higher education (IHE), ix, x,
 xiii, 82, 87, 88, 89, 90, 91, 92, 93, 94, 95,
 96, 97, 99, 100, 101, 102, 103, 104, 105,
 106, 108, 109, 110, 111, 112, 113, 115,
 118, 120, 121, 179, 180, 181, 182, 183,
 184, 185, 186, 187, 188, 191, 192, 193,
 194, 195, 196, 197, 198, 199, 200,
 201,202, 203, 204, 205, 206, 207, 208,
 209, 210, 211, 212, 213, 214, 215, 216
institutional settings, xi, xii, 129, 130, 132,
 138
institutions, viii, ix, xii, xiii, 2, 4, 6, 7, 11,
 13, 14, 16, 17, 18, 19, 20, 21, 22, 24, 26,
 32, 33, 63, 68, 89, 94, 116, 131, 134,
 141, 153, 157, 158, 161, 164, 167, 168,
 179, 180, 182, 183, 184, 186, 187, 188,
 189, 191, 192, 196, 197, 198, 199, 200,
 201, 205, 207,214, 215, 233
instructional materials, 214, 215
instructional time, 188, 189
insurance policy, 79, 80
intellectual disabilities, 190, 191

J

jurisdiction, 3, 10, 78, 133, 173, 223, 224,
 230, 231, 247
justification, 7, 13, 14, 16, 18, 47, 60, 159,
 233

L

law enforcement, ix, 71, 72, 73, 74, 78, 212
law enforcement officers, ix, 71, 72, 78
leadership development, 18
legislation, 35, 85, 224, 226, 229, 231, 237,
 246, 247, 250
line of duty, ix, 71, 72, 76, 77
loan guarantees, xiv, 217, 219
loans, x, xi, xiv, 88, 89, 90, 91, 95, 96, 97,
 99, 100, 101, 102, 103, 104, 105, 106,

107, 108, 109, 110, 111, 112, 113, 115, 118, 119, 120, 121, 122, 123, 125, 181, 186, 192, 194, 206, 210, 213, 217, 219, 239
local authorities, 10
local government, 74, 164, 228

M

medical, ix, 36, 71, 72, 73, 75, 80, 186, 199
minority students, 9, 46, 47, 53, 66

N

National Institutes of Health, 246
National School Lunch Program (NSLP), xi, xii, 129, 130, 131, 132, 133, 134, 136, 137, 139, 140, 141, 143, 144, 145, 149, 150, 152, 153, 154, 155, 156, 158, 159, 160, 161, 164, 166, 170, 173, 174, 175, 176
neutral, 12, 15, 19, 26, 28, 29, 30, 32, 42, 51, 58, 60
next generation, 61
nonprofit organizations, 164, 166
nutrition, xi, xii, 129, 130, 131, 132, 133, 134, 135, 136, 137, 138, 141, 147, 151, 152, 153, 154, 157, 160, 161, 164, 166, 167, 169, 170, 171, 172, 173, 175

O

occupation, xiii, 179, 184, 185, 188, 189, 190, 191, 192, 194
Office of Justice Programs, 73
Office of Management and Budget, 220, 221, 239, 245
operations, viii, xii, 2, 11, 90, 91, 92, 93, 101, 130, 173, 182, 199, 227, 250

oversight, xiii, 66, 171, 172, 180, 182, 195, 240

P

participants, 62, 116, 117, 147, 160, 161, 163
Pell Grant, x, 88, 91, 97, 115, 116, 118, 124, 206, 207, 213, 225, 230, 233, 237, 239, 243, 249
personal finances, ix, 87
personal injuries, ix, 71, 72
physical activity, 77, 172
physical education, 242
policy, viii, 2, 4, 5, 6, 8, 12, 13, 14, 15, 16, 20, 24, 26, 27, 28, 29, 30, 31, 32, 36, 37, 38, 41, 43, 44, 45, 46, 48, 49, 50, 51, 52, 53, 54, 55, 56, 57, 58, 59, 61, 68, 69, 96, 136, 145, 147, 164, 171, 211, 212
postsecondary education, ix, x, xii, xiii, 87, 88, 89, 90, 91, 93, 94, 96, 97, 115, 125, 179, 180, 181, 183, 184, 187, 195, 196, 197, 201, 214, 240
post-traumatic stress disorder, 76
precedent, vii, 2, 10, 12, 25, 28, 45, 46, 53
private education, x, 88, 115, 121, 192, 210
private schools, 134, 141
private sector, 104, 108
profit, 90, 157, 160, 181, 210
program administration, 182
project, 146, 147, 164, 169, 221
protection, vii, viii, 1, 2, 3, 5, 8, 9, 10, 14, 22, 34, 35, 37, 41, 65, 110
PSOB death benefits, ix, 72, 73, 78, 79, 85
PSOB disability benefits, ix, 72, 73, 80, 85
PSOEA benefits, ix, 72, 73, 82, 83, 84, 85
public education, vii, 1, 5, 6, 7, 8, 10, 27, 28, 29
public education systems, vii, 1
public officials, 28

Index

259

public safety, ix, 71, 72, 73, 76, 77, 78, 79, 80, 82
public safety officers, v, ix, 71, 72, 73, 79, 82
Public Safety Officers' Benefits (PSOB), v, ix, 71, 72, 73, 74, 75, 76, 77, 78, 79, 80, 81, 82, 84, 85
Public Safety Officers' Educational Assistance (PSOEA), v, ix, 71, 72, 73, 82, 83, 84, 85
public schools, vii, 2, 9, 11, 25, 27, 28, 30, 32, 67
public university system, vii, 1, 4, 6, 7, 11, 12, 19, 24, 26, 27, 29, 33, 64

relief, 8, 19, 32, 66, 91, 97, 99, 103, 107, 109, 111, 112, 113, 114, 115, 119, 122
repaying any loans, x, 88, 96
requirements, xiii, xiv, 5, 29, 91, 94, 108, 114, 124, 136, 151, 152, 153, 160, 162, 172, 180, 181, 182, 184, 186, 187, 188, 190, 191, 192, 193, 195, 196, 197, 200, 202, 203, 204, 205, 207, 209, 210, 214, 215, 218, 229, 241, 242
restrictions, 97, 103, 125, 182, 208, 240
rules, 10, 57, 62, 63, 132, 139, 140, 143, 145, 147, 149, 152, 158, 161, 164, 187, 191, 192, 193, 197, 200, 207, 215, 227, 228, 239

Q

qualifications, 53, 59, 101, 146
quality assurance, xiii, 180, 181, 195, 198
quality improvement, 198

R

race, vii, viii, 1, 2, 3, 4, 5, 6, 7, 8, 12, 19, 24, 25, 26, 27, 28, 29, 30, 31, 32, 33, 34, 35, 36, 37, 38, 39, 40, 42, 43, 44, 45, 46, 47, 48, 49, 50, 51, 52, 53, 54, 55, 56, 57, 58, 59, 60, 61, 62, 63, 65, 67, 68, 69
race segregation, vii, 1
racial minorities, viii, 2, 3, 4, 33, 36, 37, 58, 68
racial quotas, 45, 56, 57
racial segregation, vii, 1, 3, 5, 6, 7, 14, 25, 26, 27, 28, 29, 30, 31, 32
racism, 42
Regents of the University of California v. Bakke, viii, 2, 34
regulations, 10, 62, 63, 77, 78, 98, 101, 104, 107, 108, 109, 114, 117, 118, 136, 140, 141, 151, 183, 191, 192, 197, 200, 207, 208, 209, 214, 215

S

safety, xiii, 77, 79, 80, 82, 180, 182, 211
scholarship, 19, 20, 69, 123
school, ix, x, xi, xii, 3, 6, 7, 8, 9, 10, 11, 13, 21, 22, 24, 25, 26, 27, 28, 29, 30, 31, 32, 36, 38, 43, 44, 45, 46, 47, 48, 49, 53, 56, 58, 60, 63, 66, 68, 69, 87, 88, 90, 91, 95, 96, 97, 98, 99, 100, 101, 102, 103, 105, 110, 111, 113, 114, 115, 116, 117, 118, 119, 120, 121, 122, 123, 124, 126, 129, 130, 131, 132, 133, 134, 136, 137, 138, 139, 140, 141, 142, 143, 144, 145, 146, 147, 148, 149, 150, 151, 152, 153, 154, 155, 156, 157, 158, 159, 160, 161, 163, 164, 165, 166, 168, 169, 170, 172, 173, 174, 175, 176, 177, 178, 184, 186, 187, 190, 191, 199, 212, 215, 232, 233, 235, 241, 242
School Breakfast Program (SBP), xi, xii, 129, 130, 131, 133, 134, 136, 139, 140, 141, 143, 144, 145, 149, 150, 151, 152, 155, 156, 159, 160, 164, 166, 174, 176
school meals programs, v, xi, 129, 136, 138, 140, 141, 142, 143, 145, 157
secondary schools, 5, 7, 11, 28, 30, 141, 235

260 *Index*

segregated public schools, vii, 2
segregated university systems, vii, 2, 6
segregation, vii, 1, 3, 5, 6, 7, 8, 9, 11, 12, 13, 14, 16, 18, 19, 20, 21, 23, 24, 25, 26, 27, 28, 29, 30, 31, 32, 33, 61, 67, 68, 69
Senate, 133, 223, 224, 227, 228, 230, 231, 241, 247, 248
sequestration, xiv, 218, 235, 236, 237, 238, 239, 240
services, ix, 22, 44, 71, 72, 73, 75, 84, 93, 97, 103, 105, 160, 162, 203, 243
Special Milk Program (SMP), xi, 129, 131, 133, 134, 140, 145, 159, 167, 168, 174, 178
spending, ix, xi, xiv, 72, 85, 130, 135, 138, 139, 158, 159, 160, 171, 218, 220, 228, 229, 230, 231, 235, 236, 237, 238, 239, 243, 244, 245, 247
State Tuition Recovery Fund (STRF), xi, 89, 119, 120, 122, 125, 126
student achievement, 202, 218
student enrollment, 12, 24, 147, 182, 187
Subsidized Loan, x, 88, 119
subsidy, xii, 130, 132, 137, 144, 157, 162, 163, 173, 244
Summer Food Service Program (SFSP), xi, xii, 129, 130, 131, 133, 134, 136, 137, 139, 140, 145, 159, 164, 165, 166, 167, 174, 176, 177
summer program, 133, 134, 136, 171
Supreme Court, vii, 1, 3, 4, 5, 6, 7, 8, 9, 19, 20, 21, 23, 24, 26, 27, 28, 32, 33, 35, 37, 39, 45, 46, 49, 65, 78

T

tax base, 122
tax credits, 91, 126, 219
taxation, 122, 123, 126, 183
taxpayers, 116, 120, 123, 124, 125, 126
teachers, 24, 27, 38

teach-out, ix, x, 88, 90, 91, 92, 93, 94, 95, 100, 101
technical assistance, 131, 151, 172, 173
Title I, v, x, xii, xiii, 72, 83, 85, 88, 90, 91, 94, 95, 96, 97, 99, 102, 103, 106, 108, 114, 118, 179, 180, 181, 182, 183, 184, 185, 186, 187, 188, 189, 190, 191, 192, 193, 194, 195, 196, 197, 198, 200, 201, 203, 204, 205, 206, 207, 208, 209, 210, 211, 213, 214, 215, 216, 220, 224, 226, 234, 240, 241
Title II, 85, 106, 240, 241
Title IV, v, x, xii, xiii, 83, 88, 90, 91, 94, 95, 96, 97, 99, 102, 103, 108, 114, 118, 179, 180, 181, 182, 183, 184, 185, 186, 187, 188, 189, 190, 191, 192, 193, 194, 195, 196, 197, 198, 200, 201, 203, 204, 205, 206, 207, 208, 209, 210, 211, 213, 214, 215, 216
Title IV assistance, xii, 103, 114, 179, 181
Title V, viii, 2, 3, 5, 6, 16, 19, 32, 37, 38, 46, 61, 62, 63, 64, 65, 66, 67, 69, 104, 106
training, 77, 117, 172, 173, 184, 185, 189, 190, 201, 202, 204, 219, 231, 245
training programs, 189, 219
transfer the credits, x, 88
treatment, 15, 35, 39, 40, 92, 120, 121, 122, 126
tuition, 83, 91, 117, 119, 123, 124, 125, 127, 161, 194, 213

U

U.S. Department of Agriculture (USDA), 148
U.S. Department of Agriculture's Food and Nutrition Service (USDA-FNS), xi, 129, 132, 134, 136, 137, 140, 142, 145, 146, 149, 150, 151, 152, 153, 154, 156, 158,

159, 160, 161, 163, 166, 167, 169, 171, 172, 173, 174, 175, 176

U.S. Department of the Interior, 135

U.S. Supreme Court, vii, 1

United States, vii, ix, 1, 4, 6, 7, 11, 19, 20, 21, 24, 25, 27, 30, 31, 35, 37, 41, 62, 63, 64, 68, 72, 79, 80, 84, 120, 186, 197, 198, 199, 220, 221

United States Court of Appeals, ix, 72, 84

United States v. Fordice, vii, 1, 4, 6, 11, 31

universities, viii, 2, 4, 5, 9, 12, 13, 18, 19, 21, 22, 25, 27, 32, 33, 42, 44, 45, 48, 61, 63, 65, 67, 68, 164, 198, 246

USDA, v, xi, 129, 130, 132, 134, 136, 137, 138, 140, 142, 144, 145, 146, 147, 149, 150, 151, 152, 153, 154, 156, 158, 159, 160, 161, 163, 164, 166, 167, 169, 170, 171, 172, 173, 174, 175, 176, 177

V

vegetables, 151, 160, 169

vocational education, 245

vocational rehabilitation, 63

W

withdrawal, 3, 66, 194, 205, 206

workers, 76, 78, 81, 166

work-study, 181

Effective Teaching and Learning: Perspectives, Strategies and Implementation

Editor: Matthias Abend

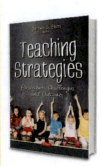

Series: Education in a Competitive and Globalizing World

Book Description: *Effective Teaching and Learning: Perspectives, Strategies and Implementation* opens with a review on the use of the term "scaffolding" in teaching, and explains the purpose of scaffolding in the context of Vygotsky's developmental theory.

Softcover ISBN: 978-1-53613-943-3
Retail Price: $82

Teaching Strategies: Perspectives, Challenges and Outcomes

Editor: James S. Etim, Ph.D. (Winston Salem State University, Winston Salem, NC, US)

Series: Education in a Competitive and Globalizing World

Book Description: The contributors, who are all classroom teachers, educators or practitioners at varying levels of the education system, propose and discuss strategies that are effective in advancing student learning.

Hardcover ISBN: 978-1-53613-588-6
Retail Price: $160

Education: Issues, Policies and Programs

Editor: Terry M. Kohan

Series: Education in a Competitive and Globalizing World

Book Description: The term "STEM education" refers to teaching and learning in the fields of science, technology, engineering, and mathematics. It typically includes educational activities across all grade levels— from pre-school to post-doctorate—in both formal (e.g., classrooms) and informal (e.g., afterschool programs) settings.

Softcover ISBN: 978-1-53614-978-4
Retail Price: $95

Leadership in Gifted Education

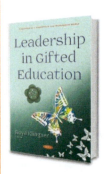

Editor: Roya Klingner (Head & Founder of the Global Center for Gifted and Talented Children, Freising, Germany)

Series: Education in a Competitive and Globalizing World

Book Description: The information and useful advice provided make this book an ideal resource for those just starting out in the gifted field as well as those who are already gifted advocates.

Softcover ISBN: 978-1-53614-287-7
Retail Price: $82